Acoutamiskan
R. Michipicoton
Cristinaux
FRAN
Sauteurs
Saut St. Marie
Saut
LAC HURON
ou
OKAREGNONDI
B. Sakinam
Hurons
Lac St. Clair
R. Outtaouack
Lac Ontari
ou de Fontenac
LAC D'ERIE OU DU CHAT
Grands Villages de
Isonnontouans
Eriechronois
Pouhatan

GREAT LAKES COUNTRY

Russell McKee
October, 1966

In striking contrast to the dune country, the colorful Pictured Rocks are a more rugged part of Lake Superior's south shoreline. A scenic attraction in this area, Chapel Rock, stands guard on a lonely bluff.

Michigan Department of Conservation

GREAT LAKES COUNTRY

Russell McKee

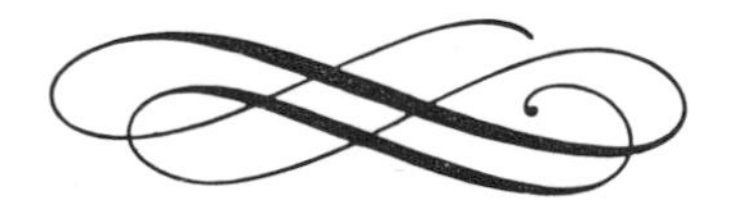

NEW YORK
Thomas Y. Crowell Company
ESTABLISHED 1834

Library of Congress Catalog Card No. 66–14943
Manufactured in the United States of America
1 2 3 4 5 6 7 8 9 10

To

ROBERT AND ADA,

my parents,

this book is affectionately dedicated.

Preface

AS ONE WRITER phrased it, books are born in debt to their times. This book is no exception. So many persons become part of such an effort that the writer feels himself merely an instrument of their work, suggestions, and encouragements. He brings together what they provide.

My own personal debt stretches in many directions: to the Great Lakes themselves for their natural strength and majesty; to Carson Hamilton and Max Salvagione for giving a slow runner his second wind; to all those special librarians of the world for whom reading is more important than overdue call slips; and to Kim and Carole Rodner and Jay and Virginia Artis for long discussions, knowledge, directions, sources, and above all else, humor and kindred spirits.

Charles Schafer is another special kind of friend who is far too sane for the times in which he lives. He is an artist where most men dabble in paint, a creator where few even construct. His counterpart with words is Kendrick Kimball, whose writing ability is still, after several decades, without any serious challengers in this entire Great Lakes region. Any man counts himself lucky to enter the lists with mentors such as these.

Certain guides and warm hearts labored mightily to relieve the early manuscript of congenital confusion. John Gray, most of all. He read and corrected from a deep interest that started years ago while serving as second cook on a doubtful-vintage Great Lakes lumber freighter.

Thoughtful suggestions on those chapters dealing with Indian life came from Drs. Moreau Maxwell, Leland Cooper, George Quimby, and James Griffin. That's a pretty formidable array of anthropologists, and any remaining flaws of interpretation there are my own sturdy form of failure, surviving all their efforts to subdue it. Robert Kelley spent kind hours clarifying early statements on geology of the Lakes, then read pertinent sections of the final manuscript.

Janet Coe Sanborn, Helen Wallin, and Orpha Charles may not realize how much of their thought and effort are contained in the illustrations, but without these helpful friends, the book you hold would be far less interesting and useful.

Many personal debts of gratitude developed along the way, for which I can only express my deep appreciation. Robert and Ellen Walhay and Donald C. Wagner, for example, held four A.M. vigils and brewed coffee when that was important to me. Charles and Ricka Dinges provided warm friendship and many thoughtful kindnesses throughout, as did Robert and Cynthia Thrasher, Frank and Liz Nall, Harry and Kay Webb, Lorayne Rodner, and R. D. Burroughs. Another special vote of thanks goes to James and Lena Gater for their help in times of need and their continued friendship, cheer, and love. Farley Tubbs, Gaylord Walker, and Gerald E. Eddy cleared many obstacles from the paths I walk, as did my good friend and compatriot, Angela Labiak.

Finally, my family has proved most helpful and interested in this work. It has been more demanding of them than most others, and they have borne their measure with grace. To Shirley, Robert, Linda, and Sally, my continuing love and appreciation.

Contents

Illustrations

Maps

GREAT LAKES COUNTRY

A stream of sun lights the shallows where the lower Detroit River joins Lake Erie. This area, noted for its islands, bays, and marshes, is a prime stopping place for waterfowl during migrations.

Michigan Department of Conservation

I

The Greatest Lakes in the World

THE GREAT LAKES—call them the Greatest Lakes! For so indeed they are, in the totality of their size and history, the greatest lakes in the world. Separately they are giants, vast sea-sized waters moving out to distant shores beyond the horizon; one, Superior, is the largest fresh-water lake on earth. Together all five form a chain of inland seas whose size and unity staggered the early explorers. They could not believe that these were lakes; they kept testing for salt water, thinking that the whole chain must form part of the ocean that would lead them to Asia. Now, after three and a half centuries of settlement, our awe of the Great Lakes has softened into acceptance. We see them; we live near them; we use them—but we have come to a time when their value is taken for granted, even neglected. We seldom see them for what they are: one of the world's unique resources.

Today our national life calls for a new understanding of the Great Lakes. We are a people in search of a history, and the Great Lakes region has provided an uncommonly large share of North American history. Look for only a moment at what the early exploration of the region represents. In 1541—the same year that Coronado was exploring the Southwest—Jacques Cartier was on the St. Lawrence River, naming Montreal and searching for a route that would lead westward into the Great Lakes. In 1618—two years before the Pilgrims landed at

Plymouth Rock—Etienne Brulé may have already penetrated as far as western Lake Superior, a point nearly halfway across our continent.

Perhaps an even earlier date is possible for the white man's arrival on these lakes. For the last sixty years, a lively argument as to whether the Vikings were not the first to reach the region has flourished around the shores of western Lake Superior. Supporters of this theory claim that a band of Norsemen journeyed overland from Hudson Bay to Lake Superior in 1362. If the evidence on which this claim is based is ever validated, the history of the Western Hemisphere will have to be revised sharply; if the evidence is fraudulent, it is one of the most splendid hoaxes ever created.

Considering the central role the Great Lakes have played in this continent's history, some have compared them to the Mediterranean; and although there are gross differences, certain interesting parallels exist. The headlands of Quebec, for example, guard the entrance from the Atlantic as Gibraltar guards the entrance to the Mediterranean. At Tobermory or Big Bay or Washington Island, one can look down into azure-blue water—the same pure blue color, although water far colder, than that in the Mediterranean.

Again, the early fur traders in the Great Lakes region were not unlike the Levantine merchants of the Mediterranean. Both groups were ruthless; both knew murder for profit; both developed into powerful political and economic forces; and both were water-based commercial enterprises. However, when we compare the amount of trade carried today through the canals man has attached to these waterways, the Mediterranean comes off a poor second. The Soo locks between Lakes Superior and Huron pour out more freight in eight months than Suez handles in a year—and some years the Soo has carried more than Suez and Panama combined.

On this continent the earliest use of metal probably took place on the shores of western Lake Superior; in Europe and Asia it first occurred on the shores of the eastern Mediterranean. Archeologists are still uncertain which continent was first in this achievement.

The changing fortunes of many wars and many empires have rolled back and forth across the Mediterranean and, likewise, across the Great Lakes. The great Iroquois Indian League, with its small bands of warriors, laid waste to an empire that touched the shores of all the Great Lakes. Though far outnumbered, the Iroquois scattered or annihilated a dozen tribes—not unlike the days of Alexander or Caesar when the Mediterranean was *mare nostrum*. After the Iroquois came the Europeans, who also tried to claim the Great Lakes as "our sea." France battled England, and England the United States, and all fought at various times with or against the Indians—who had more right to the land, but less gunpowder.

Great Lakes, Great Land. Consider the map of our continent. If Brulé did reach western Lake Superior in 1618, it was from the Atlantic a journey by water of fifteen hundred miles. That was cutting to the continental heart in a hurry, but it was an event that could only occur for very special reasons. It was explorer's luck to find together the marvelous string of lakes and the bark canoe, the ideal vehicle for traveling on them. The proper incentives also had to be there: the desire of French leaders to forge an empire, and the lure of rich commerce to spur man into courageous exploration searching for a water route to Asia.

In the thirteenth century Marco Polo had fired Europe with his tales of the magic land of Cathay. Soon after, Portuguese and Spanish coasters bumped down the west shore of Africa, up the east shore of Africa, then across to the lands of southeast Asia, where the riches they found were astonishing. If only they could be carried home to Europe. But this African route was too long and arduous. What if a shorter route could be found to the West? So Columbus and Cabot, and then Verrazano and Cartier came to the New World, searching for this route. Cartier discovered the St. Lawrence River in 1534; Brulé was exploring the Great Lakes region by 1610. Dozens of other Europeans followed Brulé in the next decades, and all were disappointed. The water they tasted in the Lakes was fresh, not salt. This could not be the sea route to Cathay. But being here, they elected to stay, and lacking an Eastern empire to plunder, they decided to build one of their own.

It was a brash decision. Within two hundred years, all the empire builders had been sacked and sent home to Europe; or they were buried here, and the region they sought to plunder was claimed by a fledgling new nation. This land of the Great Lakes was destined to be the industrial hub of the most industrialized nation on earth. Its material largess surpassed any dreams the early explorers ever dreamed or any hopes for wealth they carried to these shores among their trade goods. Systematically these explorers and their descendants, and now we, have exploited the region to build an unheralded empire. The harvest took first the animal resources (beaver), then the mineral resources (copper, iron, and coal), and finally the vegetable resources (timber).

Cathay, indeed, never offered such riches. Today the largest industrial complex on earth is on the shores of the Great Lakes, and more than 40 per cent of all the people on our continent north of Mexico live in states and provinces that border on them.

The years between discovery of the region and its present wealth contain much magnificent history. Where today broad expressways claim the land, buffalo once roamed. Tracts of housing have sprung up where violent Indian battles raged. Any Lakes-area resident may drive his lawnmower over grass where torture stakes once stood; only the trees remember the screams and pagan shouts of the victims. Creeks so small that the water does not reach above the knees were witness to furious battles for national survival. Funny-looking little forts, now assaulted only by tourists, once stood guarding vast tracts of land for Louis XIV or George III.

Three hundred years ago, Robert Cavelier, Sieur de la Salle, better known simply as La Salle, built his little ship *Griffin* beside the Niagara River and dreamed an amazing dream. His plan was to encircle what is now the eastern United States by planting a string of French forts through the Great Lakes and down the Mississippi. Ships such as his *Griffin* would supply these posts. All was then wilderness, and the amazing fact is that he nearly accomplished that dream. Had he not been murdered by his followers in a Texas swamp, we might be today a wholly French-speaking people.

You can stand on the gentle shore of southern Lake Huron and hear its waters lap softly at the sands and wonder how it could possibly have destroyed the lives and ships it has. In one storm off that shore nine large ships went to their doom with a loss of 217 lives. This was not the worst toll, however. The most disastrous Great Lakes tragedy took place on the Chicago River in downtown Chicago on a quiet morning in July 1915. No storms or strong winds were involved, yet more than 800 persons perished in that single disaster.

Or consider the strange case of James J. Strang, who on the Great Lakes a century ago had himself crowned king. The Strang kingdom was set up on Beaver Island in northern Lake Michigan, and had its own legion of followers, state religion, moral code, army, and communal economy—all in defiance of the Constitution. For six years Strang continued his rule, annually increasing his strength and authority. His political power became his strongest protection, and he might have gone on indefinitely were it not for his being murdered—like La Salle—by two of his followers. The assassination occurred as he walked up the gangplank of the federal gunboat, *Michigan*, which had arrived at the island. Some say the ship was there on a state visit, although there seems to be stronger evidence that Strang's jig was up and that the Constitution had prevailed after all. The little community where it all happened is still known as St. James.

And look at the almost incredible story of the Canadian mission of the Society of Jesus in New France. The Jesuits first came to Canada in 1611 and are still there in fair numbers. In the early days many were martyred, dying gruesome deaths by Indian torture. Despite this, they continued their work. One who escaped from the torture stake before death returned that same year to the very same tribe to continue his Christianizing; that time the Indians did not let him escape. Most suffered a hell of indignities before meeting death at the stake. Some, however, took up the trade in furs and were more merchants than missionaries. Jesuit curiosity about the New World produced some remarkable writings, providing today's reader with fascinating glimpses into travel through the Great Lakes region in the seventeenth and eighteenth centuries.

The Grand Sable dunes sprawl for miles along the south shore of Lake Superior. Their isolation, size, and beauty have made them candidates for inclusion in a proposed national lakeside park.

Michigan Department of Conservation

Today those of us who live in the middle of the continent tend to forget or take for granted how much these lakes determine our way of life. They moderate our weather. They determine our agriculture. They establish our patterns of hunting and fishing. They provide for everyone an easy escape in summer; like the French court during the reign of the Louis', we all repair to the shore in the summertime. Nobody has yet found a way to control these grand waters, and to any who have sailed on them it is impossible to believe that they will ever be tamed.

Each Lake often shows a definite personality. Superior is male: cold, moody, and mysterious. Michigan is female: generally friendly, sometimes very warm, but often squally. Huron is a back-country pitchman: shallow, a bit commercial, and far more dangerous than it appears. Lake Erie is ambivalent: very shallow and always verging on trouble. Sailors have told me at times that facing the shock of a Lake Erie storm is often worse than any actual damage it may do. Imagine your boat being lifted to the crest of a wave and seeing, in the trough beyond, rocks exposed on the bottom. The shallowness of the lake and the large waves it produces have combined to create a great many landsmen. At the far eastern end there's Ontario, lowest of the lot, closest to the ocean, and perhaps for this reason seemingly different from the others.

Often forgotten but nonetheless part of the Great Lakes are four other bodies of water which should be considered part of the chain. Most people know Lake St. Clair, near Detroit, but you need to look closely at a detailed map to find Lake George, Lake Nicolet, and Munuscong Lake—all legally considered as lakes, and all a part of that interesting complex of waters between Lake Superior and northern Lake Huron.

There are growing and disturbing reasons why a new understanding of the Great Lakes is in order. As a people, we are only beginning to appreciate the magnificent natural gift the lakes represent, but at this same moment of history, we have begun what may be the inexorable destruction of these waters.

Our recognition of their value is shown by the burgeoning use we now make of the Lakes. Prices of shore property have gone sky-high. The number of ships on the Lakes keeps multiplying. The St. Lawrence Seaway has made them a world highway. Large tracts of public land close to several of the world's largest cities have made the area a recreational as well as a commercial mecca.

This recognition of value, however, is marred by a growing pollution of the Lakes, and unfortunately pollution seems a natural consequence of greater use. There is no doubt about the problem. The questions are, How far has it gone and can we stop it before it is too late? Lake Erie is already so polluted that probably only a program of massive corrective measures, including dredging, can ever restore it. The southern end of Lake Michigan has been called an open sewer by one large Chicago newspaper, and if you disbelieve it, you have only to view the waterfront at the Chicago River or Calumet Harbor or Gary.

One study conducted by the United States Fish and Wildlife Service shows that pollution is aging the Great Lakes ten times as rapidly as normal aging action. Only Lake Superior has escaped this speed-up. All lakes normally pass through an aging process by chemical and physical reactions with the land. Soils leach out; salinity increases; water temperatures rise; and fish and other organisms change as the lake ages. But these sequences usually take centuries, and the Great Lakes are passing through them in a few decades. Trout and whitefish have been replaced in Lake Erie by carp and goldfish. Bottom-dwelling creatures like mayflies are giving way to sludge worms. The water is growing more turbid. Swimming is now prohibited at state parks that only a few years ago were placed where they are because of excellent swimming. A thousand tons of sewage solids are dumped into Lake Erie daily by cities along its shores. If pollution continues at this rate throughout the Great Lakes region, we will irretrievably pollute all but Lake Superior in a very short time, creating a national scandal and a continental stench from which there will be no escape.

Yet in the long view, there is room for optimism. The air is tinged with growing public awareness of general conservation needs. There is an increasing federal and local concern over pollution. New techniques, such as industrial re-use of water, extended filtration, and radiation of polluted water, may bring the problem under control.

At one time, the water of the Great Lakes was almost unbelievably pure. Mostly it came from glacial meltwaters and the prodigious amounts of rain that followed the retreat of the glaciers. Glaciers, however, are only one part of the story, and the Great Lakes region is a very composite example of many earth forces at work. Everything happened here, and no period in the geological history of the region has ever been dull. A sequence of massive changes has shaped the district since the world began. The Great Lakes basins are nestled against the southern edge of the rocky Canadian shield, the largest continental buttress on earth.. The shield was created in Pre-Cambrian times, perhaps four to five billion years ago, as the earth hardened from its liquid stage. Today, most of the earth's surface is covered with rock formations created within the last half billion years—since the end of Pre-Cambrian times. All continents have such ancient Pre-Cambrian deposits, but the Canadian shield is most notable because it is the largest. The shield seems to have gained its name because it lies like a protective shield over much of eastern Canada. As the map shows, it outlines the northern edge of the Great Lakes district, nearly encircling Lake Superior. The lakes were created later, out of softer rock formations that overlapped the lower edge of the shield and extended southward from it.

But while the shield is very ancient, the Great Lakes are not, having gained their present size and shape only in comparatively recent times. Ten to twelve thousand years ago, while men were tilling fields and gathering crops around the eastern end of the Mediterranean, glaciers still covered much of the Great Lakes region. Six thousand years ago,

Millions of years ago, ancient seas deposited layer upon layer of salt in the upper Great Lakes region. Beds of salt under some areas of Lake Michigan are almost two thousand feet thick. Deep under Detroit, salt is mined in these cavernous tunnels. Ceilings shown here are twenty-two feet high.

Michigan Department of Conservation

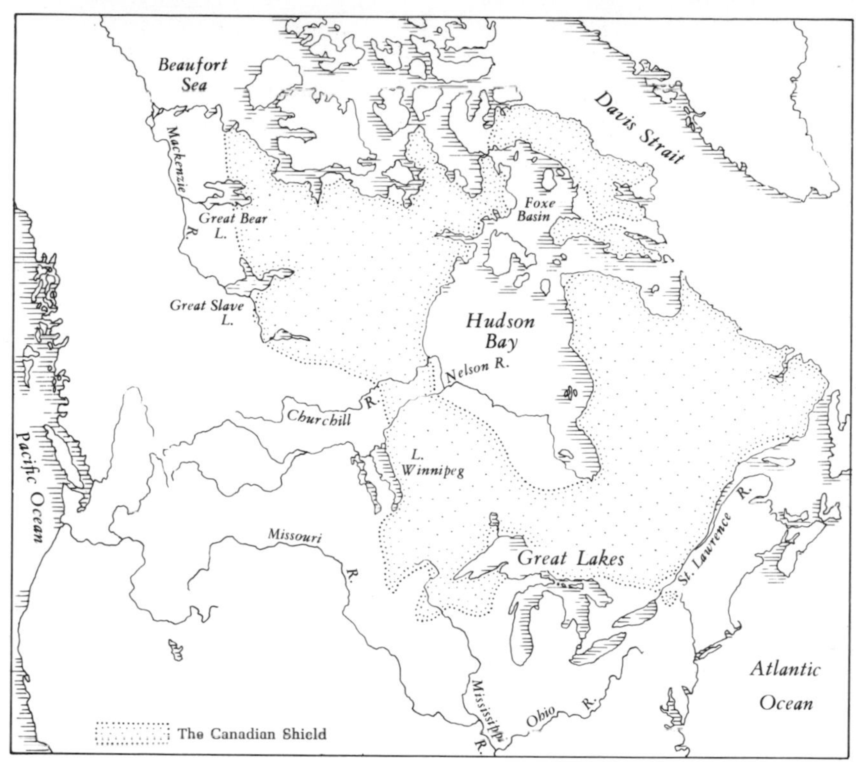

Michigan Department of Conservation

The Great Lakes lie along the southern edge of the Canadian shield, a continental buttress formed as the earth hardened from its liquid stage billions of years ago. But the Lakes themselves are comparatively young—dating back only a few thousand years.

Lake Michigan was still only a narrow lake, and men hunted in the dense forests along its shores. Today, those same shores lie in deep water thirty miles east of the Wisconsin mainland.

A geological reconstruction of the region shows that between the formation of the ancient Canadian shield and the modern Great Lakes all the known earth forces have been at work, from superheated lavas to the deep freeze of glaciers. In Paleozoic times—five hundred million to two hundred million years ago—much of North America was washed by salty seas from the north, from the south, from the east. For hundreds of centuries, shallow seas lay quietly on the land, allowing some of the world's greatest salt deposits to form in the lower Michigan and the Erie-Ontario regions. Even then, the Great Lakes region must have been basin-shaped, to catch and contain these waters as it did. Sea after sea washed over and deposited salt, sand, limestone, and other materials century after century, leaving enough pure salt alone to supply the whole world all it may ever need. In some places, the thickness of the beds of salt under lower Lake Michigan is almost two thousand feet. Deep under Detroit, where one company has nicked into this vast body of salt after years of mining, a cavernous network of underground roadways has been hollowed out, and huge trucks rumble back and forth. Enormous amounts of salt are taken yearly from such mines, yet the supply has hardly been touched.

The sedimentary rock materials beneath lower Michigan are mostly shales, dolomites, limestones, and sandstones. It is these rocks with the granites of the Canadian shield that played the most prominent part in the formation of the Great Lakes region. It came about in this way:

Picture for a moment the massive Canadian shield as a single slab of rock lying on the land. Then, against the southern edge of this rock, visualize a stack of softer rock "saucers" lying one on top of another. These saucers form the so-called Michigan Basin, the center of the stack being roughly located near the geographic center of Michigan's Lower Peninsula. For the moment, great oceans cover everything.

After the passage of many eons, the eastern half of North America begins to lift out of these ancient salt seas and assumes roughly the shape that it has today. The stack of rock saucers lying against the Canadian shield drains and hardens somewhat, but remains softer than the granites of the shield itself. Possibly great depressions, or valleys, were left along the main axes of the present Great Lakes. Perhaps the salt seas drained off the land along these depressions. Geologists do not know for certain.

More eons pass, and the first glaciers arrive. As these great ice sheets move over the land, each cuts into the softer rock of the saucers. Each time a glacier shears off material, it exposes the edge of a deeper saucer. Look at any map of the Great Lakes. The western shore of Lake Michigan curls north to form the Door Peninsula, separating Green Bay from Lake Michigan. The Garden Peninsula reaches south to meet the Door. The northern shores of Lake Michigan and Lake Huron continue this curving formation to the east, where it joins the various islands of Lake Huron. Then the Saugeen Peninsula takes over in lower Ontario, forming the east shore of Lake Huron. The general outline of all these peninsulas, shores, and islands forms an almost perfect arc. This is the exposed edge of one of the harder rock saucers in the Michigan Basin. The layer is called the Niagaran dolomite. However, after ringing the northern edges of Lakes Michigan and Huron, the Niagaran dolomite layer turns eastward to form the neck of land between Lakes Erie and Ontario—and thereby was this layer later to gain its present name from the earlier-named Niagara Falls and Niagara River.

Geologists believe that some of the saucers in this stack were weaker than others and so were more cut away by erosion and glacial action. The Niagaran dolomite was relatively tough and resistant, so it survived to form the northern outline of Lakes Michigan and Huron. But now notice how Lakes Michigan, Huron, and St. Clair form a horseshoe shape over lower Michigan. The basins of these three lakes were probably made of shale and other soft rocks. Thus they were more easily eroded by glaciers and water, and being saucer-shaped layers themselves, they each left circular basins. Similarly, a weak shale of earlier times was eroded out of Green Bay, Georgian Bay, and Lake Ontario.

North shore of Lake Michigan under winter snow. This aerial view shows the series of ancient lakeshores left behind as the lake has receded in the last several thousand years. The thin line of a highway curves along the present shore.

Michigan Department of Conservation

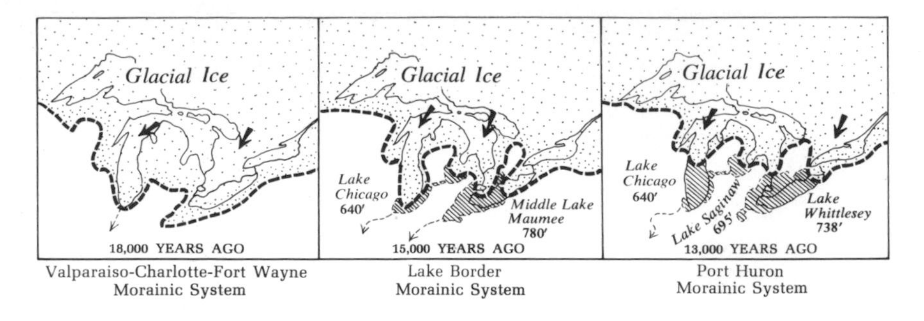

The last glacial stage, the Wisconsin, was the most important in the formation of the Lakes. As the ice melted back, water collected in the basins to form the Lakes. The map shows the Wisconsin Glacier during the period 18,000 to 3,500 years ago.

The basin of Lake Superior is formed of a far different and older bedrock than that of the other Great Lakes. Western Lake Superior lies in volcanic rock on the edge of the Canadian shield. The shield, being composed almost entirely of granite, was formed deep in the earth and then pushed up into high mountain ranges. These began to weather and gradually eroded into the low, undulating knobs seen on the shield today. In the western Lake Superior region, however, great outpourings of lava formed on the surface late in Pre-Cambrian times. It was in these formations that the copper prospectors of the 1840's sought their fortunes. Copper accumulated here in amazing quantities during this ancient volcanic period.

In a geological time sense, the Great Lakes themselves are very new. If all known time were reduced to a single hour, the Great Lakes would have been formed only in the last second. Glaciers gouged out their basins, and glacial melt-waters filled the openings. No one knows how many glacial epochs have taken place in North America, but four have occurred within the last million years. More may occur before the present series is complete, with total destruction of some of the most populated areas of North America a possibility. The first of these four great ice caps was called the Nebraskan, and it swept over the Great Lakes region from 1,000,000 to 950,000 years ago. Then the Kansan swept down from 475,000 to 425,000 years ago. The Illinoian followed, covering the area from 300,000 to 250,000 years ago. Finally, the Wisconsin glacial sheet covered Canada and parts of the United States from 65,000 to 3,500 years ago. Although the glacier had retreated from all the Great Lakes region by 6,500 years ago, it still covered large areas of Canada until 1,500 B.C.

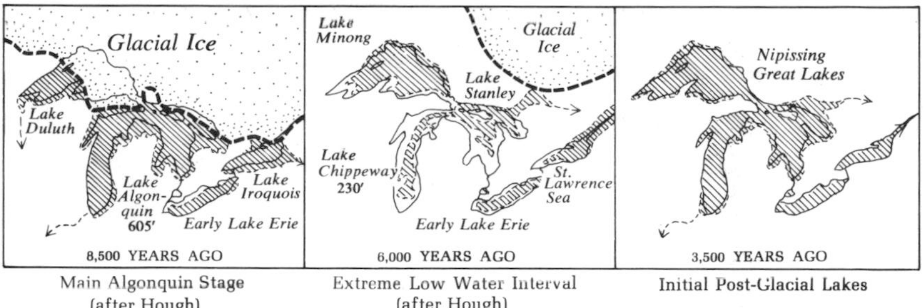

Main Algonquin Stage (after Hough) | Extreme Low Water Interval (after Hough) | Initial Post-Glacial Lakes

All four glacial periods entirely covered the Great Lakes region, under a vast sheet of ice ranging from one to two miles deep. The enormous weight, pressure, and destructive force of such ice can scarcely be imagined. All of the area's characteristic land contours, soil composition and location, rivers, lakes, and other geographic features were created by the glaciers. As each pushed down across the land, it tore out all previous features. When a warm spell ended an advance, materials carried in the glacier piled up as the ice melted and retreated. Each melt-back further confused the composition of the soil. The glacial material ranges from immense rounded boulders down to the finest-grained clay. In some places, this "overburden" of material lying on the bedrock may be twelve hundred feet deep. In others, the bedrock itself is exposed, showing deep grooves cut by the glacier's passage. Mostly, however, the mantle of glacial material is two hundred to three hundred feet deep. It provides us with the soil for agriculture, the filtration system and repository for our ground-water supplies, and the source of earth materials used for countless industrial and construction purposes.

The series of six maps shows the sequence and development of the Great Lakes during the stages of the last glacial period, the Wisconsin, which was crucial in their development. During the Wisconsin glacial advance, none of the Lakes existed, and only after melt-back started did water begin to collect in their basins.

The retreat of this last great ice cap was by no means steady; it moved forward and backward, again and again, altering the Lakes region many times. Each halt saw ridges of rock, stone, and other material pile up at its point of greatest advance. These ridges served to pool meltwater into the scooped-out areas when the glacier began to retreat. In so doing, a number of different, now extinct lakes developed. Geologists have given names to these ancient lakes, each being a crude ancestor of one of the present Great Lakes. At various times, these lakes drained south into the Mississippi or east into the St. Lawrence. When and how each drained depended on the amount of water that gathered in pools on the land; when the water was high enough, it spilled over the bedrock sills at Chicago, Duluth, and other locations. When stopped by moraines or low levels, it drained only eastward through the St. Lawrence Valley. Sometimes these lakes drained simultaneously in both directions.

Many of these early lakes were small. But great rains began to fill their basins soon after the glacier withdrew, and for two thousand years these broad valleys gained water, filling steadily. The filling action continued until about four thousand years ago when a single large three-lobed lake called Nipissing covered the entire Upper Lakes area. Lakes Superior, Michigan, and Huron then merged as one with narrow links between, and for a thousand years, this huge lake held sway over the region. But its ponderous size soon led to its gradual decline, starting about three thousand years ago. The immense amount of water overflowed its banks, causing drainage at Chicago as well as at North Bay and Port Huron. Such drainage gradually lowered Lake Nipissing's level, narrowing the channels linking it together. Also, with the tremendous weight of the glacier finally removed, the earth's crust

A cross-sectional view shows the relative depths and distances of the Lakes, and how they spill eastward off the continent.

Canadian Department of Northern Affairs and Natural Resources

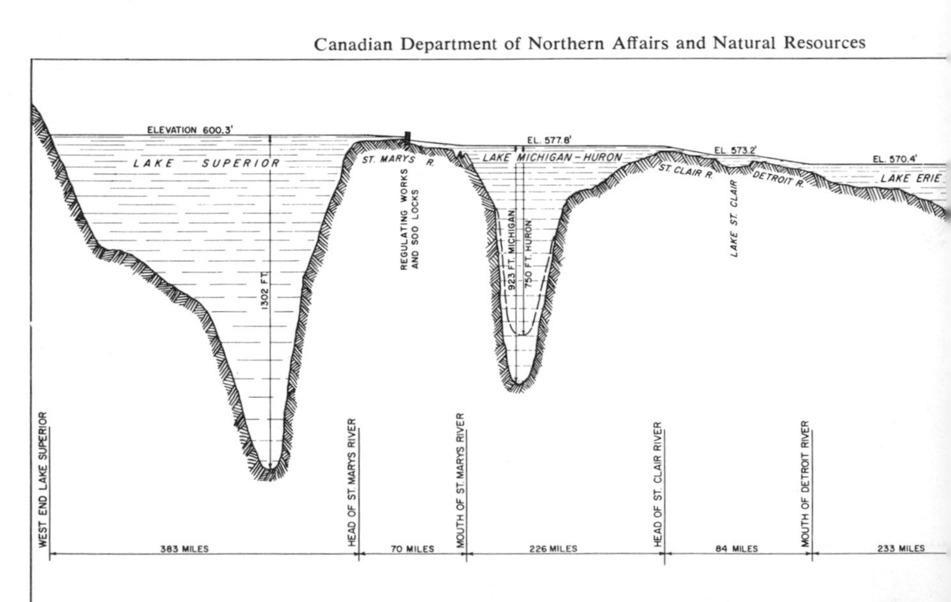

began to lift. This upward movement, known as crustal rebound, is still, as a matter of fact, occurring. In the last three thousand years it has raised this region enough to halt any further drainage through North Bay.

As the water dropped farther it fell below the level of the St. Marys River at Sault Ste Marie, and Lake Superior, being cut off from the rest of Lake Nipissing, emerged as a single, enclosed body of water. Then the Chicago outlet closed off, leaving only the Port Huron drainway, and Lakes Michigan and Huron came into being. Later rains filled the Lakes to their present levels, the only natural drainage now being through the St. Lawrence River valley. To be sure, the waters of Lake Michigan drain at Chicago into the Mississippi, but this is a man-made flow created in this present century.

Thus the Great Lakes formed as a drainage system extending deep into the heart of the continent but flowing east to the Atlantic, a unique feature of the North American landscape. The waters of Canada drain generally north to Hudson Bay and the Arctic Ocean. The central United States drains south to the Gulf of Mexico through the Missouri, Mississippi, and Ohio River systems. The divide between these two massive watersheds takes place roughly at the border of the United States and Canada, where the Great Lakes are located, draining at right angles to both. The Lakes are perhaps the single most distinctive inland feature of our continent and draining as they do toward the Atlantic and Europe, they quickly became the most important travel route during early North American history.

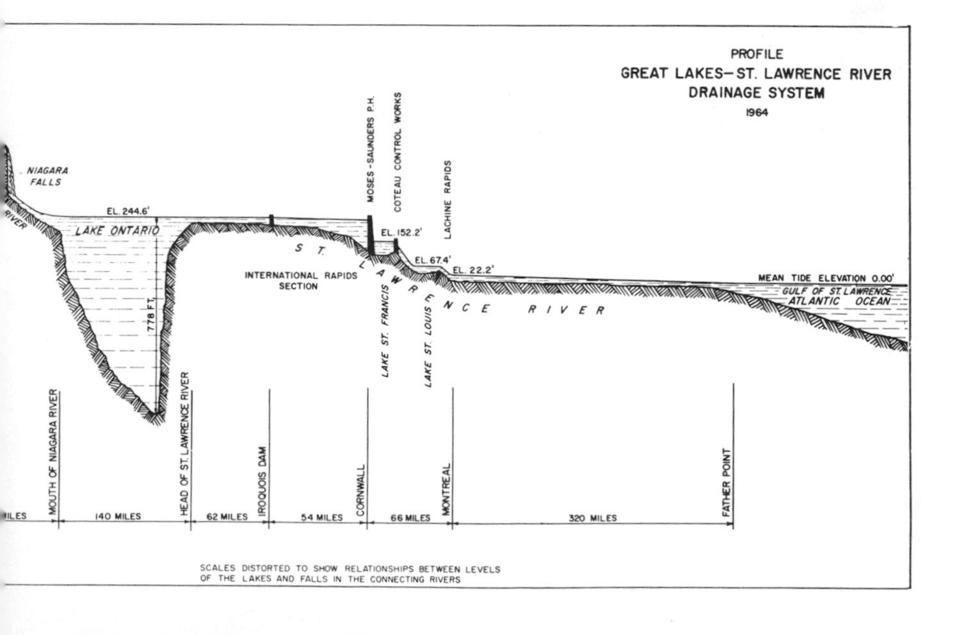

Now extinct, the giant mastodon is known to have roamed the Great Lakes region from about 12,000 to 7,000 B.C., and was hunted by early man during most of that period. The painting below is by Robert Thom.

2

The First Inhabitants

IT IS A CURIOUS and somewhat distressing fact that anthropology and archeology have invested more time and energy in the study of Old World man than in the study of New World man, that the classical college education which teaches much about the glory of Greece and the grandeur of Rome pays scant attention to our North American background. There are gross gaps in knowledge about the first North Americans. Anthropologists and archeologists still wonder when man first came to this continent, and lacking that answer, even less can be known about man's first arrival in the Great Lakes region. We are thus left with a fragment of Great Lakes history—and a very sketchy fragment at that.

Even with much time and energy archeologists can only hope to fill some of the larger voids in this history. Certain areas of detail will probably never be known. The available fragment, however, is not less interesting for the many gaps it contains. The Great Lakes area affords us a view of native North American man's development from the Stone Age through the first use of metal to the well-developed agricultural society of the mound builders—all of which occurred thousands of years ago and then disappeared long before the first white men stood beside these Lakes. The story left by these ancient peoples has only come to light in very recent times.

The North American and Great Lakes portion of mankind's story probably started some fifty thousand years ago. The last great glacial advance, the Wisconsin, was then spreading over the area now occupied by the Great Lakes. As the ice formed, it locked up a large amount of the earth's surface water. The levels of the oceans dropped accordingly, and what is now Bering Strait between eastern Siberia and western Alaska probably became a land bridge over which people could cross from Asia to North America. These Asians probably came in numerous small bands over a period of many centuries. Perhaps driven here by tribal wars or poor hunting in Asia, they gradually fanned out eastward across what is now Canada and the United States. They also drove steadily southward along our west coast into Central and South America. Just when the first migration occurred is moot and the subject of speculation. Some feel that the score of hearth oven pits near Lewisville in Denton County, Texas, are evidence of man's presence in North America fifty to seventy thousand years ago. Found at the site of these pits were charred bones and stone tips from throwing-weapons. Carbon-dating gives these pits an age of thirty-seven thousand years, although that date, near the upper limits of the carbon-dating method, might well seem questionable to some authorities.

Stone spear points and the remains of game have also been found in Sandia Cave in New Mexico, embedded in a clay layer that geologists say is fifty thousand years old. And recently, human skeletal remains found in 1916 on the east coast of Florida have been re-examined and given a tentative date of seventy thousand years ago. This dating is challenged by most authorities but does indicate the extreme range of possibilities.

While men may have been in North America fifty thousand or more years ago, there is no evidence of man's existence in the Great Lakes region even vaguely close to that date. At its greatest advance, the Wisconsin ice cap covered the entire Great Lakes region. All surface features, including any possible trace of man, were crushed, pulverized, or pushed into rubble ahead of this tremendous body of ice. The question of whether or not man might have inhabited the Lakes area before this time is thus fully confounded. The general opinion is that he did not.

Despite the oven pits in Texas, the Sandia Cave evidence, the early remains in Florida, and other similar material in Alaska, California, Mexico, and South America, most authorities believe that man's penetration of our continent did not take place until after 25,000 B.C., when several tribes or bands came in strength, crossing from Asia to North America at the Bering Strait, as earlier groups, if any, must have. Some of these later people trekked east along the Yukon River, pushed over the spine of the Rocky Mountains, then fanned out on the Great

Plains of central Canada and the United States. There they found an abundance of bison, and for many centuries had no need to move elsewhere. In all probability, the descendants of these early plains-dwelling hunters were the first men to enter the Great Lakes country. Arriving about 11,000 B.C., they lived in the shadow of the glacier, in the throes of its last and lesser push, the Valders advance. That brief surge covered all of the Great Lakes region north of the lower end of Lake Huron.

When these first people arrived, they probably hunted bison, as that species of animal was clearly present. But far larger game must soon have presented itself in the elephantlike beast known as the mastodon, which roamed over much of North America during antiquity and was present in the Great Lakes region from at least 11,000 to 7,000 B.C. Such a huge quarry was highly desirable and was hunted by these first Stone Age, Ice Age people. Mastodons were about the size of the present Indian elephant but were somewhat longer and lower, and had very large tusks. They also had long hair to protect them against the cold, and are generally known as hairy mastodons.

How these huge animals were killed by men armed only with stone-pointed weapons is unknown, but the solution to a similar problem in human survival can be seen today among the Ituri Forest pygmies in Africa, who track and kill the African elephant, using only spears as weapons. The pygmy approaches the huge beast only when it looks away, edging forward into the wind so that his scent will not reveal his presence, the elephant having weak eyes but a strong nose. When the pygmy is standing almost directly beneath the beast, he rams his spear into the animal's soft underbelly, then pulls it out immediately, and stands stock-still. The elephant roars and stamps in rage, but unless the pygmy moves out from under him, it cannot see him. The pygmy repeats this process of stab and stand until either he himself is trampled to death or the elephant is sufficiently wounded. Then the pygmy escapes as he came, following the elephant at a safe distance, perhaps for several days, until the beast dies of the wounds.

Some such method may have helped the hunters of the Great Lakes region kill mastodons a hundred centuries ago. No one knows, but the fact that the mastodon survived for several thousand years suggests that it was not an easy target.

They roamed in bands, those early peoples. They fished; they hunted; and they searched for food constantly. When the hairy mastodon was unavailable, they hunted giant beaver, deer, elk, and woodland

Chicago Natural History Museum

Nomadic tribes known as the Old Copper Indians made these copper implements in the Lake Superior region 5,000 to 6,000 years ago. The ax heads on the left were built with slots for the handles. The tool on the right is a gouge.

caribou. None of these animals is to be found in the area today except for the deer, which flourishes generally in the region, and a small band of elk which was introduced a few years ago into the northern part of Michigan's Lower Peninsula.

During the time from man's probable arrival in 11,000 B.C. down to about 4,500 B.C., the last glacier left the Great Lakes area, the earth's crust lifted, and both vegetation and climate changed radically. At one period the Great Lakes region was quite hot, and the trees shifted from conifer to hardwood, then became a mixed forest. The early people, meanwhile, absorbed all these changes and survived as nomadic hunters and fishermen.

Then around 4,000 B.C. man made a major innovation to aid him in his struggle for survival in the Great Lakes region. He began to use metal.

One can view this event in the light of subsequent events as having little importance to the history of North America. It can be argued that, unlike man's development around the Mediterranean, these primitives never fully realized the potential value of metal. And true enough, what the Mediterranean and European peoples accomplished with metal is most important in the whole sweep of human history. Certainly the North American Indian, though he knew and used metals as long as the Asian and European, failed to develop any use beyond a low cultural level. In Europe the opposite was true, with work in metal being rapidly carried to a sophisticated level. By the time white men penetrated the Great Lakes region in the sixteenth and seventeenth centuries, the difference in the knowledge of metal was crucial; it allowed the newcomers from Europe to dominate the native North Americans.

That is one side of the argument. The other side is that man's situations in Europe and North America were so basically different that no comparison should be made. Homo sapiens originated in Africa and Asia, and migrated to North America. Agriculture began for all mankind around the eastern end of the Mediterranean, and it likewise was imported or, at least, was developed in the American continents somewhat later. The first use of metal in the Old World occurred in an agricultural society. In the Great Lakes region the use of metal began at about the same time, but it was grafted onto a hunting, nomadic way of life. These early Great Lakes people had no need for agriculture. The Lakes region was well endowed with game, and they used metal as they used stone; it served as a superior form of material with which to make the same implements that they had always made. The story of the first North American use of metal is thus unique, quite amazing in itself, and provides one of the most interesting glimpses into North American prehistory. But it cannot be compared and should not stand comparison with the use of metal in the Old World.

The first use of metal in North America almost certainly occurred on the Keweenaw Peninsula in the west end of upper Michigan. A vast lode of native copper lay throughout the peninsula, deposited during one of the last great volcanic upheavals of the region. Native copper was also to be found at several other points around Lake Superior, notably north of Sault Ste Marie, on Isle Royale, and on the south shore of the lake, west of the Keweenaw Peninsula. But the greatest supply was on the Keweenaw, where it could be seen, exposed in the bedrock, in large and small veins. It could also be picked up as "float" copper—chunks that had been dislodged and moved away from bedrock by glacial action and erosion.

Why so many thousands of years should have passed between the arrival of man in the Great Lakes area in 11,000 B.C. and the first use of copper around 4,000 B.C. is a mystery. Copper was in common abundance and must certainly have been known to the early inhabitants. Actually they may have tried to use it, then cast it aside when it refused to chip into the shapes of their familiar stone weapons. Or they may have worshiped the red metal as part of some ancient ritual and religious system, as did certain Indians in the seventeenth and eighteenth centuries. For whatever reasons, copper was probably not used before about 4,000 B.C., and there is precious little evidence that it was used to any extent before 3,000 B.C.

How copper was first used is also unknown. Lumps of it may have served as mallets. Pieces with jagged edges may have been used as crude knives or spear points. But although the men who first hammered this metal with stones, hoping to make spear points, must have marveled at its refusal to break or crack, the practice of hammering irregular chunks of metal into projectile points, axes, adzes, chisels, knives, wedges, punches, drills, fishhooks, gouges, needles, awls, and other utensils gradually spread throughout the district. Probably many nomadic bands around Lake Superior carried copper from place to place, so that knowledge and use of the metal spread.

The exact mining methods of these people, known as the Old Copper Indians, are unknown, being inextricably entangled with the mining operations left by later Indian peoples. For example, the mound builders mined copper in the region from about 600 B.C to A.D. 800. Also, the Indians after 800 are known to have used copper to a lesser degree, thus adding the traces of their mining activities to those left by both the Old Copper and mound-building Indians.

But all the remaining traces indicate that the methods used in mining the copper were generally simple, though laborious. The Indians seem to have originally sought veins of the metal where it was exposed at ground level. Then they cleared away the surrounding dirt and stone, using heavy rocks to crack out as much of the copper as they

Copper's resistance to breaking and cracking made it an ideal metal for ancient craftsmen. The spear points pictured here, found in the area of Lake Superior, were made by the Old Copper Indians.

Chicago Natural History Museum

were able. As the work progressed downward, a point would come when the ore could no longer be chipped out with stone hammers. The Indians then built fires over the work area and, when the surrounding stone became hot, cracked it away by douses of cold water. This method has been used all over the world in primitive mining operations. The Indians preferred the smaller pieces or thinner veins of copper, for they could pound such pieces into the desired shapes, being unable to cut out the larger blocks of metal. When the Old Copper people found a mining area, they worked it systematically, cutting into the bedrock wherever the metal appeared. Henry Gillman, an archeologist from Detroit, visited one of these ancient mining areas on Isle Royale in 1873, and described the site as follows:

"The works, generally pits of from ten to thirty feet in diameter, and from twenty to sixty feet in depth, are found scattered throughout the island, wherever examined, being sunk through the few feet of superincumbent drift, where it exists, into the amygdaloid copper-bearing rock. They invariably are on the richest veins; and the intelligence displayed in the tracing and following of the veins when interrupted, etc., has elicited the astonishment of all who have witnessed it—no mistakes having apparently been made in this respect. These excavations are connected underground, drains being cut in the rock to carry off the water. Stopes [tunnels] one hundred feet in length are found. A drain sixty feet long presented some interesting features—having been cut through the surface drift into the rock, it had evidently been covered for its entire length by timbers felled and laid across. When opened, the timbers had mostly decayed, and the centre portions had sunk into the cavity, filling it for nearly its entire length with the rotted wood.

"At a deep inlet known as McCargoe's Cove, on the north side of the island, excavations such as are described extend in almost a continuous line for more than two miles, in most instances the pits being so close together as barely to permit their convenient working. Even the rocky islets off the coast have not escaped the observations of those ancient miners, and where bearing veins of copper are generally worked. The stone hammers, weighing from ten to even thirty pounds, the chief tool with which the labor was performed, have been found by cart-loads. They are either perfect, or are broken from use; and the fragments of large numbers of them are found intermingled with the debris on the edge of the pits, or at their bottom. These hammers are occasionally found grooved for the affixture of the handle, but are oftener without this adaptation. Tools made of copper, and consisting principally of chisels and knives, have also been taken from such of the pits as have been explored. Arrowheads of copper have also been picked up, both in the vicinity of the pits and scattered over the island, at the surface, as if lost in the chase. The tools, though injured from oxidation, appear to have been of fair workmanship, and were evidently hardened, apparently through the action of fire. With the exception of stone hammers, no other tools formed of stone have been observed."

After the copper was cracked free, the Indians hammered it into the shape they wanted. Then to reduce brittleness, they heated and chilled it, this probably serving as man's first use of the annealing process.

These mining methods were at least as good as any used elsewhere until the Middle Ages. The early North American Indians also displayed a broad knowledge of sound engineering methods. The explorers and copper prospectors of the region in the nineteenth century reported finding several huge chunks of copper raised off the bedrock and supported on cribwork in some of these ancient mine pits. In a number of cases, these copper lumps weighed many tons. One such prospector, Samuel Knapp, reported finding in 1848 a lump of solid copper ten feet long, three feet wide, and two feet thick, "weighing over six tons." (A nugget that size would actually weigh about sixteen tons.) Knapp said that the lump was raised on cribwork about five feet above the bedrock. He gave the location as a mine pit near the present village of Rockland, Michigan. The copper was supported, he said, on a platform of timber which had long since decayed to a mush, but dirt and debris continued to support the huge metal lump. How the Indians were able to lift such a mass several feet is a fascinating question suggesting, as it does, a sound working knowledge of pry bars, levers, and wedges. Of course, Knapp's tale may be exaggerated, and there is no knowing which Indians were responsible. Despite this, other finds by other searchers indicate that Knapp's story contained a kernel of truth and that the early Indians, from whatever period, were surprisingly good mining engineers. The great variety of weapons and utensils and the general excellence of workmanship are also astonishing when one considers that these Indians used only stones as anvils, stones as hammers, and stones as tools to shape the metal.

The ability of these Indians to mine and manufacture copper has led to many unwarranted conclusions about their other abilities and activities. One statement given wide currency is that prehistoric mining operations on Isle Royale would have taken ten thousand men a thousand years to perform. This is at best a moot question, better left unexplored. Another writer has estimated that five thousand ancient mine pits can be found in the copper regions around Lake Superior, but inasmuch as no one has ever carried out a careful survey, that estimate can be little more than a guess. One student did count about a thousand mine pits in the McCargoe Cove area of Isle Royale, which certainly indicates considerable prehistoric effort by the Indians—not to mention a fair amount by the student himself. At this date, however, no one knows how extensive the work actually was.

Another popular unsubstantiated story is that the copper was mined and shaped by a slave people, subjects of a strong and unified culture farther south. According to this version, none of these people stayed in the copper region for longer than a summer at a time, this being one way of accounting for the general lack of such cultural remains as dwelling and burial sites.

There is also a popular belief that Michigan copper from this early period has been found throughout the southwestern and southeastern United States, as well as in Central America. It is assumed that such copper implements, found in Georgia or New Mexico or Mexico, indicate an extensive system of early trade between the Old Copper Indians and other groups spread throughout the Americas. This seems highly unlikely. The world of the Old Copper Indians centered around Lake Superior and may have extended as far west as the Mississippi, northwest into central Manitoba, and east to eastern Ontario. They pushed south around Lakes Michigan and Huron, and perhaps entered peripheral areas around the other Great Lakes. Possibly tribes and bands traded within this locale, but there is no evidence that copper implements from that period ever found their way outside this defined region.

Living all around the Old Copper Indians at that time were other tribes known as the Boreal Archaic Indians, and their use of copper was much less extensive. Copper utensils found in other parts of North and Central America derive from later trade activity, probably carried on by the mound builders. That was a period of North American prehistory replete with earthworks, ceremonies, extensive trading and warring expeditions, and a well-defined social structure. It all grew and died hundreds of years before Columbus arrived on these shores.

Finally, there is an intriguing puzzle about a prehistoric townsite on the south shore of Isle Royale. In writing about his visit to the

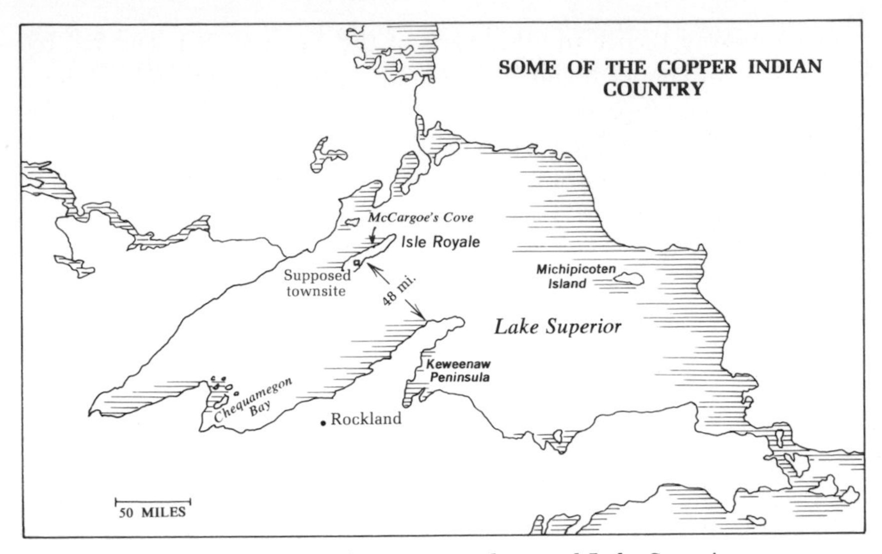

Mine sites and copper implements found around Lake Superior suggest that Indians mined the area as early as 4000 B.C. They may have carried the copper from mines on Isle Royale to the Keweenaw Peninsula on the south shore of the lake.

island in 1873, Henry Gillman told of seeing the remains of this ancient village:

"At an indentation of the coast on the south side of the island, where a stream about forty feet in width had cut a passage through the rocks, and formed quite a fall of water, was discovered what is taken to be the site of the town, or the habitations of these people. It occupies an elevated slope, giving an extensive view of Lake Superior, and overlooking the intervening point of land which makes the little bay an excellent harbor. The remains consist of a series of shallow excavations, generally about four feet in depth and occupying the successive terraces of the slope. Some of these pits are circular, others are quadrangular, and they vary from ten to thirty feet in diameter. Indications suggest that timber or bark was used in their construction, the soil being thrown up around them to a sufficient height. But time did not permit a satisfactory examination of this interesting locality, which, with other points on the island, it is hoped, will afford, on a thorough exploration, many valuable facts connected with the life of this remarkable people. They, doubtless, shipped the copper, the object of their toil, to the south shore of Lake Superior, the wonderful metal finding its way thence to other parts of the country, as is testified by the articles of copper found in the burial-places of the mound builders. This point, therefore, was well selected as a town-site. The good landing, the admirable harbor, the abundant stream and fall of water, the sheltered and yet commanding hillside, which enabled them to watch the departure and return of their copper-laden flotillas, were all strong recommendations even to these semi-savage inhabitants."

In 1923 William P. F. Ferguson also explored what he called an ancient townsite on the south shore of Isle Royale. With a work crew, he excavated five big pits and several smaller ones. He called them "pit dwellings," and wrote at length about subsurface walls of stone, fire platforms inside the foundations, and so forth. But J. B. Griffin, director of the Museum of Anthropology at the University of Michigan, has stated that he could find absolutely nothing of this nature at the site described by Ferguson. Griffin has worked on the island extensively since the late 1940's. George I. Quimby, formerly of Chicago Natural History Museum, who also spent considerable time on the island, agrees. Both men question whether in fact such a town ever existed, and suggest that both Gillman and Ferguson may have been victims of misinterpretation.

If a village site was established on the island, either at the location indicated by Gillman or elsewhere, it must almost certainly have only been used during the summer months. Winter's cold, the reduced availability of game, and the treacherous waters of surrounding Lake Superior would have prevented habitation of and traffic to the island during winter.

Yet even here there remain intriguing questions. What boats were used for the journey to this and other islands in the Great Lakes, and how were these waters navigated? One way to reach Isle Royale today is to take a large, diesel-powered National Park Service vessel from the Keweenaw Peninsula. The trip takes five hours, and the boat is detained frequently by the severe storms which rake that part of the lake. The north shore is closer to the island, can be seen from that shore, and was probably the jumping-off place for many prehistoric island excursions. But there is also good evidence that early navigators traveled the southern route, from the Keweenaw to the island and back again, as most visitors do today. How was this accomplished by these early peoples? As we shall see, the development of the bark canoe probably occurred quite early in this region, and was one of the chief influences in the history of the entire Great Lakes area.

Mound builders carrying dirt to a burial mound in slings, pouches, and baskets of bark and twigs about 2,000 years ago. Drawing by William E. Scheele.

Illustration from *The Mound Builders* by William E. Scheele (© 1960 by The World Publishing Company, Cleveland and New York)

3

High Culture and Strange Mounds

STARTING WITH THE EARLIEST NOMADS, man has lived in the Great Lakes region for more than thirteen thousand years, and for more than half that time he had only a few stone tools to aid him. Roaming continually in search of food, starving in winter, and hammered by the weather at all seasons, the earliest bison and mastodon hunters somehow managed to eke out an existence and hold on.

When the Old Copper Indians arose about 4000 B.C., they were able to make life easier through the use of copper implements, working this material into their culture. But the Old Copper people faded into history about 1100 B.C. Many moved north, as the sort of forest they were accustomed to retreated, following the glacier. Others were absorbed by other tribes around the Great Lakes, to the west and north. Old Copper tools and weapons also faded from sight about this time, and the use of copper declined.

In short, these people failed to profit from their ability to work metal. While metal was giving the Mediterranean peoples a powerful thrust toward modern life, the Old Copper Indians used it in traditional ways until even these values were lost, and the tribes themselves fell apart or disappeared. Perhaps the available supply of copper was exhausted, so that knowledge and methods of working it died out and were buried with the artisans of better days. In any case, with the decline of these people a distinctive phase of Great Lakes history ended; copper would not again be used for several centuries.

But as the steady action of the waves has changed the Lakes themselves, so have wave after wave of people changed the social history of the region. The rise and disappearance of the Old Copper Indians was only the first in a steadily quickening stream of tribes and peoples. Next came invasion by a new and vigorous people who built their own culture, lived many centuries, and like the Old Copper Indians also fell into decline. These groups were the various mound-building peoples.

The first speculations about who these people were came during the American colonial period, when early writings about our continent were interlarded with notes concerning the material found in the mounds. Among others, Thomas Jefferson excavated a mound, pondered its age, and called its creators "the Mound Builders." For many years the mound builders were generally believed to be a single ancient race of people, different from Indians, who disappeared long before the coming of the white man. Since the colonial period, hundreds of mounds in the eastern United States have been cut open, the land on which they stood has been systematically converted to real estate, and some confusion has been dispelled while more has been generated.

Experts are divided on the origin of the mound-building habit. Some say mound-building first developed in Asia, the practice coming to these shores with the early migrations. They point to the mounds found in eastern and northern Siberia. Pottery came from Siberia; the first Americans came from Siberia. Why not mounds also? Others theorize that mound-building originated in the Americas, that it is an ancient social activity indigenous to our hemisphere, that it occurred first in Mexico and Central America, where it became well developed, was imported into the southern, central, and eastern parts of the continent, and finally entered the Great Lakes region. They point to the pyramids of the Toltecs and Aztecs and Mayans in Mexico. All of those "mounds" are very old, far older than any in eastern or northern Asia and older than any found in this country.

Whatever the solution, it is clear that the first mound builders began to penetrate the Great Lakes region about 1,000 B.C., soon after the Old Copper peoples began to decline. Who these people were and where they came from originally is unknown. The first wave may have set out from the Mississippi and Illinois River valleys, and pushed eastward along the Ohio River. Groups of them gradually settled in Illinois, Indiana, and Ohio, where they were established by 800 B.C. They are sometimes known as the Adena people, Adena being the

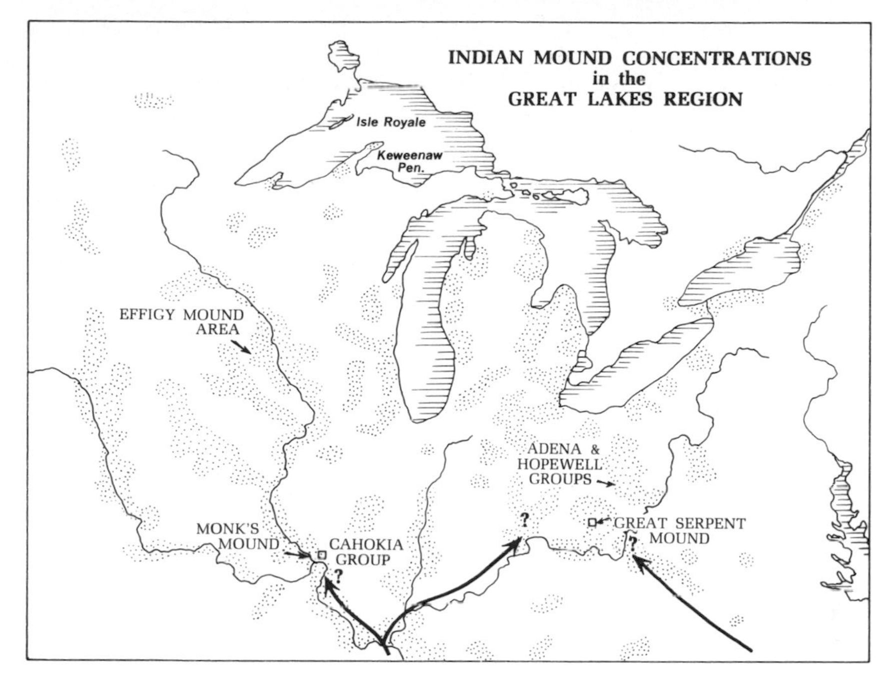

Mound-building peoples came to the region about 1000 B.C., *as the Old Copper Indians began to decline. They may have traveled along paths indicated by the arrows, but their actual origins are unknown. The first groups settled in Indiana, Illinois, and Ohio. Gradually the mound builders became established in all the states bordering the Lakes.*

name of the landowner of the property near Chillicothe, Ohio, where their mounds were first opened and studied.

A few centuries later, another invasion brought a new people to the region. These were the Hopewells, also a mound-building group, who soon established themselves in the Ohio River valley. (Like the term *Adena* in its origin, the name Hopewell is derived from the thirty-eight mounds excavated in Ross County, Ohio, on lands once owned by a Captain M. C. Hopewell.)

For centuries, the Adena-Hopewell mound builders flourished throughout the southern Great Lakes region, from the Mississippi east to western New York. Hundreds of mounds have been found in all the states and in those parts of southern Ontario bordering on the Great Lakes.

Some of the mounds were used for burials, these being generally round or conical in shape. Buried with the dead were found great quantities of axes, knives, pottery, stone utensils, baskets of seeds, ornaments of shell, bone, and copper. Presumably, these provided for the dead mound builders on their journey to whatever Nirvana these Indians envisioned.

The purpose of the other mounds is more speculative. The round burial mounds seldom measure more than twenty or thirty feet in height. But from St. Louis to the Gulf of Mexico are found far greater mounds that look like pyramids with their tops lopped off. Monk's Mound of the Cahokia group in Illinois is a hundred feet high and covers nearly sixteen acres, being larger at its base than the largest pyramid in Egypt. A path led up the sides of these mounds, and because some form of temple was apparently constructed atop them, the group are generally known as the temple mounds.

A third curious group, found mainly in southern Wisconsin, northern Illinois, and eastern Iowa, are the effigy mounds, which have been shaped to resemble birds in flight, snakes, deer, bears, turtles, eagles, and foxes. The largest of these is in southern Ohio, where the Great Serpent Mound wriggles along a creek for a quarter of a mile, averaging twenty feet in width and two to five feet in height. Effigy mounds were not usually used for burial, although the dead have been discovered, usually located at the head or heart of the animal depicted.

Mounded geometric embankments in the shape of hexagons, circles, squares, octagons, and semicircles have also been found. Some enclose as much as a hundred acres, and many surround the burial-mound clusters. Some of these embankments have been built with amazing precision. One circle mound in Ohio has a diameter of 1,045 feet, and is so nearly perfect that it diverges at most only four and a half feet from this diametrical distance. Other geometrical mounds were laid out with similar accuracy, yet these people are not known to have had any knowledge of mathematics.

Finally, there are a wide variety of ring mounds, platform mounds, fortification mounds, and so-called garden mounds. Scattered over the Great Lakes area, as well as elsewhere, they appear to have served a number of different purposes.

The various kinds of mounds probably represent the work of different tribes, all part of the mound-building culture that developed throughout the southern reaches of the Great Lakes. The tribes were similar but displayed some differences, as in the mound variations they created. Thus, it is misleading to think of all mound builders as Adena Indians or Hopewell Indians. What developed was an array of Adena-like, or Hopewell-like peoples who were not necessarily of the same tribal unity. Thomas Jefferson wrote of "the Mound Builders" as though they were a single, unified people, but they were probably not organized into a definite society. Very little is known about their wars, travels, and religious ceremonies, though much is surmised.

Of all the prehistoric groups to inhabit North America, only two have left substantial evidence of their cultures. These are the Pueblo peoples of the Southwest and the mound builders. Some magnificent cliff dwellings still exist and tell much about the Pueblos who built them. Their dwellings provided for shelter, protection, and communal activities—all purposes concerned with life itself. Their dead were given scant attention, often being buried in rubbish heaps. But the mound builders chose to emphasize death and the hereafter, and paid scant attention to life on earth. Where the Pueblos built dwellings of permanent stone and adobe, the mound builders used sticks, matting, skins, bark, and other flimsy materials. But for their tombs, the mound builders used more permanent matter: earth, most of all, but also stone and wood. Items of great value were buried in the mounds, draining the society of much wealth. Construction of the mounds themselves called for tremendous communal energy. Each community must have also supported a large class of priests and religious leaders, so of the total energy available to a mound-building community, a large percentage was engaged in satisfying the requirements for death and the life thereafter.

It is difficult to visualize the extent of this involvement, but some measure is shown by the amount of work required to build a single mound. One authority estimates that a hundred thousand mounds were built in twenty eastern states, and that the Ohio mounds alone contained thirty million cubic yards of earth. Little is known about where this earth came from, but presumably it was dug up somewhere not far from the mound sites. The flimsy baskets available to the mound builders could have held no more than twenty to twenty-five pounds, about one fourth of a cubic foot. Carrying such a load on his shoulders or in his arms, each man traveled on foot from supply to construction site. Digging at the supply point, placing the earth at the construction site, and returning for another load, all consumed time. Yet Monk's Mound in Illinois contained 2,500,000 cubic yards of earth, or 250,000,000 individual basket loads.

Though mound-building must have been an enormous drain on their energy, these people also found time to develop a variety of utensils, weapons, ornaments, clothing, and other items useful to them for purposes of life and death. They knew and used pottery widely, many excellent examples of their ware having been found. Generally, these pots are less than a foot high and range from open bowls to enclosed containers to bottles. Most are decorated, and many were used only in religious or burial ceremonies. All were constructed by rolling the clay into coils, then placing coil on top of coil until the desired height had been reached. The pot was then patted with the hand or a wooden paddle to join the coils together. As it dried, it was incised with decoration, and when thoroughly dry, it was baked to hardness, generally in an open fire. Crude kilns have also been found, but the principle of enclosed-atmosphere firing was not widely used.

Most of the mound builders' weapons were made of flint, argillite, obsidian, and other highly prized stones. How highly they themselves prized these materials may be measured by the distance they traveled to obtain them. Obsidian is found in North America only in the western mountain areas, such as Yellowstone Park. This is nearly two thousand miles from the Ohio Mound Builders and even farther from the more easterly groups, yet obsidian artifacts have been found throughout the eastern United States. Obsidian is a black stone that splits like glass and makes razor-sharp implements. There are two theories of how this material reached the mound builders: one is that it was traded from one tribe to another, reaching the most easterly tribes last; the second is that each tribe sent its own expeditions to Wyoming to carry home the supplies required. The expedition theory is generally favored, because obsidian was little used by peoples between Yellowstone and the mound-building area, thus tending to rule out the trade theory.

But if long expeditions were used, other abilities of these amazing people come to light. To gather such supplies as obsidian, they must have sent out expeditions to explore as well as to collect. They must have traveled in force for protection when invading new territory. They must have known how to travel guided by the sun, moon, and stars. And the whole idea of such expeditions suggests a people many stages removed from that of nomadic hunters who travel only so far as the need for food demands, or from a simple sedentary agricultural people who live in villages, hunting or farming only nearby territory.

Obsidian was not the only material obtained by the mound builders. In Isle Royale and northern Michigan they gathered copper, overlooked or unused by the Old Copper Indians. Sheet mica came from the mountains of North Carolina. Pearls, sea shells, and other marine forms were obtained from the Gulf of Mexico. Grizzly-bear teeth, only available in the Rockies, came from various sites in that area.

To gather these materials also required knowledge of mining, trapping, and collecting, as well as a knowledge of how to work them once they had been collected. Copper from Isle Royale was used for everything from axes to delicate tubes of curled sheet copper strung as ornaments on thongs or hair. Knives, mallets, awls, beads, needles, and other utensils were also made of copper in a surprising array of

Copper axes, awls, needles, and jewelry from burial mounds in lower Michigan and northern Indiana. The copper was mined near Lake Superior, then carried south by the mound builders.

Chicago Natural History Museum

sophisticated forms. These people even introduced inlay, decorating rings and helmets with pearls and mica. All this industry was accomplished by first cold-hammering the copper to the desired shape and thickness, then annealing it in open fires.

Sheet mica was mined to make magnificent ceremonial figures with human bodies, bird-claw hands, and stylized heads used for burial and religious purposes. Obsidian likewise was shaped into ceremonial knives and other tools buried with the dead. It was seldom used in military, hunting, or other daily activities. Skilled artisans created all these implements and artistic objects, many fine examples of their work having been found in the mounds. In all this work, a division of labor was practised, again attesting to the advanced state of these people. A man who made stone knives or arrowheads made them for the entire village. Some were priests; others, builders of mounds; still others traveled to collect the materials needed for the artisans.

But of all the arts and activities of these amazing people, agriculture was the most important single practice they brought to the Great Lakes region. Agriculture was new in the area, and was the key difference that allowed freedom for religion, crafts, and other activities. While Indian groups farther north continued their nomadic hand-to-mouth existence, the mound builders established permanent settlements and supplemented hunting and fishing with crops, setting aside enough dry food for times of need. Little is known of their actual farming methods, but they raised corn, beans, gourds, squash, melons, tobacco, and perhaps other crops as well. Their mainstay was probably flint corn, a kind of maize common at that time in Mexico and the American Southwest. It is not well suited to the Great Lakes region, but it evidently grew and they harvested enough to help them through the winter. Storage pits were dug outside the mound builders' dwellings, and successive layers of boulders, corn on the cob, shelled corn, twigs and bark, ashes, sand, and clay, and finally leaf mold were placed in the pits until filled to ground level. Farming was mainly along rivers in well-watered areas. Garden crops were supplemented by wild roots, nuts, and berries, as well as by food obtained from hunting and fishing.

These food-gathering methods were so successful that mound-building communities became quite permanent and developed sizable populations. In effect, it was agriculture that allowed the mound builders to live in small cities, to develop religious ceremonies and complex burial practices, to create a class system and division of labor.

Taken as a whole, the world the mound builders made for them-

The National Geographic Society. Courtesy *National Geographic Magazine.*

Effigy mounds in the shapes of sacred animals form curious patterns on the Midwestern landscape. The largest of these, the Great Serpent Mound in southern Ohio, curves along a stream for a quarter of a mile, averaging twenty feet wide and two to five feet high. Mounds of this type were seldom used for burial, though some have contained graves below the animal's head or heart.

selves comprised a virtual social revolution. They gained great control over their environment through agriculture, then turned their surplus energy to preoccupation with the soul and life after death. A glimpse into this past is seen in the Feast of the Dead, as practised by the Huron Indians of historic times. The Hurons and other indigenous Great Lakes tribes may have inherited such practices from the early mound builders. The ceremony, viewed by early French missionaries, was described by Father Brébeuf in 1636. The Hurons, he said, believed men's souls traveled to soul villages in the sky after their deaths, each going to a separate village according to his kind. Warriors killed in battle went to one village, old women and children to another, chieftains to a third. To assure the soul a swift and successful journey, the Huron practice was to place ordinary tribal members in bark coffins raised on wooden scaffolds several feet above ground. Warriors killed in battle were buried in a flexed position, their knees against their chest, in shallow graves. Children were buried on the trails between villages, so that their soul might find rebirth easily by rising up and entering some passing woman's body. Such methods of burial assured to each a proper destiny.

Once every eight or ten or twelve years, the whole Huron nation would celebrate the Feast of the Dead. At this time the bodies of all those who had died since the last feast were disinterred or taken down from burial scaffolds.

Father Brébeuf describes the scene: ". . . having opened the graves, they display all these corpses long enough for the spectators to learn what they will be some day. The flesh of some is quite gone, and there is only parchment on their bones; in other cases, the bodies look as if they had been dried and smoked, and show scarcely any signs of putrefaction; and in still other cases they are still swarming with worms. Finally, after some time, they strip them of their flesh, taking off the skin and flesh by handfuls which they throw into the fire along with robes and mats in which the bodies were wrapped. . . ."

After this, the cleaned bones were placed in beaver-skin bags or strung together as skeletons and dressed in fine robes and ornaments. All were then carried on a slow, ceremonial journey, perhaps lasting several days, to a central place for mass burial. There, a large grave was dug. The bones were hung on poles around the pit while lengthy rituals were conducted. Finally, all were buried together with a great quantity of robes, utensils, weapons, and ornaments of the finest quality.

The mound builders almost surely held similar ceremonies centuries earlier in at least roughly the same fashion. Other customary activities practiced by the Lakes Indians in historic times probably also originated with the mound builders; for example, the barbaric practices meted out to captives; tribal, religious ritual ceremonies; methods of hunting, fishing, and farming; a style of life based primarily on stone implements and weapons, and rudimentary agricultural methods.

The mound-building people seem somewhat too advanced and strangely out of place when viewed against the whole sweep of prehistory in the Great Lakes region. When their culture came to an end around A.D. 700, the mound builders left behind a legacy of social custom, arts, and artifacts which would never be developed to higher levels by any of the other tribes in the region. They attained a peak, a summit of Great Lakes Indian culture. Had they survived, they might have attained the level of civilization found among the Incans and Mayans. But the mound builders failed to survive, and their way of life, advanced as it was, gradually gave way to other groups. Perhaps famine or pestilence brought the end; perhaps an intrusion of new people from east and west caused their downfall, as some evidence indicates. Perhaps strains caused by an all-powerful priesthood or the burdens of mound-building proved too much, bringing on revolt and dissolution from within. For whatever reasons, the mound builders declined and left in their wake scattered tribal communities, agriculture, preoccupation with the dead, and thousands of mounds for later peoples to discover and excavate and view with wonder.

With the mound builders gone, the period from 800 to 1600 saw numerous new tribes inhabiting the area. These were divided into three major language blocs. In western Wisconsin and Minnesota, tribes speaking the Siouan language established themselves. On the eastern borderlands, around Lake Erie and Lake Ontario and up the St. Lawrence River valley, lived the tribes of the Iroquoian language bloc. Down through the center, including much of Ontario, Wisconsin, Michigan, Illinois, and Ohio were the Algonquians, one of the most widespread language groups in North America. These peoples, arranged in many different tribes, stretched solidly from Labrador on the Atlantic Coast to west of Hudson Bay and southward down the Mississippi River valley. They knew both Arctic tundra and the bayous of Louisiana. They farmed the river valleys of Illinois, of southern Michigan, and of Ohio; they hunted the woodlands of the northern Great Lakes.

Little is known of these people before 1600. Various tribal locations have been determined, but the early inhabitants are understood principally from the diversity of stone implements, pottery, dress, and other artifacts found by archeologists. Of their various travels, wars, alliances, social structure, and religion, little is known. Much, however, is surmised. The earliest white men on this continent made a haphazard collection of tribal legends, myths, and observations. Some students speculate that Indian legends heard in 1600 may refer to actual happenings that occurred as early as 1400. Perhaps so—but even this loophole does not permit much of a glimpse of these early people. Ultimately we are left with a period of eight centuries, a sort of Great Lakes Dark Ages, heavily marked by gaps and guesses. What little is known, however, is important.

The Siouan, Iroquoian, and Algonquian Indians were split into a dozen or more tribes in the Great Lakes region long before the whites arrived. With numerous exceptions noted, the tribes of a given language bloc did not steadily war on each other. Confederations of tribes which were common by the early historical period were probably equally common in the prehistoric period also. Most of their methods of warfare, travel, torture, agriculture, and religion probably came from earlier indigenous tribes in the region. Others came with the early Iroquois peoples who moved from the southeastern U.S. north into the Alleghenies, differing in many respects from the mound builders and their descendants. And finally, some of the practices and activities found by white explorers were devised by Indians then living as a result of environmental pressures.

About a hundred thousand Indians were living in the Great Lakes area in 1600, at the opening of the historical period. This represents 10 to 15 per cent of all Indians living on the continent north of Mexico. The population was thus generally light, ranging from one person every two square miles around Green Bay to one every twelve square miles south of Lake Michigan.

Agriculture was common in the southern reaches of the Lakes region, while hunting, fishing, and other food-gathering practices continued in the northerly areas. Travel was by dugout or by birchbark canoe in those areas where the paper birch tree was to be found. Elmbark canoes were used where birch trees were less available, especially among the Iroquois in New York. In the winter, travel in deep-snow areas was on snowshoes, so that hunting and trapping could continue.

When the white explorers arrived, the Five Nations of the Iroquois already had formed into their confederacy, standing solidly in command of western New York and parts of southern Ontario. The Algonquian tribes, meanwhile, occupied the middle ground; the Siouans held the western flank of the Lakes.

This, then, was the scene when the white man arrived. The people in the Lakes country were living in fair harmony with the land. Theirs was a scene more of industry and peace than of war and desolation.

The richness of legends, the complexity of religious rites and ceremonies, the extent of handicrafts, and the expansion of agriculture—all tell of a time when existence, if not rich, was endurable. The tribal lands were held by virtue of force, a pattern of ownership maintained by incessant small raids, but this sort of warfare did not cause much change in the amount of land a tribe controlled. In effect, it produced balance and stability.

It is interesting to speculate how our national history might have changed if the earlier mound builders had unified and maintained control over this area. When Pizarro invaded the Incan empire in the 1530's, he captured that entire nation with a few men simply by conquering the central religious and governmental leaders. Had a centralized religion and government dominated the Lakes peoples, the whole area might similarly have fallen under control of the first French or British or Dutch colonizers to arrive—with drastic significance for our national destiny. As it was, the mound builders went the way of history and left behind various small tribes. These were not completely dominated until white settlers, carrying firearms and themselves closely knit together, came in sufficient numbers to subdue them. The Indian tribes joined the English or Dutch or French side of the fight, or they warred on one another. They never really took their own side in a unified fight against the whites. They suffered mightily from the white man's smallpox. But their presence did help keep the political situation fluid for nearly two centuries.

It is to that feuding tribal atmosphere that we now turn, a time of violence among Indians and of national rivalry among whites, a time that saw Indian turned against Indian while the white man conquered all through smallpox, whiskey, trinkets, and religion. The Indians of the Great Lakes seemed bent on self-destruction during the seventeenth and eighteenth centuries, while the white men pushed steadily deeper into the continent. The white men generally preferred to keep the Indians alive for use as guides, trappers, traders, and mercenaries. The French missionaries, particularly the Jesuits and Recollects, also tried to eliminate Indian warfare, torture, and sacrifice. They wanted to stabilize the population for conversion to Christianity.

But the Great Lakes Indians during the seventeenth and eighteenth centuries seemed almost methodically bent on destroying themselves. Tribes fought pitched battles against one another, and the steady encroachment of the white man's ways undermined the old life. By 1650 the decline and fall of the Great Lakes Indians was already in sight.

In this seventeenth-century drawing, by a Frenchman who traveled to the New World, the hunter looks more like a cupid than a brave, walks on snowshoes, and tracks down "elks" with very large horns.

Baron de Lahontan, *New Voyages to North-America*

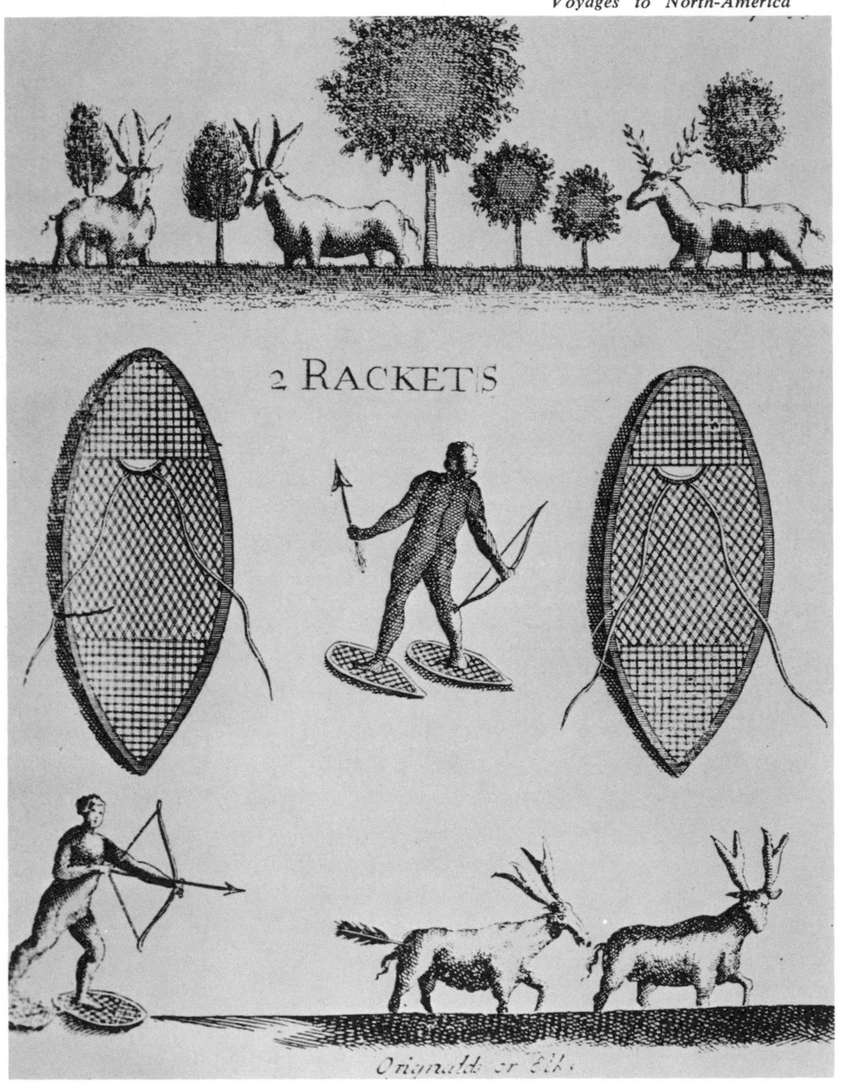

4

The Savage Life

THE AMERICAN INDIAN of the Great Lakes region survived only two centuries of contact with the white man; then he was swept aside and his way of life forgotten.

Those two centuries, from 1600 to 1800, saw a series of desperate struggles for control of the new continent. On the Great Lakes and in the forests that surrounded them, the Dutch fought the British, and together they fought the French. Farther south, all three fought the Spanish. These wars continued for scores of years in many corners of North America. Meanwhile, the fledgling United States grew slowly stronger as the European nations exhausted themselves. The basis for the colonies' success in the Revolutionary War began to take shape a hundred years before Concord and Bunker Hill. It gained momentum on the Great Lakes, down the Mississippi, in the Gulf of Mexico, on the treacherous waters of Hudson Bay.

Almost overlooked in this struggle was the life of the resident Indian, a pagan, brutal, and sometimes beautiful pattern of human activity. To the white man, the Indian was viewed mainly as an obstacle to national ambitions. The Indians lived a fleeting and precarious existence, seeming by contrast to the Europeans both bizarre and unreal. Their lives were steeped in superstition. Where our Midwestern cities now stand, strange rituals and fantastic tortures took place. Though anthropologists have reconstructed the Indian way of life, the white man's history is often the only one seen or heard.

The Indian position during the seventeenth and eighteenth centuries was pivotal between French, English, and Dutch. Their supply of

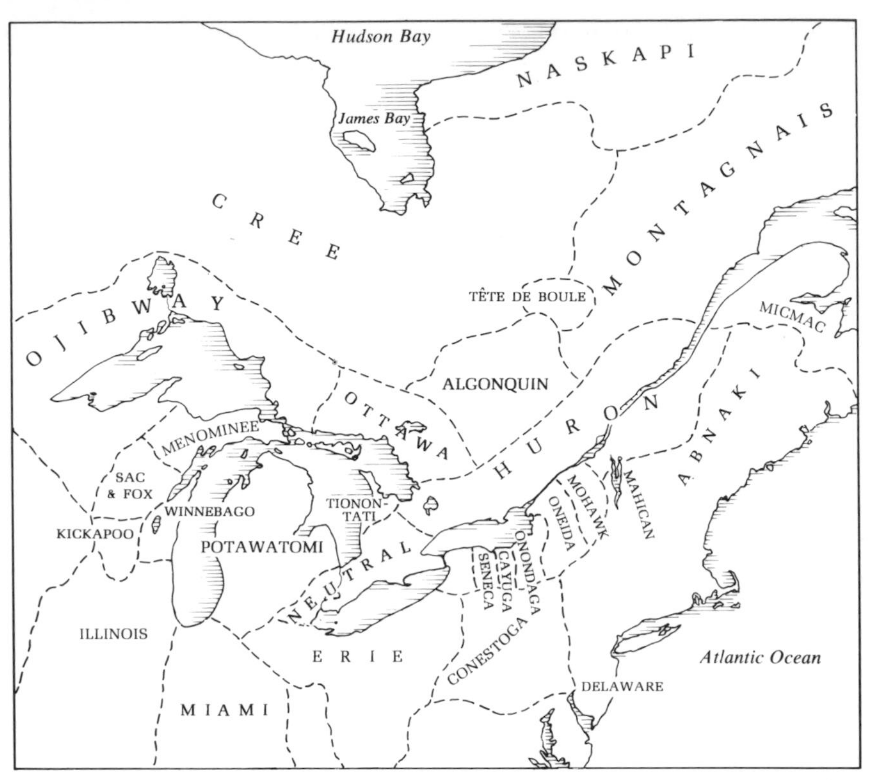

Location of Indian tribes, A.D. *1600. At the time of the coming of the white man, more than 100,000 Indians populated the area.*

furs was one of the main prizes to be won. Theirs was the land on which the wars were staged and battles lost. The Indians long held the balance of power during the early years of settlement, even though that power was seldom used with much effect.

When the first Europeans arrived, around 1520, they found Indians living in a jigsaw pattern of interrelated but independent tribes. Each controlled a certain segment of land. A balance of power was in force, crudely and not without frequent challenges, but it was there.

No one knows how long this situation had existed. But by 1600 many of these tribes had sizable populations, indicating that a general state of peace and growth must have prevailed for some time. The tribes, the area they commanded, and their populations at the time of the white man's arrival have been estimated as follows:

ALGONQUIAN PEOPLES OF THE GREAT LAKES REGION

Tribe	*Land Area*	*Population*
Algonquin, Ottawa	78,900 sq. mi.	7,300
Potawatomi	35,500 sq. mi.	4,000
Menominee	9,800 sq. mi.	3,000
Sac (or Sauk) and Fox	12,000 sq. mi.	6,500
Kickapoo	5,900 sq. mi.	2,000
Ojibway (Chippeway)	140,000 sq. mi.	33,000
Miami	48,000 sq. mi.	4,500
Illinois	118,300 sq. mi.	9,500
TOTAL	448,400 sq. mi.	69,800

IROQUOIAN PEOPLES OF THE GREAT LAKES REGION

Tribe	*Land Area*	*Population*
Seneca, Cayuga, Onondaga, Oneida, Mohawk — The Five Nations	28,300 sq. mi.	5,500
Erie	38,600 sq. mi.	4,000
Neutral	29,000 sq. mi.	10,000
Conestoga (Susquehanna)	27,100 sq. mi.	5,000
Tionontati (Tobacco Huron), Huron (Wyandot)	53,700 sq. mi.	18,000
TOTAL	176,700 sq. mi.	42,500

SIOUAN PEOPLES OF THE GREAT LAKES REGION

Tribe	*Land Area*	*Population*
Winnebago	5,400 sq.mi.	3,800

Some Santee Dakota Indians of the Siouan Language group were also found in western Wisconsin, but most of their range was west of the Mississippi.

In the northern reaches of the Great Lakes, the Indian supported himself by hunting, fishing, and gathering berries, nuts, and roots. Farther south, fish and game were supplemented by planted crops.

For some Indians, particularly the Iroquois, agriculture became extremely important. The Iroquois raised fifteen varieties of corn, sixty kinds of beans, eight sorts of squash, in addition to tobacco and probably other foods as well. Their cornfields sometimes stretched for miles along streams, the corn growing to a man's height, with squash planted between the rows. The kinds of corn grown included flint, dent, flour, and pop, with flint and flour corn producing several colors of seed.

The men cleared the fields by slashing and burning, but it was the women who did the actual planting. Partly this was because they believed that women's reproductive powers were magically transmitted to the crops, partly because in the Iroquois world the women owned the fields. Planting started in early spring. For corn, the earth was hilled to help the roots take hold—a practice the early colonists learned from the Indians. Several seeds, usually four, were planted in each hill. "One for the beetle, one for the crow, one for the cutworm, and one to grow" was an old Northeastern saying muttered by farmers and farmers' sons in the days before modern equipment ended hand-planting. Some speculate that the saying originated with the Indians and was transferred to the colonists along with the corn.

Indian farming areas in the Great Lakes country included much of western New York, Ohio, the Lower Peninsula of Michigan, Indiana, Illinois, Wisconsin, and parts of Minnesota. Southern Ontario between Lakes Huron, Erie, and Ontario was also used extensively. The Indians obtained a large portion of their food from these lands, most of which are still under cultivation today. Besides providing sustenance, farming tended to stabilize tribes within a given area—a fact that augured well for peace and the increase of population. Farther north, where short seasons prevented cultivation of crops, Indians continued to live by hunting and gathering. This kept them on the move and also worked to check population growth.

Apart from these differences, the tribes around the Great Lakes had many points in common. Everyone depended on the canoe for transportation, so travel routes normally followed the water closely. The Great Lakes, for example, were heavily traveled. When the white man arrived, the main weapon was the bow and arrow, which probably had been known to the Indians for about a thousand years. Many religious rites and ceremonies were observed, most based on worship of ancestral or animal spirits. A widespread reverence for the dead was observed.

Where the snow was deep in winter, snowshoes were commonly used. Implements and weapons were made of stone or bone, copper having nearly disappeared from the region. Pottery was used as it had been for centuries, although decoration was less ornate than on the pots of the mound builders. Universally, the Europeans stated that deer and beaver were hunted or trapped for meat and hides, and that fish were either hooked or speared, or caught in nets and weirs. In the single term "deer" they included moose, elk, and white-tailed deer. Technically, of course, moose and elk are members of the deer family, but current popular usage separates the three. And depending on locale, the Indians trapped or hunted a wide variety of other animals and birds.

For dwellings, the Great Lakes Indians built several kinds of bark- or skin-covered structures. The long houses of the Iroquois were often one hundred feet in length and housed from eight to ten families. These contrasted with the small, circular wigwams of the Algonquian tribes, generally housing only one family. The long houses were a framework of poles lashed together and covered with elm bark or woven reeds. When occupied, fires were built down the center of these large dwellings, one fire for every two families. The smoke was supposed to rise through holes in the roof, although we learn from the Jesuit missionaries that this was more the exception than the rule, more theory than practice. Smoke, the Jesuits reported, was one of the three major horrors of life in the long house, the other two being dogs and noise.

The wigwams of the Algonquians were dome-shaped, the circular framework being made of saplings set firmly in the ground so that the tops could be bent in toward the center and lashed together. This frame was covered with bullrushes, cattails, grasses, cedar bark, or birchbark, or some combination of these. A hole in one side allowed entrance, and a smoke hole was left at the top.

But if the physical world of the Great Lakes Indians was simple enough, the spirit world was not. In the realm of fantasy, the Indian displayed vast imaginative powers and produced remarkable visions and superstitions. *Gluskabe*, or *Gloscap*, a mythical benefactor of mankind, made the world fit to live in, but he could also play tricks and jokes on deserving Indians. Not so friendly was *Witigo*, a cannibal monster who lived in the forest, ate lone hunters, then spat them out to rove and ravage the land as cannibals. Longfellow took the name Hiawatha for his Indian hero from northern Michigan, the land of

Gitchi-Gumi, but the real Hiawatha was an Iroquois leader. He it was who traveled from tribe to tribe, urging the Five Nations to unite. Legend adds that he combed snakes from the hair of Atatarho, a fierce Onondaga leader; by this he won Atatarho's support and assured the unity of the confederacy.

Such tales were part of the spirit world of the Great Lakes Indians, a world peopled with many diverse elements. Two streams of spiritual thought were evident, with the farming Indians preferring one and the hunting Indians the other. The Iroquois and other agricultural Indians had a class of religious officials who led ceremonies, generally at prescribed times of year. But the northern hunting Indians made a wide use of dreams and visions; their shamans induced trances to bring success in hunting or fishing or to restore health. The Iroquois also placed great stock in dreams, but the communal nature of their ceremonies differed from the individualistic rites of the hunting Indians. Some leaders from both groups worked as individuals, but others organized into secret societies with memberships carefully restricted. Two of the most interesting were the Midewiwin, or the Grand Medicine Society, of the Algonquians and the False-Face Society of the Iroquois.

The Midewiwin, as it was called by the Indians, originated among the Ojibway, then spread to the Winnebago, and then to the other neighboring tribes. It had an extremely secretive and complex structure, with various grades for initiates. Symbolic drawings on birchbark had meanings known only to the membership. Part of the ritual called for members to dance around a mat-covered lodge, alternately "killing" and reviving each other with various magic objects. One scholar believes the Midewiwin developed after the first French missionaries arrived among the Algonquians and that Indian leaders used it to oppose Christianity with their own brand of spirits. Overtones of Christian beliefs are apparent in the Winnebago Midewiwin. Their ritual supposedly gave eternal life through the soul's transmigration. Also, their main religious figure was Earthmaker, the Giver of Life, "who loved us and therefore brought us into connection with life."

The False-Face Society of the Iroquois tried to cure sickness or break evil spells cast over tribal members. The Iroquois believed that evil spirits lived in the forest, ghoulish heads without bodies, the so-called False Faces. Sometimes these spirits caught Indians walking in the woods, causing sickness or spells of madness. To break such a hold, the Iroquois developed their False-Face Society. The society included certain tribal members who carved magnificent wooden masks in the likeness of the False Faces. These masks were worn during ceremonial dances to break evil spells. The False-Face Society also held a mid-winter festival, a kind of New Year's ceremony, usually taking place toward the end of January. This ceremony involved a contest between the spiritual Master of Life who desired spring to return for his people and an enemy who opposed its coming. The entire tribe took part, with members of the False-Face Society dancing their strange ritual in the winter night. The Iroquois also believed that dreams had special significance during this ceremony, and all present were encouraged to tell theirs publicly. During the year dreams were told only to chosen experts in strict confidence, lest secrets and personal desires be betrayed. Dancing, feasting, playing games, and clowning accompanied the festival, the whole often lasting several days. Winter's end was approaching when this ceremony was held, giving everyone a boost toward the long-awaited springtime.

Confederations of tribes were common among the Great Lakes Indians. Algonquians confederated against Iroquoians, and Siouans against Algonquians. Within each language group, alliances formed against other tribes of the same language. Most were loosely held agreements, often rupturing over minor slights. But the one that survived many years and proved its worth against every opponent was the League of the Great Peace, commonly called the Five Nations of the Iroquois. The Five Nations were by all odds the most influential Indian group in the Great Lakes region. Had it not been for this great alliance, our national language today might well be French. As a force in history, this confederation made the crucial difference as to whether the empires of France or Britain would gain control in the eighteenth century.

The Five Nations was probably a new confederation in 1600. Some speculate that it was not even formed until after that date. The alliance included five small tribes strung out along the hills of what is now western New York State, as if in a great open-air long house. In Iroquoian terms, the Mohawks at the eastern door, held "the place of flint"; next to them came the Oneida, "of the boulder"; and in the center, keepers of the central flame, were the Onondaga, "on the hills." (The Onondaga were the largest in number and the most influential.) Next came the Cayuga "of the marsh"; and finally the keepers of the western door, the Seneca, the "great hill people." These five tribes maintained a working military alliance for more than a century. They developed a new method of mass-attack warfare, and used it to

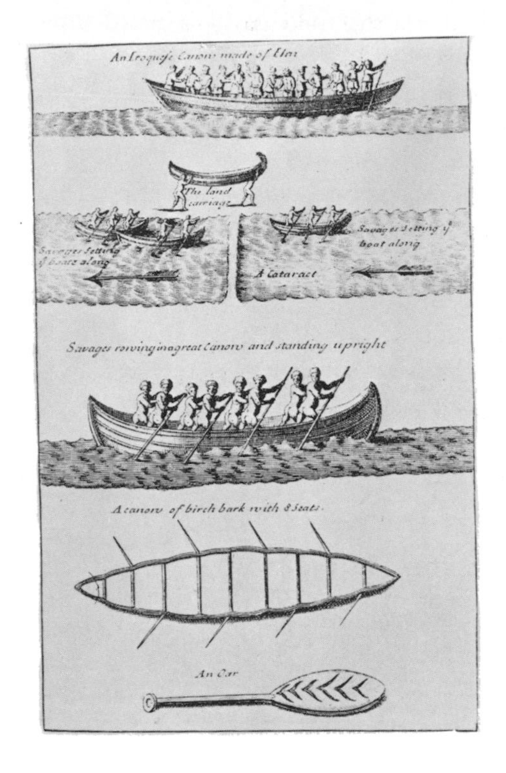

Indians of the Great Lakes region. French adventurer Baron de Lahontan drew this fanciful sketch of Indian canoes in Canada in the late seventeenth century. The top canoe was supposedly made of elm, common among the Iroquois who lived outside the area of the birch tree. The bottom canoe is the more familiar birchbark version.

Baron de Lahontan, *New Voyages to North-America*

conquer nearly the entire Great Lakes region. In the early years, they suffered several defeats, but they learned their lesson well, and by the 1640's the towering strength of this league was able to lay waste to the territory of every opponent. The Iroquois were never large in total population, but what they lacked in numbers, they made up in ferocity. Their most serious failure was never against an enemy; it was in underestimating the designs of their white allies, the British.

This powerful federation provided most of the grisly history of war and torture that fills the journals of the first traders and missionaries. The Iroquois were without question the best warriors in the region. At first they struck in small raiding attacks—a principle of warfare known to all the Great Lakes tribes. Although these sporadic ambushes and retaliations seldom produced much change in tribal dominance, they did provide warriors with their chief interest in life—proof of personal courage in combat. Warriors might kill an enemy or take him prisoner or—a very high act of courage—simply touch him on his own home ground and then escape. All warriors carried the bow and arrow for ambush attacks, but the Iroquois were also renowned in-fighters. They liked to use the tomahawk—a word borrowed from the Algonquian—to bash in enemy skulls—usually Algonquian. Iroquois warriors also had matted reeds or woven sticks as armor and carried wooden shields for protection. In enemy territory, the Iroquois frequently resorted to ambush, and describing the Iroquois on the warpath, one French explorer said: "They approach like foxes, fight like lions, and disappear like birds." These were very different tactics from those learned by the white invaders in Old World military academies.

The torture of prisoners is described frequently in writings of the period. The *Jesuit Relations*, in particular, are spiced with gruesome narratives. The Europeans generally deplored torture and often tried to prevent it but were seldom successful. They tended to regard torture merely as unnecessary barbarism, overlooking the part it played in the whole Indian way of life.

Usually after a raid only men were tortured, though if no men were captured, women might be used. However, women and children taken captive were usually given to families who had lost sons or husbands, and they were then considered to be members of the family. Such an adoption was accepted for life, and when children grew to adulthood, they were expected to fight as tribal members. Even men were sometimes adopted and kept alive to replace lost family members.

The Iroquoian tribes seemingly were more brutal than the Algonquians, but both groups tortured their prisoners. Among the Iroquois a prisoner often had his fingernails pulled out or his fingers cut off as soon as he was captured. His captors would next slash his shoulders and back, then bind him and lead him to their village. It was suggested that he sing during this journey, and bravery demanded that he try, though his fate was certain and known to him. Outside the village, he would be stripped naked and made to run the gauntlet of villagers brandishing thorny clubs, knives, tomahawks, firebrands, and other weapons.

After entering the village, he was ceremonially adopted into a family that had lost a member to the enemy. The women of that and other families then were placed in charge of the torture. The victim might be spared for several days or might be tortured soon after capture. When the time came, he might again be made to run the gauntlet inside one of the long houses. Firebrands or hot hatchets were then forced into his wounds. His fingers, if any were left, would be crushed or cut off. Later, tied to a stake or low platform, the captive would

Michigan Historical Commission and the Great Lakes Historical Society

Building a dugout canoe. Long before the arrival of the white man, Indians traveled the Great Lakes in canoes. This engraving shows how they burned down trees, then gouged and burned them into hollow shapes.

have the skin removed from the top of his head and hot pitch poured on the opening. If he fainted, the torturers stopped and revived him with water, then again repeated the process. Women, who were judged the more expert torturers by the observant Jesuits, were often very solicitous in their comments. Saying "Are you cold, my son?" or "Here, let me warm you," they would then place a torch under the victim's armpit. They often cut off strips of his skin, cooked it before his eyes, then made him eat it. Tradition required that he do so with stoical bravery. The tortured Indian tried to avoid crying out, for supposedly this would bring misfortune to his captors. If he could curse them, this too would add to the woe of his tormentors.

After the cutting and burning had proceeded as long as possible and the victim seemed near death, the consumption of his flesh got under way in earnest. However, it was important that the victim be finally killed by the knife, and at the end he was cut into pieces before he died otherwise. All then took part in a cannibalistic feast, and if he had been particularly brave, the Indians ate his heart and blood. The head itself might make a separate feast for the village chief.

This grim activity has often been considered to be a form of religious ceremony. The Iroquoian tortures have been compared to those of pre-Columbian Mexico, with similarities noted between the two including cardiac emphasis, knife-inflicted death, cannibalism, use of a platform for torture, and sacrifice to a sun- or war-god. It also has been suggested that the ferocity of the women resulted from the tensions of long-house-life, from the prolonged absences of husbands and sons, and from the drudgery of their daily tribal existence. Whatever the modern explanation, the use of torture was obviously widespread, embedded deep in the Indian way of life, and having enough similarities from tribe to tribe so that a pattern or ritual seems to have existed. The victim also knew his role and his fate. He had viewed the same activities in his own village, and he knew he must turn the tables on his tormentors by showing as much courage as he could summon.

When the white man arrived, his deepest early penetration into the continent was made in bark canoes along the chain of Great Lakes and the Ottawa River. He moved from the St. Lawrence River directly inland, reaching the Mississippi in a relatively short time. Samuel de Champlain, Etienne Brulé, and some of the Jesuit missionaries—if not other Frenchmen as well—had seen two and possibly three of the Great Lakes by 1615. Brulé may have seen western Lake Superior by 1618, a point nearly half the distance across our continent.

All this wide-ranging travel was made possible by the canoe. Europeans first saw this frail and flimsy craft along the St. Lawrence. On the Great Lakes it earned comment in most of the early journals, proving so able that a kind of mythology grew up around it, persisting in popular belief to this day. Perhaps because white men first saw the bark canoes around the Great Lakes, they assumed that it was indigenous to the Great Lakes Indians. Actually, the bark canoe had its origins elsewhere and was brought to the Lakes by early migrants.

Just where and when the idea of a canoe came to man is unknown. It may have occurred to many primitive peoples, scattered over the globe and the centuries. The earliest-known version was the dugout, used by prehistoric lake dwellers in Europe. Egyptians used the canoe form for their papyrus arks, papyrus being a reedy hollow-stemmed plant. A vague Chinese record of 2000 B.C. carries the notion that every form of boat was derived from the log dugout. Greeks and Romans around the time of Christ copied the form of the Egyptian ark, and their vessels were basically canoe-shaped.

But while the earliest examples were found in Europe, the canoe almost certainly came to our hemisphere from Asia, during the migrations that began two hundred centuries before Columbus arrived in the Caribbean. By then canoes apparently were being used everywhere in this hemisphere, from the Arctic north to southernmost South America. Columbus saw log dugouts and heard the Caribbean peoples call them *canow* or *cano.* He took the word home as *canoe*, and it went through Europe, and later came back to North America, as *caano, cano, canno, canoo, cannoe*, and *canoe*. The latter form finally became fixed in the English language; a bastardized form of a South American Arawak Indian word, it had nothing to do with the Algonquian or Iroquoian Indians. Both the word and the canoe itself are therefore immigrants, neither originating in North America as is frequently believed.

Here in the Great Lakes region, we have grown accustomed to the Chippeway birchbark canoe as a prototype or model for all canoes. But around the world and over the centuries, canoes have been built from all manner of trees, tree barks, reeds, leaf bundles, and skins. Sizes may vary from a one-man shell less than ten feet long to a double log dugout a hundred feet long.

In its heyday, the Great Lakes Chippeway canoe came in two basic sizes. The fifteen- to eighteen-foot family or hunting canoes were most numerous, and served as models for today's popular metal canoes. A second and larger version was used for freight or for carrying large

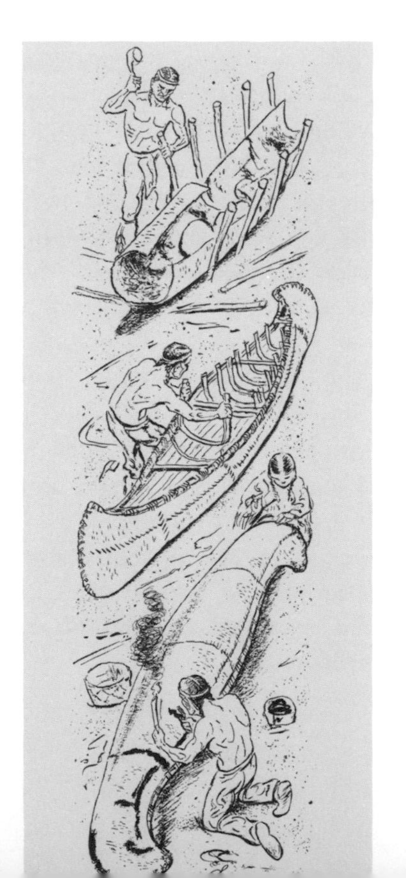

More advanced in construction, the Chippeway hunting canoe was seen most frequently on rivers and small lakes. It was made from sections of birchbark, supported by stakes, then fitted to a wooden framework. Seams were sewn with roots or wood fiber and sealed with tree pitch.

Michigan Conservation magazine

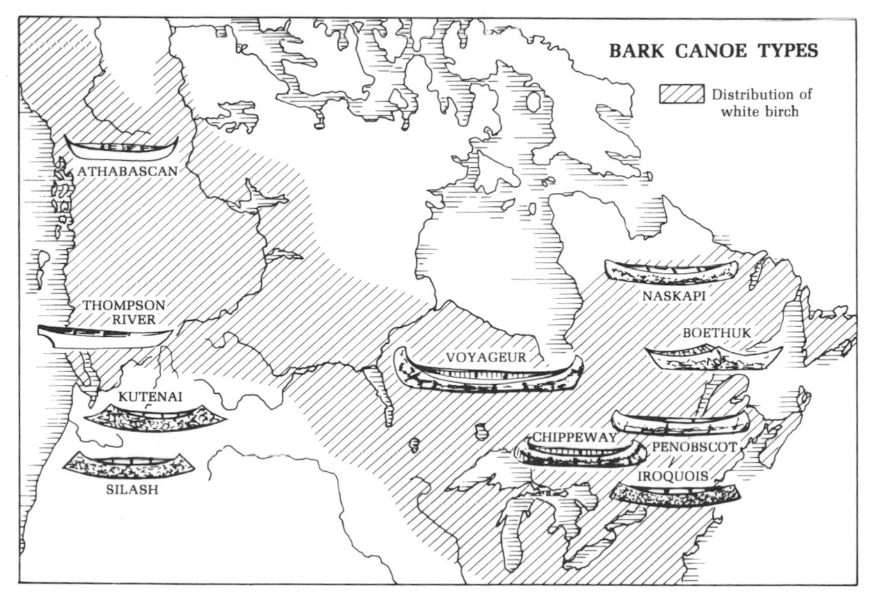

Indians navigated the inland waterways of North America in many sizes and types of canoe. Above are characteristic bark canoes of the region.

war parties. The family or hunting canoe was most commonly seen on rivers and smaller lakes. It portaged easily—one man could handle it—was easy to build, could be loaded heavily, and needed but a few inches of water for passage. The bigger canoe was more frequently used on the open Great Lakes, often holding several tons of freight or carrying fifty or more warriors. These canoes had higher sides and were much longer, possibly thirty-five to forty-five feet.

With the coming of the white man, the tapestry of Indian culture was irreparably rent. Primitive man first came to this continent some twenty-five thousand years ago. He found his way to the Great Lakes by 11,000 B.C. From 4000 to 1100 B.C he found and used copper in the Lake Superior region. From 1100 B.C. to A.D. 800 he developed a higher culture, with burial and religious mounds, art, and agriculture. From 800 to 1600 he diversified into tribes and clans, keeping ways of life learned over the centuries and slowly adding to the whole. But now, within two and a half centuries, the white man crushed all this, scattered the Indians, took what was useful, and destroyed the rest. A whirlwind was coming among these people—and they thought it was only a few white men bringing trinkets, axes, and whiskey. Naturally, the period opened with scenes of welcome.

For more than a half century scholars have debated the authenticity of a thirty-inch stone found near Kensington, Minnesota. This tablet, known as the Kensington Rune Stone, bears a crude Scandinavian inscription and is dated A.D. *1362. Together with some rusted weapons found nearby, it is the basis for claims that Vikings penetrated the continent as far as western Lake Superior.*

Drawing by Charles Schafer

5

A New World Beckons

NO ONE KNOWS for certain who were the first white explorers to reach the Great Lakes. The evidence is still so fragmentary and controversial that the truth may be forever out of reach. The first problem concerns the Vikings. Despite heroic efforts by some to prove that the Vikings came to the Lakes first, an equally industrious group has charged, often with passion, that such a notion is absurd. This controversy has bubbled around the west end of Lake Superior for more than half a century and is one of those fascinating, if fiery, arguments that may never be settled.

The dispute centers around a tablet of stone bearing a runic inscription, several rusted axes, halberds, "fire steels," a sword, and a few other items of metal. The inscribed stone, known as the Kensington Rune Stone, is roughly rectangular in shape; it stands about three feet high and is sixteen inches wide and five or six inches thick. The various pieces of metal were found at several points in west-central Minnesota, where the Kensington Stone was also discovered. A Viking-type sword, an ax, and a shield boss or handle were supposedly found a few miles east of Lake Nipigon on the north side of Lake Superior. The heart of this controversy is the Kensington Rune Stone itself, the subject of several books and much vexatious discourse. The inscription, which is hacked into the stone in a crude form of Norse-Swedish, reads:

We are 8 Goths [Swedes] and 22 Norwegians on [an] exploration journey from Vinland round about the west. We had camp by [a lake with] 2 skerries [islets] one day's journey north from this stone. We were [out] and fished one day. After we came home [we] found 10 of our men red with blood and dead. AVM [Ave Virgo Maria] save us from evil. We have 10 men by the sea to look after our ships, 14 days journey from this island. Year 1362.

This stone was discovered in 1898 by Olaf Ohman, a farmer living near the village of Kensington, Minnesota. He said he found it entangled in the roots of an aspen tree, which he had removed in clearing a portion of his land. Ohman carted the stone into town and for some time it stood in the window of the town bank, where it gained fame as a local attraction. Word of it spread, and the stone became the subject of several sensational newspaper stories. A copy of the inscription was sent to Scandinavian scholars who translated it and unanimously denounced the whole thing as a crude hoax. After this verdict was published, the stone was lugged back into obscurity; it lay forgotten in farmer Ohman's barnyard for nearly nine years.

Then Hjalmar R. Holand, an historian and antiquarian, heard of the stone while traveling in the region. He visited Ohman, and after much discussion, the farmer gave the stone to Holand, thus launching a search and a study that have spanned half a century, taken Holand to Scandinavia several times, and resulted in several books. Throughout all this time and labor, Holand has never entertained any doubt about the Kensington Stone, believing fully that a party of Vikings penetrated to the Lake Superior region in 1362, and that they were probably severely mauled, if not wiped out, by resident Indians during this journey. He supports this view with a vast array of physical evidence and speculation, forcefully convincing the reader that Columbus has been falsely named the discoverer of the Western Hemisphere.

Holand believes that these first white explorers—all devout Christians—came on a sort of western crusade to discipline a group of apostate Norsemen, said to have entered North America somewhere west of Greenland. Of the apostate Norsemen, nothing further is known, but according to Holand, the crusaders, searching for their countrymen, sailed into Hudson Bay, coasted south into James Bay, and continued on along rivers and lakes to the Lake Superior region. It is indeed true that a line drawn from southern James Bay to the Kensington Rune Stone's location passes near the north shore of Lake Superior, and such a route, Holand believes, was used for this fourteenth-century Viking journey.

Evidence opposing the stone's authenticity is quite overwhelming but not conclusive. Certain early chronicles in Scandinavia indicate that such a mission to the west was planned, but none says that it was ever carried out. Most scholars simply dismiss the expedition on the grounds of improbability. They concentrate their attacks on the inconsistencies in Holand's work and particularly on the vagueness surrounding the Kensington Rune Stone's discovery. They point to conflicting statements about the size and age of the aspen tree under which the stone was supposedly discovered, the location of the tree in Ohman's field, the lack of suitable witnesses, the fact that flecks of metal were found in the stone's chiseled inscription. They claim that a book of runic characters was available in the Kensington neighborhood and conclude by calling the whole affair a crude attempt to validate the Vikings as the first discoverers of America.

Holand fields all these charges with swift-footed ease. Concerning the aspen tree and the stone's discovery, he simply obtained affidavits from all those concerned, then fitted them into the story he has presented. The microscopic flecks of metal, he states, came from a nail that Ohman used to clean dirt out of the text. The question of a local book of runic characters is at best circumstantial evidence and proves nothing. Holand characterizes Ohman as a farmer of modest education and notes that even American runic experts were uncertain what to say about the text, until they sent copies to Scandinavia for evaluation. Furthermore no runic expert had ever been known to be in the Kensington countryside. Holand's conclusion is inescapable: without a capable hoaxer, there can be no hoax; ergo, the stone must be authentic.

The skeptics have never been convinced, and in recent years have enjoyed bringing up the question of the so-called Beardmore relics, which include the already-mentioned sword, battle-ax, and shield handle from a presumed Viking burial site east of Lake Nipigon. As the story of the discovery of these relics is reconstructed, a Canadian National Railway trainman named James Edward Dodd had taken out a mining claim on a piece of land near Beardmore, Ontario. Dodd, a part-time prospector, said he was digging on this claim in May 1930 when he came upon some rusty iron objects. Thinking them Indian relics, he took them home to Port Arthur and tried unsuccessfully to sell them. In 1936 C. T. Currelly, curator of the Royal Ontario Museum in Toronto, heard of the find and invited Dodd to Toronto. The upshot was that Currelly saw the relics, became convinced of their authenticity, and bought them from Dodd for five hundred dollars. They were then put on display in a prominent place in the museum.

The first dissenting note was heard in January 1938 when Eli

Ragotte, a brakeman on the CNR, stated that he had seen the relics in Dodd's basement in 1928, two years before they were "discovered" at Beardmore. Though Ragotte retracted this statement under fire, other equally disquieting declarations were soon made. That same month a Port Arthur Norwegian named M. J. Hansen claimed that he had lost a similar set of relics from a house he had rented to Dodd. Later another prospector came forward and signed an affidavit that he had worked the claim where Dodd said he made his find. The prospector said that at no time had they found any relics and added that they could not have been found by Dodd. Hansen, meanwhile, kept issuing conflicting statements about Dodd and the relics, none of which proved the Viking story's validity.

Finally, in November 1956, Dodd's foster son Walter appeared at the Toronto museum to tell museum officials his story, which was reported the following spring in *Maclean's* magazine, published in Toronto.

"I was twelve or thirteen years of age in 1930 or 1931," Dodd stated in an affidavit—1930 being the supposed date of the reputed find—"when my stepfather (actually his foster father) found some rusty pieces of iron in the basement of the house we then lived in. One week end I went with my stepfather from Port Arthur to Beardmore. My stepfather had the iron pieces with him. He laid them on the ground at a spot where he had been blasting some time before. . . . We returned to Port Arthur and . . . later on . . . my stepfather made a trip to the claim by himself and brought back the weapons, and upon his return told the story that he had found the weapons while blasting."

Soon after this statement was signed by the younger Dodd, the Beardmore relics were removed from their place in the Toronto Royal Ontario Museum, and never since have they been displayed.

But if a valid case against the Beardmore material has been rather firmly established, this is not yet true of the Kensington Rune Stone. Not that attempts have not been made. At least one strong, well-documented attack against the stone has been published in recent years, and scholars periodically take pot shots at Holand's position. But no admitted forger has ever come forward or been located, and no affidavits against the validity of the stone by any of the principals have ever been made. The skeptics have mounted an array of strong, if circumstantial, evidence, but they are unable to blow away the fact of the stone's existence. The Minnesota Historical Society investigates the matter at seemingly regular intervals, but it has not yet produced any conclusive proof either way. Some of those who are convinced that the stone is fraudulent have reasoned speciously in their obvious desire to end the matter conclusively—which has not helped their cause.

This delightful argument has now flourished for more than sixty years in the Great Lakes region. Either the Kensington Rune Stone represents a very serious and important piece of North American history, or it represents a wonderfully outrageous hoax. Whatever its final outcome, the whole story will continue to be part of Great Lakes history.

But if indeed they were the first white men to reach the region, the Vikings failed to follow up their lead. Effective discovery, exploration, and use of the Great Lakes did not begin until after the arrival of the French. Perhaps the French came later, but they explored steadily and methodically, keeping at least partial records of their journeys. Their part in the Great Lakes story begins in the sixteenth century with the early navigators who came searching for a sea route to the Orient. These men plotted their course and sailed, gradually mapping out the northeast coastline and finally penetrating to the vast central watercourse of the Great Lakes themselves.

The first North Atlantic navigator was the brilliant Italian mapmaker and explorer who took the English name of John Cabot. He sailed from Bristol Harbor with eighteen men in his little ship *Matthew* one spring day in 1497 and after a passage of fifty-two days came to the northeastern headlands of our continent. He roamed the bays and peninsulas of that region before returning to England, fat with tales of the New World. His voyage stirred interest throughout the seaports of Europe and led others to speculate further on the elusive route to Cathay. It must, they reasoned, lie somewhere west of where Cabot sailed.

Giovanni da Verrazano, a Florentine navigator sailing under the French flag, was next. He left Dieppe in January 1524 in the small bark *Dauphine,* and after a stormy passage, made landfall in North Carolina, near the mouth of Cape Fear River. Verrazano explored northward, mistaking Chesapeake Bay for the route to Asia, and then returned to France. His tales, too, stirred the interest of sailors, merchants, and ambitious leaders.

The quest continued, and in 1534 Jacques Cartier, sailing from St. Malo, France, explored Newfoundland and the bays in the Gulf of St. Lawrence. The following year he returned and, spending the winter, explored the lower end of the river. In 1541 he again came with a much larger expedition, hoping to find the Great Lakes themselves. He had heard from Indians about the vast lakes that spread on and on westward, offering endless travel by boat, and he wondered if here, at last, was the elusive route to China. But the Indians also said that warlike tribes guarded the western land, that many rapids would keep his boats from passing. They warned that the journey was long, that they themselves would not attempt it.

Cartier tried the rapids with longboats, but found them unpassable. He named the white water *La Chine* (China) in the hopeful belief that Asia lay just beyond. He climbed the highest hill along that part of the St. Lawrence to look far to the west. This hill the Indians called Hochelago, but Cartier renamed it Mont Royal—now Mount Royal in Montreal—in honor of his king. From where he looked, the land rolled away out of sight, everywhere green-forested, laced with rivers and lakes. He could see the Ottawa River where it turned into the St. Lawrence, while below to his left lay the white billows of the Lachine Rapids.

While he temporized about the trip inland, his crew stumbled on what seemed to be deposits of gold and diamonds along the shores of the big river. Elated, they gathered a large horde of the precious material and decided to stay the winter—a decision that was very nearly their undoing. All hands came down with scurvy and might have perished had not a few in desperation decided to try a remedy suggested by an Indian. The Indian urged them to brew a tea using fir-tree needles. The needles must come from a special sort of fir tree, the Indian told them, but he would show them one. Off the group went into the forest, scratching their sores and scuffling along behind the Indian. No doubt insanity seemed the last throe of this foul affliction, and a mad tea party offered a fitting beginning to a miserable end. The tea was brewed and consumed. Their other shipmates croaked out some dying jeers, and down they lay waiting for the end.

But, behold, within two days the tea drinkers showed sharp improvement, and a scramble by the others was made in search of the tree. The poor sapling was denuded after which, aboard ship, steaming tubs of fir-tree tea were brewed and drunk. The laxative effect combined with the therapeutic effect. For days the St. Lawrence echoed with their moans and groans. Finally, normal body processes prevailed, bringing glimmers of health back to the troop.

When spring came, they searched for more of the gold and diamonds before setting out for France, their fortunes in the hold and visions of glory in their heads—only to learn upon their arrival in Paris that the gold was pyrite and the diamonds worthless quartz. This misadventure plunged Cartier's journey into oblivion, dulling French interest in the New World's colonial development for more than sixty years.

Individual merchants, fishermen, and coastal traders, however, continued to push back and forth across the Atlantic to the Grand Banks, Newfoundland, and the Gulf of St. Lawrence. Their motives were simple. They sought immediate riches, not colonial empire nor the discovery of the Northwest Passage nor the redemption of pagan souls. Fishermen and traders had been busy along this coast before Cartier, and they certainly came in growing numbers after his last voyage. An English explorer, searching for the Northwest Passage in 1527, wrote that the harbor of St. John's, Newfoundland, contained, ". . . eleven saile of Normans, and one of Brittaine [Breton] and two Portugall Barkes, and all a-fishing."

By 1608 when Samuel de Champlain arrived with his scout Etienne Brulé, many advances had been made. Some routes were charted, so coastal maps were available. The lower St. Lawrence was known to many sailors. Yet despite this early accumulation of information, colonization had to await the arrival of Champlain. Champlain was the driving force that established the colony of New France on these shores. No one before him had been able to develop such a colony. And as sponsor of Brulé's travels during this period, much of the credit for Great Lakes exploration must go to Champlain, even though he personally was not their discoverer.

Champlain made a dozen voyages to the New World over a span of thirty-four years. His first trip was to the West Indies in 1599; his last, upriver to Quebec in 1633. He pushed French influence inland from Quebec and Montreal to Lakes Huron, Ontario, and Erie. Possibly he sent Brulé across other more westerly lakes, including Superior and Michigan.

Unfortunately Brulé did not keep a journal on his travels; fortunately, Champlain did. From these journals, much of our knowledge of early Great Lakes exploration is derived. But it is often thin information contained in chance comments when it happened to occur to Champlain to write of Brulé—or sometimes when he only mentions "my lad" or "my servant" under conditions that seem to refer to Brulé.

Etienne Brulé was born in Champigny, south of Paris, in 1592. At the age of sixteen he left farm life forever, journeyed to the port of

Samuel de Champlain founded the first French settlement in the New World at Quebec (shown here in the background). An able explorer and administrator, he made twelve voyages to the American continent and encouraged explorations to the Great Lakes.

Based on a sketch in Champlain's journal, this engraving shows Champlain and a party of Hurons attacking the Iroquois near Ticonderoga, New York. The Iroquois canoes at right are supposedly made of oak bark; those of the Hurons, of birch. In this battle, unlike some later ones, Champlain and his Indian allies were victorious.

Honfleur, and sailed with Champlain on his voyage of 1608 when he founded Quebec. It was Champlain's sixth trip to the New World, but already he was planning long-range policies to strengthen and spread French influence and trade. One of his plans was to place young men among the Indians for extended stays. They would thereby learn the language and the ways of the red men, making French colonization easier.

Brulé accepted eagerly the challenge of wilderness life. He was quick-witted, felt at ease among Indians, had insatiable energy and curiosity. He was not burdened by the fur merchant's acquisitive sense, nor did he show more than vague interest in religion. He was in many ways the complete adventurer, living for today rather than tomorrow or the hereafter. Today he would hunt, fish, and travel with the Indians. Today he would enjoy the Indian women attracted by his fair complexion.

The sort of life he liked was daily fare for the Indians. They traveled at length, often on whim; they explored and hunted and fished; they were always quite open about their sexual activities. Festivals were held in times of plenty or on visits to other tribes or in victory over

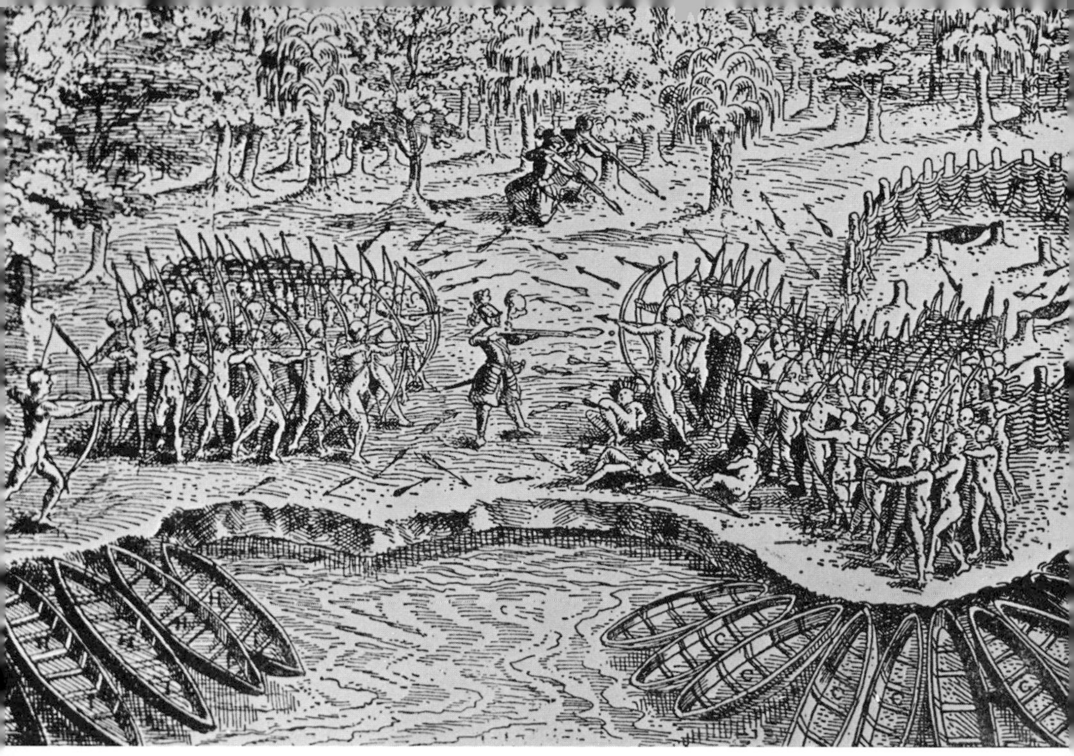

Justin Winsor, *Cartier to Frontenac*

the enemy or at a captive's torture. The red men seemed to enjoy many happy times. When two tribes visited, according to Champlain, the warriors and women gathered in a meadow with the women lined up in front, the men behind. All sang together. Suddenly, the women stripped naked except for their ornaments while the singing continued. After a pause, the women began to dance in place, stamping up and down. Gifts were exchanged, and were placed in the lodges when the dancing ended. Then athletic contests, including races and feats of strength, took place.

The missionaries, of course, disapproved of the Indians' sexual mores. Father Gabriel Sagard wrote in his *Long Journey to the Huron Country* that the boys ". . . are at liberty to give themselves over to this wickedness as soon as they can, and the young girls to prostitute themselves as soon as they are capable of doing so. Parents are often procurers of their own daughters." Men could live with girls without marriage and "without reproach or blame," he reported. Trial marriages were common, often being broken off even though certain formal preliminaries had been undertaken. After marriage, divorce could occur at any time if either partner renounced the other. Champlain wrote that it was not uncommon "... that a woman spent her youth in this fashion, having had more than a dozen or fifteen husbands, all of whom were not the only men to enjoy the woman. After nightfall, the young women and girls run about from one lodge to another, as do the young men for their part on the same quest, possessing them whenever it seems good, yet without any violence, leaving all to the wishes of the women. The husband will do the like to his neighbor's wife, and the wife of her neighbor, no jealousy intervening on that account, and no shame, disgrace, or dishonor being incurred."

Missionaries frequently were invited to join the frolic, maintaining their celibacy with difficulty in the face of determined Indian offers. Finally, wrote Sagard, "... they admitted the justice of our reasons and no longer importuned us, finding it right that we should do nothing contrary to the will of our good Father Jesus. In these importunities the women and girls were beyond comparison more insistent and plagued us more than the men themselves who came to petition us on their behalf."

Into this milieu came Etienne Brulé, unmarried, a long way from home, bearing his quota of earthy desires uncluttered by any great burden of European morality. Champlain chose him to live among the Indians. He agreed to the proposition eagerly, apparently enjoying himself throughout if the laments of the missionaries are any indication. They felt that his libertine ways detracted from their efforts to Christianize the savages. Champlain scolded Brulé who responded by turning more and more toward the Indians.

As the years passed, Brulé grew steadily less interested in the French and their New World efforts. He traveled extensively with various Indian tribes, either on Champlain's orders or on his own initiative. He wrote nothing of these travels, and his name appears only occasionally in journals of the period. But these very unrecorded travels are what really beg the question, did he discover the Great Lakes? And if so, when?

Champlain's journals indicate that Brulé stayed in the New World from his first arrival in 1608 until his death in 1633. He lived with the Indians almost constantly. In 1610 he ascended the Ottawa River, passed through Lake Nipissing and on into Georgian Bay in Lake Huron, thus becoming the first white man to see that lake.

His activities from then until 1615 are virtually unknown, but he seems to have spent some time among the Hurons, north of Lake Erie and east of Georgian Bay. During that period he may have visited the

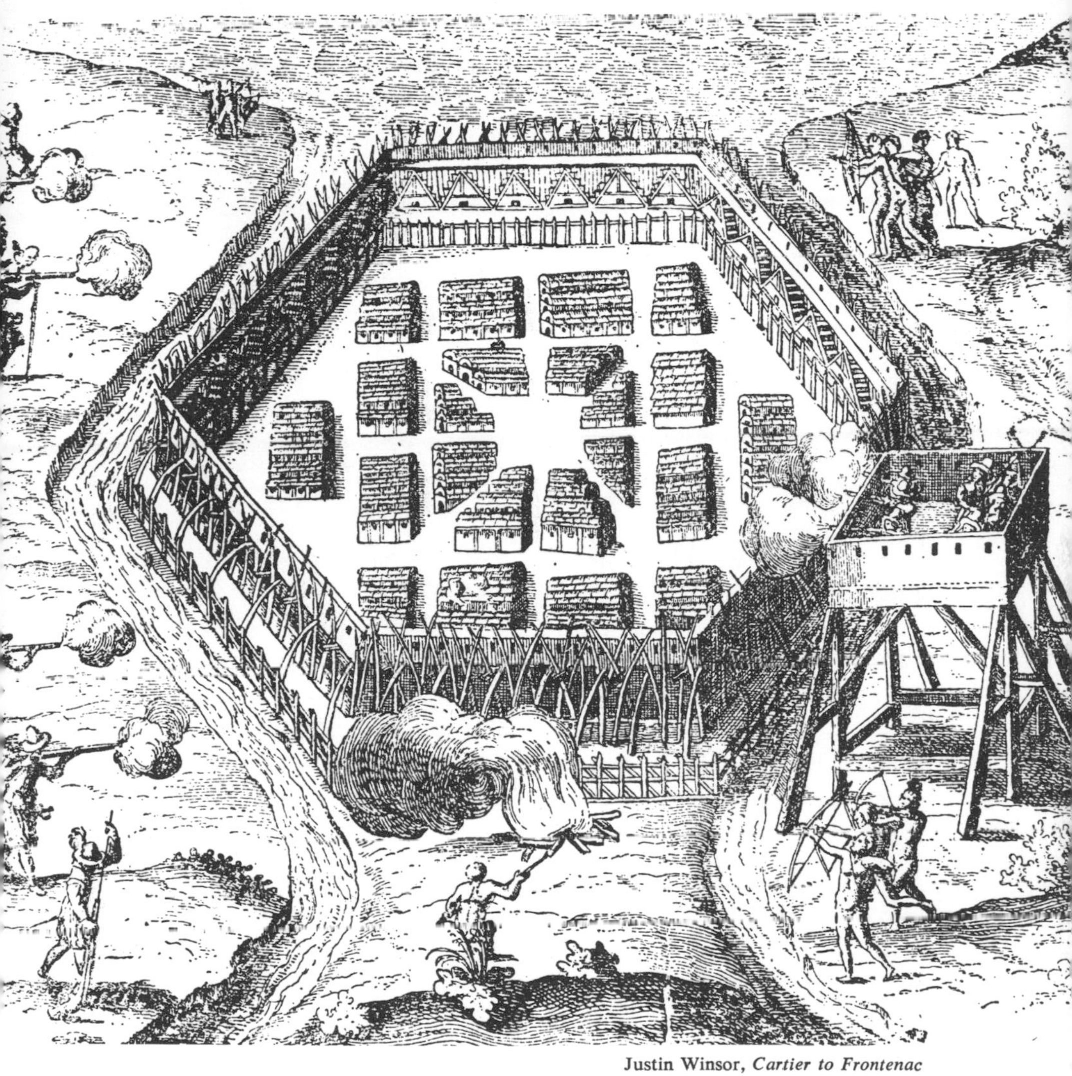

Justin Winsor, *Cartier to Frontenac*

Not always the winner, Champlain sometimes had trouble controlling his Huron army, which in turn lost to the Iroquois. One unsuccessful attempt was made on an Iroquois fort in western New York. Champlain was wounded, and the Hurons had to retreat without breaching the enemy walls. Above, an engraving of the battle made from Champlain's sketch.

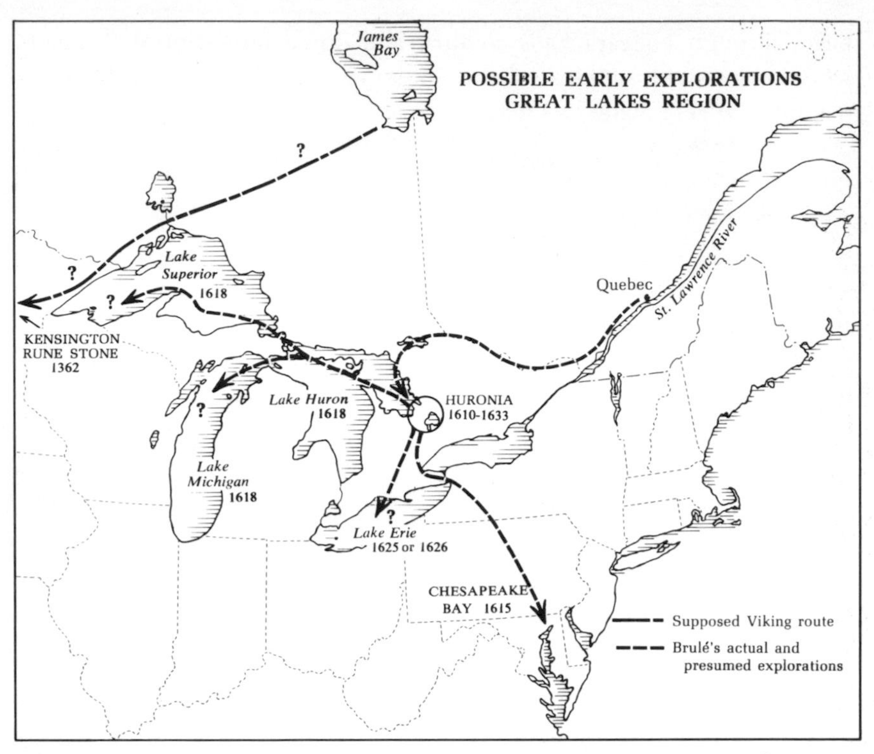

In the early seventeenth century, under Champlain and Brulé, the French developed their strength in the Great Lakes region. But some historians claim that they were not the first Europeans to see the Lakes. Three centuries earlier, Viking adventurers may have traveled as far as western Lake Superior.

north shore of Lake Ontario with the Hurons. Given his adventurous nature, this seems entirely likely, and if so, he was the first to see that lake also.

His journeys continued in 1615 when Champlain with a party of French pushed up the Ottawa River and entered Georgian Bay to meet Brulé. The Hurons were being harassed by the Iroquois, creating difficulties in taking furs down the St. Lawrence. This had interrupted the French fur trade, and Champlain planned to lead the Hurons and French against the Iroquois, crush the confederacy, and restore the fur trade. His mixed troops began a march south to Lake Ontario, passing around the east end of the lake toward the present city of Syracuse where the Iroquois maintained a palisaded fort. Meanwhile, Brulé was to lead a small party of Indians around western Lake Ontario, through Niagara Falls country and down into central Pennsylvania to gain the support of the Andastes, who hated their Iroquois neighbors. Brulé made this journey in good time, but when the Andastes refused to send any warriors, he decided simply to forget the war. He stayed there through the winter of 1615–16, traveling with the Andastes to Chesapeake Bay before returning to the Susquehanna Valley in the spring.

Meanwhile, Champlain's war did not go well. He made contact with the Iroquois, but he was unable to control his Huron allies, and they in turn were unable to conquer the Iroquois. After an inconclusive battle the French and Hurons retreated to Georgian Bay, Champlain wounded and the Hurons still faced with the threatening Iroquois.

The following summer, Brulé returned from Pennsylvania to Huronia by the same route he had taken on his journey south. On the way he was captured by the Iroquois, tortured, and very nearly killed. With the help of a sympathetic Iroquois, he escaped to live among the Hurons until 1618, when he again made contact with—or was finally found by—Champlain. The French leader was irate over Brulé's defection, but Brulé was eloquent in his own defense, overcoming Champlain's wrath with the story of his torture. Brulé had scars to prove his point. This seems to have satisfied the French leader, for he again sent Brulé west with some Hurons to explore the country farther.

On this journey, Brulé probably passed along the north shore of Georgian Bay and Lake Huron, into the St. Marys River, then along the south shore of Lake Superior for a distance. How far a distance he journeyed is not known, but he may have gone to the far end of Lake Superior. While returning, he may also have seen the north end of Lake Michigan. After this long western venture, he returned to Huronia.

In 1625 or 1626, he again went traveling, this time to the land of the Neutrals, a powerful group that traded with both warring factions—the Hurons and Algonquians on one side and the Iroquois confederacy on the other. The Neutrals lived north of Lake Erie, near Lake St. Clair. Probably on this journey Brulé also visited Lake Erie, though he may well have first seen that lake during his Niagara travels ten years earlier. The journey to the Neutrals completed Brulé's important explorations, and he returned to live among the Hurons until 1629, when he made a mistake that was to cost him his life.

Throughout the 1620's, the British envied the French their territory along the lower St. Lawrence, coveting the fur trade in particular. The

British, who had settled farther south along the Atlantic Coast, like the Dutch supported the Iroquois, the Indian allies of the French being the Hurons, Algonquians, and Montagnais. When the British and French were not feuding, their Indian allies stirred with their own discord. Piracy on the high seas was common, and skirmishes inland frequent. Finally, in 1628, war broke out between France and Great Britain.

Champlain, at Quebec, laid his defenses for a siege, but he was woefully short of men, guns, and supplies. To help defend the colony, he called in from their outposts all the French available, including Brulé. The first winter of the war was desperate, and the colony nearly starved. In the spring of 1629, a convoy of French ships bringing supplies was due to arrive, but July came before the ships were reported. In desperation Champlain sent Brulé with three companions downriver to speed the ships on their way. Unfortunately a flotilla of English privateers caught the French fleet in the lower St. Lawrence, sinking several and capturing the remainder. The ships that greeted Brulé as he paddled down the river were not friendly French but hostile British.

Sizing up the situation and knowing the weakness of Champlain's colony at Quebec, Brulé decided on the spot to throw in with the British. With Brulé as pilot, the English ships sailed upriver to capture Quebec easily. Champlain was taken as a prisoner to England, and the colony was seized by the British.

Brulé gained nothing from his treachery. The British allowed him to stay at Quebec but showed no enthusiasm for his presence. After a time, he went back to live with the Hurons. Champlain was held a prisoner in England until the following year when the war ended. Under the terms of the peace settlement, he was then released, and Quebec was restored to French possession. In 1633, Champlain returned to New France as governor.

The problem of Brulé's treachery, smoldering during the war, now came to the fore, and his fate was soon sealed. He was caught between the French and their Huron allies, without even nominal protection from the British. Even while Champlain was making plans to capture and try Brulé, a small group of Hurons turned on him. They bound, tortured, quartered, and ate him. This probably occurred in June 1633, barely a month after Champlain's return to New France. The murder is believed to have taken place near Penetanguishene Bay on the lower end of Georgian Bay.

Thus ended the life of Etienne Brulé, discoverer and explorer of the Great Lakes. He was the first white man to see Lakes Huron, Ontario, Erie, and possibly Lake Michigan. If the Vikings were not the first to visit Lake Superior, Brulé was the first on that lake also. His accomplishments are stained by his treachery and beclouded by his failure to record them. At the end he was an outcast with neither the French nor those Indians who were once his friends interested in bringing his murderers to justice. But Brulé had opened the Lakes to French penetration, and the effect of his discoveries was to be felt throughout the colonial period.

Champlain, the great French colonial leader and administrator, died only two years after Brulé. He was stricken with paralysis at sixty-eight, dying at Quebec on Christmas Day 1635. The colony he founded continued to prosper, gradually beginning to shape the early development of eastern Canada. Today, about a third of Canada is still French-speaking, and Canada has long since passed from being a French to a British colony to a dominion, and finally to being an independent nation. Yet France has not given up all her territory in this part of the world. France still owns Big Miquelon, Little Miquelon, and St. Pierre Islands on the south shore of Newfoundland in sight of Canadian soil—a token of the days when the fleur-de-lis fluttered over Quebec and the French claimed dominion over much of North America.

In the early months of 1679, La Salle led a party of men above Niagara Falls to build a trading ship. This drawing of their arrival was made by Louis Hennepin, a Recollect friar who accompanied them and later wrote of their adventures.

Louis Hennepin, *A New Discovery of a Vast Country in America*

6

Opening the Continent

THE OPENING WEDGE that Brulé and Champlain drove into the Great Lakes region soon attracted other French empire builders, missionaries, explorers, and traders. The empire builders saw the trickle of highly prized furs imported from Quebec, and these called more eloquently than words for new investments of money and men. But words were important, too. Many of the clergy in France read of the New World and saw in it a fertile field for the Roman Catholic Church. Their information came from letters written by the early missionaries to their superiors, relating facts about the Indians, life in the wilderness, and their religious activities. Hundreds of these so-called relations were written, and they found an eager audience in France. The collected *Jesuit Relations*, numbering seventy-three volumes, are today the prime source of historical information about the Great Lakes Indians and French colonial life. Most of the men who clambered aboard ships at Havre or Cherbourg had read or heard discussed some of these relations, and from them, each had gained his own bright vision of the New World. Whether on secular or sacred quest, such men were soon crossing the Atlantic in growing numbers—all tumbled together in the ship's hold, but each in search of his own particular form of fortune in France's new colony.

The pattern of growth was unsteady but unmistakable: unsteady because New France was never able to control the hostile Iroquois, who constantly opposed the growing French colony; unsteady, too, because long periods passed when French interests in Canada lay dormant; but unmistakable because the whole French endeavor grew despite Indians, wilderness, and colonial restrictions.

Various forms of Christianity were tolerated in the British and Dutch territories to the south: Puritans, Quakers, Catholics, and Presbyterians established settlements in Massachusetts, New York, Pennsylvania, and Virginia. In New France, only Catholicism was permitted until growing Huguenot power forced the rule's relaxation. The French court was very restrictive in its trade allowances also, providing only a limited number of traders with fur licenses. France's kings generally failed to back exploration and at best gave only qualified approval. An example of this regal frugality is the "gift" of Fort Frontenac that Louis XIV bestowed on La Salle. The construction of the fort, which was located where the St. Lawrence River starts its descent from Lake Ontario to the sea, had been started in 1673, and was half finished when the king gave it to La Salle. In return for this generosity, La Salle had to pay the crown ten thousand livres for the construction work completed up to that point, had to rebuild the entire structure in stone, had to maintain it at his own expense with a garrison equal to Montreal, had to agree to form a settlement at the location, had to build a church when the number of colonists reached one hundred, and had to retain one or more Recollect friars at the post. Such requirements limited New World investment to a wealthy few, and most who were wealthy preferred a more easy life than wilderness exploration. La Salle was an energetic exception.

The geographical position of New France also helped to keep it from growing steadily. Entrance to North America was blocked by Spain in the Gulf of Mexico, by British colonies on the eastern seaboard, by dense forests and a harsh climate in the north. This left only two pathways open to the rich, fur-bearing interior—one through the St. Lawrence River valley, the other through Hudson Bay. Both were cold at all seasons and icebound in winter. Both called for tricky navigation, in addition to a large measure of luck. For all these reasons there were thirty thousand French in Canada by 1690, whereas there were three hundred thousand in the British colonies.

Other differences worked against the growth of New France. The British colonies were settled, stable communities, supported by agriculture, hunting, and trade. In New France, very little farming was carried on, and that limited mostly to the vicinity of Quebec and Montreal. In the forest and wilderness Frenchmen lived like nomads, eating off the land. They seldom remained in the tiny settlements more than briefly. This in itself was remarkable, for the French traders came here with no preparation for wilderness life. The British virtually brought their community life with them, transplanting it to the New World; the French left their communities behind in Europe to become wanderers in the wilderness.

Two highly interesting cultural units developed in the Great Lakes region as a result of the fur trade: coureurs de bois and the voyageurs. Each had its own distinctive way of life. The coureurs de bois, who ranged the forests, either led solitary lives or joined Indian bands, often taking Indian wives. They lived and journeyed throughout the Great Lakes country, hunting, trapping, and bartering for furs. Normally they left Montreal in the fall, suffered a harsh wilderness existence throughout the winter, then returned to Montreal with their furs in spring or summer. Such men were expert woodsmen and highly capable, often enduring unbelievable hardships. Some operated legally with a government license; others worked for licensed traders; but many were outlaws who sold their furs illegally to the British or Dutch, or dealt with corrupt French officials.

The voyageurs were boatmen. To survive as a voyageur, a man had his work cut out. He had to paddle a large canoe all day in unison with others, had to carry ninety-pound packs at a jog-trot over mile upon mile of portage, had to sing, to brawl, to be able to build a canoe, to live on thin rations and group reliance.

No such unusual and self-reliant groups developed in the British Colonies until the late seventeenth century when woodsmen and farmers began to push over the Alleghenies to become the pioneering frontiersmen of mid-America.

But the French boatmen and rangers paid for their daring. Many were killed by Indians or their forest-crazed compatriots. Many drowned, negotiating river rapids or crossing the Great Lakes, or they perished in the wilderness from exposure or starvation. Some, like Brulé, were eaten by the Indians. They were individuals who lived hard and often died alone, and the only legacy they left is a skein of rousing tales of courage and adventure. Most, of course, never wrote or kept journals. They had been farmers, artisans, sailors, soldiers, or petty merchants, and in keeping with the general pattern of that day, they were mostly illiterate. Their story was left for others to tell.

The history of these early colonials shows that the Great Lakes country was not won by a sudden sweep but by alternate probes and withdrawals. Unlike the British settlements, the French used Indian allies in their probing exploration of the Great Lakes region. The

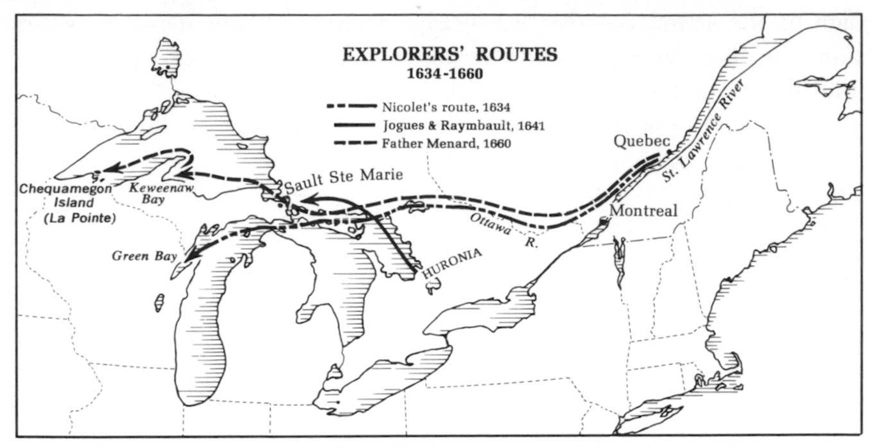

Early explorations pointed up the importance of the Great Lakes as an inland water route. Nicolet, in his search for Asia, got as far as Green Bay, Wisconsin. Jesuit priests, such as Jogues, Raymbault, and Menard, sought converts among the Indians.

English for the most part destroyed resident Indians or took their lands by force.

Though essentially correct, this distinction is crowded with exceptions. The French were friendly with the Algonquians and Hurons, but warred with the Iroquois steadily. The English exterminated many coastal Indians but were allied with the Iroquois. The French spread out rapidly along the Great Lakes waterway, while the English were walled against the coast by mountain ranges. Settled communities developed naturally in one but not in the other. The English coming to settle as colonists needed ownership of the land outright, but the French were traders, not settlers, needing peaceful relations with the Indians. The French ranged deeper into North America than the English, and their exploration was earlier and more thorough.

The first of these probes of the Great Lakes region began with Brulé's explorations, which took place from 1610 to 1633. Then in 1634 Champlain, still hoping to find the Northwest Passage, sent Jean Nicolet into the Lakes region. So hopeful was he of success that Nicolet carried a resplendent silken robe in which he planned to greet the khan of Tartary. Nicolet, traveling westward for weeks, kept hoping to reach Asia but met only more naked savages, no civilized Chinese. When he arrived in Green Bay, his western journey ended with no sign of the khan. To salve his disappointment, he sent messengers to announce his arrival, donned the silken robe, then entered the nearest Indian village, shooting pistols in the air. The natives thought it grand. But after a feast or two, Nicolet returned to give Champlain the sad news: all the water was fresh; there was no ocean; and Asia still lay elusively beyond the horizon.

Next came Isaac Jogues and Charles Raymbault, two Jesuits, who spent the summer of 1641 beside the St. Marys River, where that stream plunges down from Lake Superior to Lake Huron. They noted many details about the countryside, commented on the journey in their relation for that year, and preached to the Indians who worked the river for whitefish. In the fall, the two priests returned to their Indian villages east of Lake Huron.

Father René Menard ventured west on Lake Superior in 1660, established a mission at Keweenaw Bay, then pushed on to the far end of the lake. At Chequamegon Bay, he set up another mission. His journals, too, told of the country. Such energy might have developed French influence steadily throughout the region, but unfortunately Father Menard was lost that winter while traveling in the wilderness south of Lake Superior.

In 1667 the powerful French intendant Jean Talon, having had his fill of Iroquois depredations, called up a regiment of French regulars to deal with the refractory tribesmen. As fiscal officer of a French province, the intendant sometimes wielded more power than even the governor, and this was particularly true in Talon's case. The colonial governor at that time was Daniel de Courcelles, an ineffectual counter-weight to Talon's dynamic energy. The regiment was unable to eradicate the Iroquois, but it caused enough damage to extract a peace treaty that for the first time assured French safety on the lower Great Lakes.

In 1668 Fathers Jacques Marquette and Claude Dablon set up a Jesuit mission at Sault Ste Marie. The next year, Marquette pushed on to Chequamegon Bay to re-establish Menard's mission. While there, he first heard of the great river, "Michissipi," and made notes about it in his relation for that year. But he found no time to search for the river and by 1671 was back at the Straits of Mackinac. There he established the mission of St. Ignace.

In 1669 the new peace treaty with the Iroquois was so successful that Adrien Jolliet was able to use the Lake Erie route for his return to Montreal. This was the first time this lower Lakes route had been used with any measure of safety. He was returning from a search for copper in western Lake Superior and came down Lake Huron, along Lake Erie, and across Lake Ontario to Montreal. For the first time, an open-water route to the West had been established.

From all these explorations France developed a strong proprietary attachment to the Great Lakes and in 1671 laid claim to the territory. The king sent a special representative, François Daumont, who took possession at Sault Ste Marie on June fourteenth. In the name of Louis XIV, he claimed for France all of the Great Lakes, Manitoulin Island, ". . . and all other countries, rivers, lakes, and tributaries contiguous and adjacent thereunto, as well discovered as to be discovered, which are bounden on the one side by the Northern and Western seas and on the other side by the South Sea including all its length and breadth."

After the ceremony, the French descended to their encampment to sing the *Te Deum*. They felt much better, now that France owned the entire continent. Unfortunately, a pair of drunken Indians marred this great occasion by stealing the king's escutcheon, which Daumont had tacked on a cedar post. Without this to hold the claim, the whole continent became once again open to all comers.

One onlooker at this quaint ceremony was Louis Jolliet, the younger brother of Adrien, and already a capable woodsman and explorer. In 1672 Intendant Talon asked him to find the great river "Michisippi," mentioned by Père Marquette and often described by the Indians. There was still hope that it might lead to salt water which would ultimately lead to China. The following spring, Jolliet started west on his great venture. At St. Ignace, Marquette joined him with five companions. The expedition pushed west into Green Bay, then floated down the Fox and Wisconsin Rivers to the Mississippi. Full of hope, they paddled south, but as days lengthened into weeks, discouragement began to creep in. The river held steadily to its southern course. They continued on, to where the Arkansas joins the Mississippi, before admitting reluctantly that the big river must flow only to the Gulf of Mexico; it could not possibly reach the Pacific. Discouraged, they turned back, traveling up the Mississippi to the Illinois River, then following the Des Plaines north to Lake Michigan. They coasted north on Lake Michigan to Green Bay, where Marquette spent the winter at the Jesuit mission. Jolliet went on to Sault Ste Marie, where he stayed till spring; then he returned to Quebec.

In 1701 Sieur Antoine de La Mothe Cadillac, a proud, quick-witted Gascon, sailed from Montreal with fifty French soldiers and a hundred

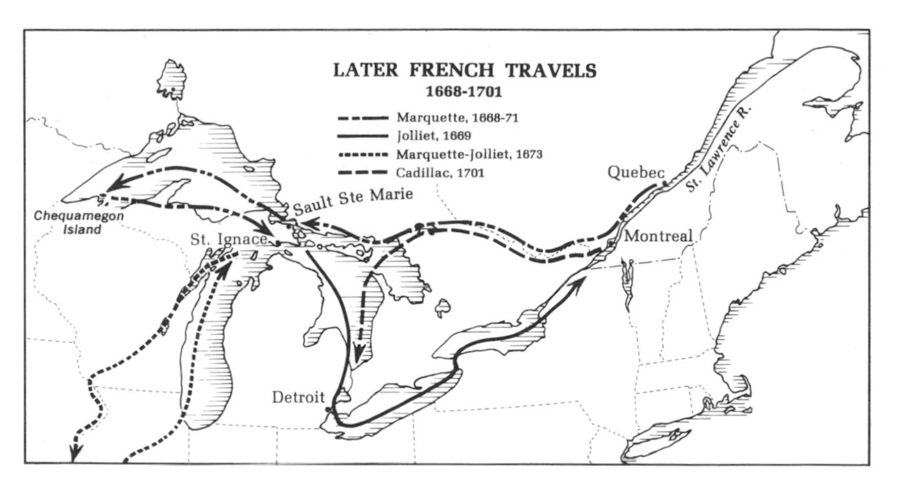

In the last half of the century, the French strengthened their hold over the Lakes. Marquette established a mission at Sault Ste Marie and re-established the French Jesuit mission at Chequamegon, "the Island of the Golden-Breasted Woodpecker." Jolliet opened the water route on the lower Lakes. Marquette and Jolliet explored the Mississippi Valley. Later, Cadillac built a fort between Lake Erie and Lake St. Clair, thus founding the city of Detroit.

loyal Indian warriors. His mission was to build a fort at the *détroit*, strait, between Lake Erie and Lake St. Clair. Because the Iroquois were being difficult around Lake Erie, Cadillac followed the old Ottawa River route west to Lake Huron, then south through Lake St. Clair to the Detroit River. Here, on July 24, 1701, he made camp and next day began construction of a fort, destined to become a French stronghold and fur-trading center. It is today, of course, the city of Detroit.

All these exploratory probes served primarily to gather information about the Great Lakes, and if we accept the record at face value, they accomplished their purpose. But the record can be misleading. We tend to think of these explorers as the first to arrive on the Great Lakes, and perhaps they were. But French traders were scattered throughout the Great Lakes area in the seventeenth century, and no doubt preceded some of these "discoverers." Being illiterate, those traders wrote nothing and their discoveries remained unknown until some later explorer found words for the landscape.

La Salle is generally called an explorer and discoverer, yet most of the country he traveled was seen by white men years earlier. Nevertheless, of all such adventures, the story of La Salle's life in the Great Lakes region typifies the raw courage such a land required. His story counts as one of the most important to come from this period of North American history, whether it included any actual discovery or no.

René Robert Cavelier, Sieur de La Salle, was born at Rouen, France, on November 22, 1643. He came to the New World in 1666 when he was twenty-three years old.

La Salle had two gifts: great energy and an absolutely unbendable will—traits which his enemies termed lust for power and stubborn obstinacy. His enemies were numerous throughout his life, so although there is some dispute what to call his other attributes, there is general agreement about his ability to make enemies. He was very good at this; his enemies worked against him at the French court, at Quebec, at Fort Frontenac, on the Great Lakes, and along the Mississippi. The record hints darkly at frontiersmen hired to spread trouble in his path, at deals entered into behind his back, at powerful forces seeking to disenfranchise him. His murder by his followers in a Texas swamp proves the final power of these machinations. But the years he survived and explored our continent also prove something to weigh in the balance. He was by all counts the most audacious, driving, determined French explorer to appear during the entire colonial period. Though his personal ambitions were doomed to failure, more than any other man he opened the way for French colonization in the heartland of the continent.

La Salle had a thorough French education in a family of moderate wealth. He was trained as a Jesuit, but soon left the priesthood for secular life. His brother, an abbé of the Sulpician Order, had been sent to Canada as a missionary, and in the spring of 1666 La Salle followed. After a stormy two-month voyage, he arrived in Montreal with some money, a vaguely formed determination to make his fortune, and a boundless youthful energy. Through the good offices of the Sulpician Superior at Montreal, La Salle received a patent to a tract of land near the old village of Lachine. There along the St. Lawrence he busied himself for three years, building a dwelling, a palisaded fort, and a trading house. He leased most of the land to settlers, thereby developing a modest but steady income. This done, he began to look for new adventure.

In 1669 La Salle accompanied a Sulpician priest, Father René de Brehan de Gallinée, on an exploration throughout the Lakes region. They were afield until 1671, a trip that saw La Salle's dreams soar. He began to visualize the need for a string of forts so that trade could be carried on along the Great Lakes and rivers farther to the west. Jolliet, known to La Salle, did not explore the Mississippi until the following year, but when he did, La Salle simply included that river in his plan. Through his fortified trading posts he would build a successful commercial enterprise so the colony of New France itself would prosper and become the center of French empire. The French court, however, still only thought of the New World as a place to exploit, maintaining a restrictive tariff on fur, designed to keep prices high. Under such controls, a black market had developed among French traders, who roamed the country collecting and selling furs illicitly. La Salle wanted the unlicensed trade stopped, partly from loyalty to his king, partly because he himself wanted a fur monopoly. The line of fortified posts would make such controlled growth possible.

That fall La Salle tried to convince Talon of his plans. The intendant heard, but he did not heed, and La Salle had to wait until his friend Frontenac was named governor the following year. Frontenac was also inspired with La Salle's vision of empire, and in 1674 he had him presented at the French court. He also arranged for La Salle to receive the seigneury of Fort Frontenac on Lake Ontario. La Salle would control the area, but as noted earlier, he had to build a fort and settlement, maintain a garrison, and carry out other pledges.

To perform these obligations, he had to resort to moneylenders. Some were friends; some were usurers; but within two years, he had built the fort and village, carried out the other terms of his bargain, and was in a commanding position to intercept any illegal fur traders headed toward Montreal. This success aroused much jealousy. The Jesuit hierarchy, in particular, was not loath to fan discord, because the young trader was a protégé of Frontenac, an old foe of the Jesuits. Frontenac had long felt that the Jesuits were too narrow and personally ambitious in their plans for New France; the Jesuits in turn thought Frontenac too secular a governor.

Despite the rift, La Salle's fortunes continued to improve. In 1677 he was again in Paris, receiving permission to establish a string of trading posts along the Great Lakes, the Ohio River, and the Mississippi River. He also was commissioned to apprehend any unlicensed traders and to develop the fur trade beyond Niagara Falls. This success at court brought the Jesuits out in open warfare. They had planned to establish their own colony along the Ohio, plans which were now wrecked. The number of La Salle's enemies increased markedly.

In 1678 La Salle returned to Canada, bringing shipwrights, carpenters, blacksmiths. He also brought Henry de Tonti, or Tonty, a

French army officer as his lieutenant. "Tonty of the Iron Hand," as he became known along the frontier, had courage, endurance, and ability, although the name itself originated from the metal hand that replaced his own lost campaigning in Italy.

La Salle's immediate plan was to move his men above Niagara Falls to construct a sizable trading vessel, which he would use as an itinerant fur trading post on the upper Lakes. On outward voyages he would carry men to build forts along the Great Lakes, and return trips would see the hold filled with furs. He planned to build another similar ship for the Mississippi. His was a grand scheme for empire, full of enterprise, daring, and insight. If La Salle could make it stick, the rewards would be great. The key, of course, was the ship itself. To construct it in the wilderness would be difficult. Already it was autumn, with cold weather hampering activity in the Niagara Falls area, the closest point to the upper Lakes. Nevertheless, La Salle and Tonty led their party of men and a Recollect friar named Louis Hennepin to establish a camp beyond the Falls. There, where Cayuga Creek joins the east bank of the Niagara River, through the early months of 1679, they labored to construct a ship of some forty-five tons.

Clearing fresh snow from their work each morning, the little knot of shipbuilders hacked down and hewed out lumber from the forest, while living largely in the open, surrounded by hostile Indians, two

Right above
Another sketch by Father Hennepin shows La Salle's ship, the Griffin, *under construction just above Niagara Falls.*

Right below
While the English settled in communities, many French immigrants lived like nomads, wandering in the wilderness. René Robert Cavelier, Sieur de la Salle, realized that French influence in the New World depended on the development of trade. He dreamed of a chain of forts and trading posts connecting the St. Lawrence, Great Lakes, and Mississippi Valley, and actually built forts from Lake Ontario to Texas. But before his dreams were realized, he was murdered by his own men.

The Great Lakes Historical Society

Justin Winsor,
Cartier to Frontenac

hundred miles from the nearest habitation. The habitation itself was only a wilderness fort. None of these men had any preparation for such a life. Then the small boat used to bring supplies and fittings from Fort Frontenac was wrecked on Lake Ontario—some claim it was sabotaged—with nearly all the equipment lost. Hostile Senecas lurked nearby, hooting at the worried shipbuilders. Sometimes they stormed into the little shipyard, howling wildly and waving tomahawks, and thus ". . . express'd some Discontent at what we were doing," wrote Father Hennepin. "One of them in particular, feigning himself drunk, attempted to kill our blacksmith, but was vigorously repuls'd by him with a red-hot Iron-barr, which together with the Reprimand he receiv'd from me, oblig'd him to be gone." The French did not dare fight off the intruders for fear of bringing down a general attack. All these troubles conspired against the project, nearly causing the men to mutiny. Only the toughest leadership by La Salle and Tonty kept the work going. The external threat of the Indians and the dangers of the surrounding wilderness also helped La Salle keep his company intact.

By late spring or early summer—the date is uncertain—the ship was launched, and Hennepin noted that the men, ". . . immediately quitted their Cabins of Rinds of Trees, and hang'd their Hammocks under the Deck of the Ship, there to lie with more security than a-shore. We did the like, insomuch that the very same Day we were all on board, and thereby out of the reach of the Insults of the Savages."

The ship was named the *Griffin,* or as it is sometimes written *Griffon,* an allusion to Governor Frontenac's coat of arms. La Salle said the *Griffin* was a bird that would fly above the ravens, a sarcastic allusion to the black gowns of his Jesuit opponents.

For some months the fitting out continued. Then La Salle, fearing trouble from his creditors, returned to Fort Frontenac and thence to Montreal where he found all his holdings under government interdict. His foes had spread enough rumors to cause the new intendant, Duchesneau, to seize his property. Duchesneau had not needed much persuasion, being an old rival of La Salle's friend Frontenac.

To most men, such a loss would have meant disaster. To La Salle, it was merely another obstacle to overcome. Through the summer, he wheedled one creditor after another into extensions of time, mollified or overcame other objectors, and by midsummer started walking overland to the Niagara camp, where he hoped to find his ship ready to sail on its journey. The way passed through the lands of the Iroquois, but he arrived safely early in August. The ship quickly was made ready, and on August ninth set out across Lake Erie, the first vessel larger than a canoe ever to ruffle the waters of the upper Great Lakes.

The strange sight must have amazed the local Indians. Spreading her large white sails, with an emblazoned griffin, the ship coursed along steadily. After an idyllic three days, the *Griffin* entered the low, marshy narrows now known as the Detroit River. The surrounding country was open, marked by patches of walnut, oak, chestnut, and wild plum trees. Game was abundant along the way. La Salle's two Indian guides were soon able to hang the rigging with quantities of meat including bear, so that the company moved up the river in high spirits. "Those who will one day have the happiness to possess this fertile and pleasant strait will be very much oblig'd to those who have shown them the way," Father Hennepin wrote sanctimoniously of this advance guard of civilization.

The little company continued northward. They discovered and crossed Lake St. Clair, then after much search found the main channel of the St. Clair River which led them into Lake Huron. This "Lake of the Hurons" was named for the Indian tribes on its eastern shore, the word *Huron* coming from the French word *hure*, meaning the head of a wild boar, for to the French the way these Indians wore their hair in ridges was like a wild boar's bristles.

The lake also proved quite bristly, the ship being very nearly wrecked in a gale—an ominous harbinger of later events. The gale hit the ship while off the mouth of Saginaw Bay, causing all hands to offer many prayers and promises to the deity. All hands, that is, except the Danish pilot, Lucas, who cursed his fate. Hennepin wrote: ". . . everybody fell upon his Knees to say his prayers, and prepare himself for Death, except our Pilot, whom we could never oblige to pray; and he did nothing all that while but curse and swear against M. la Salle, who, as he said, had brought him thither to make him perish in a nasty Lake, and lose the Glory he had acquir'd by his long and happy Navigations on the Oceans of the World." However, fortunately for the Christians, the heathen stuck to his tiller, guiding the *Griffin* through the storm to reach safe anchorage at Michilimackinac. There was a trading post and a Jesuit mission located at the starits, beside a palisaded Huron village. The log houses of the French traders were clustered near the shore. Many of these men were unlicensed to trade in furs, so La Salle's arrival brought with it the unhappy authority of the French crown. Though heavily outnumbered, La Salle decided to land in style and march his company to the chapel to hear Mass. He carried this off without incident, afterward firing one of the *Griffin's* cannons. At this, the Indians howled in amazement, while the unlicensed traders stood by glumly. By these activities, La Salle soon dominated the village.

The next day he discovered new evidence of his Montreal rivals' tampering. Most of the band of fifteen men, whom he had sent out to the trading post earlier, had been lured away or had deserted. Some who were still at Michilimackinac were promptly arrested; others fled to the woods. All the trade goods sent with these men were gone, adding another loss to La Salle's financial ledger.

Several of the men were still believed to be loyal, however, and to be waiting with their collected furs in Green Bay. In expectation of this, La Salle sailed the *Griffin* west along the north shore of Lake Michigan, then skirted the Garden Peninsula to drop anchor at Washington Island in Green Bay. Here, as he had hoped, was the advance party with furs for the *Griffin's* hold. His men were living among the friendly Potawatomies. Trade goods, a forge, shipbuilding materials, and other needs were placed on shore immediately, and the furs were stored in the *Griffin's* hold.

La Salle planned to send the *Griffin* back to Niagara, where the furs would be unloaded and dispatched to Montreal to satisfy his creditors. Then the ship would be reloaded with trade goods for its return, to the ". . . Southern Parts of the Lake [Michigan], where we should stay for them among the Illinois," as Hennepin writes. La Salle, meantime, would proceed south to Illinois to construct that winter the boat for navigation on the Mississippi River. The plan sounded reasonable, but it turned out to be disastrous.

The first ship larger than a canoe to navigate the upper Lakes, the Griffin *made a historic trip to Green Bay, on the western side of Lake Michigan, in 1679. Here it is shown passing near what is now Detroit.*

George A. Cuthbertson, *Freshwater*

On September 18, 1679, the *Griffin* set sail from Washington Island bound for Niagara. It was lost on this return voyage, apparently in a storm which arose soon after the ship left the island. The discussion over what actually happened to the ship would fill volumes, but evidence favoring any one theory is meager—at best. La Salle's own belief, which grew into conviction, was that the boat was scuttled soon after leaving Washington Island, the crew taking its valuables west to join Daniel Greysolon Duluth, the celebrated leader of the coureurs de bois in western Lake Superior. In a long letter La Salle wrote to the colonial governor in 1683, he related the story of an Indian guide, who told La Salle that three years earlier, in 1680, he had seen a man who looked like the *Griffin's* pilot, held captive in a Sioux village on the Mississippi River. The Sioux told the guide they had caught the man and four companions paddling up the Mississippi. Their canoes were loaded with trade goods, and the other four men were killed during the skirmish. La Salle, filling his letter with the story and its details, seemed convinced that the *Griffin* met its end as he suspected.

Another story explaining the *Griffin's* fate is based on evidence unearthed by a Mississagi lighthouse keeper on western Manitoulin Island. In 1890 he found four skeletons in a cave near his lighthouse; and not far distant two more skeletons, a watch, a chain, and seventeenth-century coins were also discovered. Nearby was part of an ancient ship hull, and a bolt taken from it was pronounced similar to those used in La Salle's days. Supporters of this find believe that the *Griffin*, with its crew of six, passed through the Straits of Mackinac but was wrecked on the island. The crew, they say, got ashore but probably died of starvation the following winter.

Another similar tale is based on a wreck located on Find Out Island, off Tobermory in Georgian Bay. This wreck has been known to local residents for many years, but it is only since 1955 that it became a matter of wider public interest. Those who think that this wreck is the real *Griffin* have for some time carried on a lively debate with those who support the Manitoulin version.

But there are holes in both of these stories. Those who favor either Manitoulin or Find Out Island as sites believe that the *Griffin* somehow negotiated the Straits of Mackinac without being seen, and that the ship was then wrecked or scuttled at one or the other of the Lake Huron locations. But the record is silent on this point. Shortly after the loss, Tonty asked at St. Ignace if the *Griffin* had been seen to pass the straits on the return trip. It had not been, or he would have certainly reported the fact to La Salle. La Salle's detailed letter of 1683, after all available evidence had been collected, makes no mention of the ship passing St. Ignace. Could those at St. Ignace have missed seeing the *Griffin* in a storm or at night? They could, but the chance of an inexperienced pilot attempting to thread that shoal-bound strait in storm or darkness, with a square-rigged ship, is slim indeed. Also, according to Father Hennepin, the storm which hit Lake Michigan occurred soon after the *Griffin* sailed from Green Bay. After waving the *Griffin* on its way, La Salle, leaving Tonty behind to round up the remainder of the advance party, coasted south by canoe with Hennepin and the rest of the men. They passed along the Wisconsin side of Lake Michigan, but were soon forced to put ashore because of a storm. This same storm must have also hit the *Griffin* before it passed through the straits. Father Hennepin wrote the following account of the *Griffin's* departure from Washington Island:

"They sailed the 18th of September with a Westerly Wind, and fir'd a Gun to take their leave. Tho' the Wind was favourable, it was never known what Course they steer'd, nor how they perish'd; for after all the Enquiries we have been able to make, we could never learn any thing else but the following Particulars.

"The Ship came to an Anchor to the North of the Lake of the Illinois [Lake Michigan], where she was seen by some Savages, who told us that they advised our Men to sail along the Coast, and not toward the middle of the Lake, because of the Sands that make the Navigation dangerous when there is any high Wind. Our Pilot, as I said before, was dissatisfy'd, and would steer as he pleas'd, without hearkning to the Advice of the Savages, who, generally speaking, have more sense than the Europeans think at first; but the Ship was hardly a League from the Coast, when it was toss'd up by a violent Storm in such a manner, that our Men were never heard of since; and it is suppos'd that the Ship struck upon a Sand, and was there bury'd . . . ."

After the violent storm that "toss'd up" the *Griffin* and drove La Salle ashore, his party continued south through foul weather, then rounded lower Lake Michigan to stop at the St. Joseph River near what is now the Michigan-Indiana boundary. By this time it was November, and the men were sullen and worn. La Salle elected to wait for Tonty to arrive from Michilimackinac. The men clamored to push on; La Salle was iron-willed as ever, saying he, at least, planned to wait with Father Hennepin and the Mohegan guide. Afraid to venture into an unknown wilderness without their leader, the men decided to stay, and La Salle set them to building a palisade, later called Fort Miami, near the river mouth. It was well along when after twenty days Tonty and his band appeared from the north. He had traveled overland down the lake's Michigan shore—a routine journey, passed over lightly in La Salle's journal. Together, the two groups continued south along the St. Joseph River about as far as the present site of South Bend, then southwest overland to the headwaters of the Kankakee. They paddled south on that river to the Illinois where they soon came to a large village of Illinois Indians, near the present site of Utica.

La Salle named the place Fort Crèvecoeur and began the construction there of his second sailing vessel. The Indians proved friendly, and the work progressed rapidly. However, by January 1680 La Salle, who had run short of supplies, was fretting over the *Griffin's* whereabouts. The hull of the new ship was nearly constructed, so anchors, rigging, and other materials were now needed. On March first, fearful that the *Griffin* was lost, La Salle placed Tonty in charge of the fort and taking four other men and his Mohegan guide, he set forth on the long journey to Montreal.

This was a journey of a thousand miles through the wilderness, but La Salle made it in sixty-five days. He traveled first to his post, Fort Miami, on the St. Joseph River. Leaving the canoes, he continued on foot across southern Michigan to Detroit, then southeast from there to Point Pelee on Lake Erie. Here canoes were built for the trip to Niagara, from which point he walked overland to Fort Frontenac, then traveled the remaining way by canoe.

The amazing abilities of La Salle can be seen from this journey. A succession of difficulties had interrupted his plans before he even started for Montreal. He traveled through unknown, hostile Indian territory. Being late winter, the water in the streams and marshes was frozen too tight for travel by canoe but not enough to support a man. So they slogged along, dragging their canoes, through icy mud, sometimes up to their chests. At other times they walked through deep, drifted snow. Of the six men, only La Salle and one other man made the entire journey without ever being sick.

At his station above Niagara Falls, La Salle learned the *Griffin* had been lost, thus confirming his deepest fears. But worse was yet to come. Another ship from France, freighted with twenty thousand livres of his goods, had been lost in a storm on the St. Lawrence River. Of the twenty shipwrights aboard, only four awaited him in Montreal;

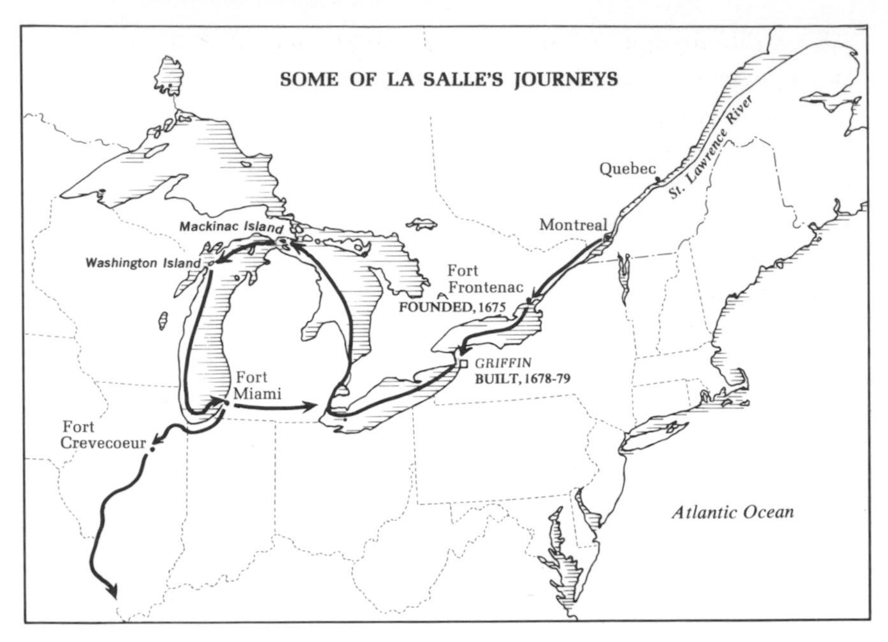

La Salle dreamed of a vast French empire in the New World held together by a string of forts. He actually established forts from the St. Lawrence to Texas and built the first ship larger than a canoe to sail on the Lakes.

the others had returned to France. His creditors believed him dead; his finances were in ruinous shape. In a whirlwind week at Montreal, he rebuilt the trust of his creditors, reported to the governor, and then set out again with supplies to return to Tonty and the Illinois party.

At Fort Frontenac two messengers met him with a letter from Tonty. Tonty wrote that soon after La Salle left Illinois, and while he himself was out hunting one day, about twenty men—nearly the entire group—deserted. They destroyed Fort Crèvecoeur, where the boat was being built, threw most of the arms and stores in the river, and carried off the rest. There was a report, Tonty wrote, that they had also destroyed Fort Miami before heading toward Montreal. The messengers who brought this letter told La Salle the deserters were now on Lake Ontario, close behind. With nine of his most trusted followers, La Salle set a trap by lying in wait along the shore. He surprised the deserters near Fort Frontenac, killing two in the ambush and capturing the rest.

Even this attempt at justice caused trouble. La Salle's enemies soon called these deaths murder. The captured deserters complained bitterly of La Salle's rigorous, autocratic ways. They claimed that he had made promises that had not been kept, that they had not been advised of the hardships of wilderness life. They said that La Salle's iron will kept them shut in a virtual prison, so that they had to rebel to escape the wilderness. Showing no concern over these charges, La Salle continued west, this time taking the River Severn north to Lake Huron, then paddling along the shore to Lake Michigan and Chicago. From there he continued south, completing the journey through spring-swollen streams to finally arrive at the land of the Illinois. He was shocked at what he found. Everywhere was carnage, devastation, and death.

As La Salle traveled east to Montreal, an Iroquois war party had pushed west from New York on a march of conquest. This band had attacked all the Illinois Indians they could find, dug up all their dead, and killed all they could capture. All along the river carrion birds fed on corpses; skulls were planted on pikes. At one point, La Salle saw several upright motionless forms along the bank. Investigating, he found that they were the remains of Indian men and women, still bound to the stakes where they had been tortured to death, then half eaten by the Iroquois. La Salle had the presence of mind in this grisly scene to examine the skulls for Caucasian hair or for any other sign that his faithful friend Tonty had been murdered. He found none.

Standing amid the carnage, La Salle must have wondered what had brought him to this hell in the wilderness. During his entire four-month journey to and from Montreal, the urbane French aristocrat had not had one piece of good news nor one stroke of luck. On the contrary, at every point, ruin stared him in the face. Amazingly, his courage and determination had not failed, and he had continued to push his plans despite every obstacle. But now the idea of Tonty's death truly shattered him. Still desperately hoping he lived, La Salle followed the Illinois River south to the Mississippi in search of his friend. There he saw the great river for the first time. The Iroquois had driven the Illinois Indians down to that point and scattered them beyond the river. No one was in sight. The river lapped along quietly, and La Salle finally began to accept the thought that Tonty was dead. The shock of this loss dashed his ambitions, and he decided to winter at Fort Miami on the St. Joseph. If any of Tonty's followers were alive, they would eventually turn up at the fort. La Salle waited, hoping for news.

Tonty was not dead. He had been captured during the Illinois warfare, trying to persuade the Iroquois not to attack. He reminded them of the French-Iroquois peace treaty of 1667, adding that the Illinois were allies of the French. During a wild battlefield conference just before the attack, Tonty was stabbed deeply near the heart and taken prisoner with the remaining Frenchmen. Later, all were freed to make a desperate, starving journey of thirty-four frozen days, until at last they reached the sanctuary of some friendly Indians at Green Bay. For a time they lingered there to recover. Then Tonty pushed on to Michilimackinac where he was recovering his strength when one spring day La Salle arrived from the south. It was a joyous reunion! For La Salle in his depressed state of trouble, bitterness, and frustration, the delight of seeing a friend long given up for lost must have been overwhelming.

The two men immediately began to lay new plans. With a few faithful followers, they soon were paddling east to Fort Frontenac, where they loaded canoes with supplies and trade goods before once again starting west. This time they were determined to make the fur trade yield real profits. They followed the Humber River out of Lake Ontario, pushed north to Georgian Bay, then crossed northern Lake Huron into Lake Michigan. From there they followed the Wisconsin shore south to Illinois. The summer and fall were occupied by these goings and comings, so it was midwinter before they arrived on the Illinois River once again. The party had grown during the journey until now it numbered twenty-two Frenchmen and thirty-one Indians.

Passing the wreckage of Fort Crèvecoeur, where stood the unfinished hull of La Salle's second ship, the party pushed on down the river. La Salle's plan was to follow the Mississippi to the Gulf of Mexico, so for several weeks the party paddled steadily southward. Finally, standing on the mud of the delta, La Salle planted the fleur-de-lis, proclaming the entire Mississippi valley a province of France and, in honor of his king, naming it Louisiana.

But La Salle's success on this trip was short-lived. After his return journey up the Mississippi, he learned that his friend Frontenac had been replaced by a new governor, La Barre, a friend of the Jesuits. This meant he was also an avowed enemy of La Salle. At Montreal, La Salle's fears were confirmed. Realizing he could accomplish little without firm backing, he soon set sail for France to gain the king's ear.

This time Louis XIV paid heed when La Salle spoke. The explorer captured the court with his New World tales, and trapped the king's interest with information about the vast colonial empire awaiting

French development. Louis supplied a small army of soldiers and settlers, telling La Salle to move his colony into the Gulf of Mexico. With four ships, the company sailed in the fall of 1685. In the Gulf, La Salle knew he was in danger both from the Spanish, who claimed the adjacent land, and from hostile Indians. Without meeting either, he established a colony in December 1685 near the present site of Galveston, after failing to find the Mississippi on the coastal journey west.

The settlement was a disaster. La Salle landed with 180 soldiers and settlers, and in little more than a year, the total had dwindled to 40. Those who remained were mutinous. Heat, barren land, poisonous snakes, and the failure of expected supplies, all cut steadily into the colony. Realizing his only hope was in French Canada, La Salle decided to push east to find the Mississippi. He would go up that river, he decided, to obtain help for the colony. With a small force, he started east. In mid-March, the company divided into two groups to secure sufficient supplies of game before pushing on. La Salle now could trust almost no one, having to drive his men to carry out the simplest orders. When the company split in two to forage for food, he placed his trusted nephew, Moringet, in charge of one group while he took the other.

On the night of March 16, in La Salle's absence, Moringet was murdered in his sleep along with two loyal followers. On March nineteenth, La Salle himself was shot in the head, while joining this group. The murderer concealed himself in tall grass near the encampment and caught La Salle by surprise. Stripped naked, his body was left to the vultures.

So ended the life of one of the most intrepid leaders and explorers the French ever sent to this continent. Despite his constant frustrations, La Salle accomplished much, making his presence felt from Quebec to Texas. His dream of a line of French fortified trading posts connecting the St. Lawrence, the Great Lakes, and the Mississippi into a vast inland empire, had not been realized, but the shape of his design was clear to all. He constructed forts and trading posts on Lake Ontario, at Niagara, on Lake Michigan, on the Illinois River, and in Texas. He built and sailed the first ship on the upper Great Lakes. He did all this against overwhelming opposition from hostile Indians, from his followers, from members of the French colony, and from the Spanish. Had he lived, it seems certain La Salle's determination would have carried the day, and French influence on latter-day America might have been far stronger than it was.

La Salle and Father Hennepin in council with the Indians. This painting was done in the early nineteenth century by American artist George Catlin for the king of France to commemorate La Salle's discovery of the Mississippi.

National Gallery of Art

7

The Martyrs

THE PRIESTS AND MISSIONARIES who came to the Great Lakes region in the early years of French rule were neither explorers like Brulé nor colonizers like Champlain nor empire builders like La Salle. Yet they were to become all three before the end of the seventeenth century.

The first members of the Society of Jesus in New France, known more commonly as the Jesuits or Black Robes, arrived in Canada in 1611, when it started its Canadian mission, and its members are still there in fair numbers. They explored with Nicolet, Jolliet, and others. They plodded through the wilderness in search of pagan souls, amazing the Indians by their consummate courage. Filled with a zeal that to a later generation seems to border on insanity, they endured rejection, torture, and murder. Yet Gabriel Lalemant, Jean de Brébeuf, and Isaac Jogues were not mad but men of great faith and determination.

The story of the Jesuits in Canada begins in Paris at the court of Henry IV, where the king's confessor was a Jesuit, Father Pierre Coton. Coton, perhaps after hearing reports of the New World from Champlain and his friends, suggested to the king that Jesuit missionaries should be sent to accompany the next expedition to Canada. Henry liked the idea, although this may have been for mixed reasons. The Jesuits, openly distrustful of the king's politic conversion from Protestantism to Roman Catholicism when Henry gained the crown, had been banned from France from 1595 to 1603. Some of the king's Huguenot advisers, feeling that it was a mistake to have lifted the ban, believed he should transport the whole Jesuit order to Canada—the sooner the better. The judgment of the great historian Francis Parkman is kinder; he says that it was piety that drove the king to wish three thousand miles between himself and his confessor's companions. Henry's Medici queen was also in favor of a Jesuit mission to Canada. She believed every French enterprise should be accomplished with acts of piety, a virtue not much in evidence at court and therefore very necessary for others.

The first opportunity to send a Jesuit missionary to Canada came in 1607 with the petition of a merchant explorer, the Sieur de Poutrincourt, for permission to return to his colony in Acadia. Father Pierre Baird was chosen for the post, the cleric immediately speeding from his theology class at Lyons to the port of Bordeaux. But apparently no one had asked Poutrincourt how he felt about transporting a Jesuit, and as it turned out, Poutrincourt and his Huguenot partners did not take to the idea at all. Accordingly, he laid his plans carefully. In the winter of 1607–08, he gathered his baggage in Dieppe where, on February 26, he sailed away to the New World, neatly avoiding Father Baird at Bordeaux.

Wise in the ways of politics, Poutrincourt did take along a priest, a Father Jesse La Flèche. Like many another Catholic cleric, La Flèche distrusted the relatively liberal theological thinking of the Jesuits and welcomed any chance to hinder the widening of their influence. When Poutrincourt suggested that if Father La Flèche converted hordes of savages, perhaps the court would no longer feel it necessary to send Jesuits to Canada, La Flèche agreed enthusiastically.

On landing at Port Royal in Acadia, the priest went to work and was soon busy converting the Indians and conducting baptisms. The first Indian chieftain to be converted was leathery old Membertou, described as a centenarian. Among other manifestations of faith, this ancient agreed to divest himself of all but one wife. All his kin, numbering in the dozens, were also converted to Christianity, being rewarded by presents from Poutrincourt for doing so. By July, the list of converts was long and the supply of presents exhausted.

But the plans of Poutrincourt and La Flèche were swept away on May 14, 1610, when King Henry was assassinated in the streets of Paris by a religious fanatic. Many people blamed the murder on the Jesuits, some of whom had preached the dangerous doctrine that the law of God was higher than the law of kings, and that it was not wrong to kill an unjust—or heretical—king. The queen regent, however, protected the Jesuits, and their power at court became stronger than ever. There now was no question but that the Jesuits should go to Canada, and Poutrincourt's able young son, Biencourt, who had returned to France for supplies for the colony, was the person designated to take them.

Father Baird, who had been left waiting in Bordeaux previously, now was sent to Dieppe to join Biencourt. Accompanying Baird was another Jesuit, Father Massé, described as a man of oxlike patience. Unfortunately no one told the Huguenot shipowners, partners in Poutrincourt's venture, that Jesuits would now be included. At Dieppe this confrontation occurred in a drafty waterfront warehouse one January day in 1611.

The Huguenots made their position quite clear. They disliked and feared papists in general and Jesuits in particular. Furthermore, as French patriots, they regarded the Jesuits as Spanish agents who were attempting to undermine the French government. Either the Jesuits returned to Paris, or they wanted no further part in the venture.

Religious toleration improved and European unity was restored when money began to appear from under the folds of Father Baird's black robe. He was instructed, he said, to invest 3,800 livres in the settlement, making the Jesuits equal partners with the merchants. Also, if necessary, he would be willing to loan another amount to aid the venture. It *was* necessary. Another 737 livres changed hands. And finally, if the fitting out was delayed for any financial reason, that too could be remedied. Yes, in the fitting out there were such delays; the sum of 1,225 additional livres changed hands. The preparations for sailing now proceeded apace. On January 26, 1611, the ship was ready; Jesuits, Huguenots, and adventurers all set forth together, eyes on the horizon and thoughts aloft on religion, profit, and adventure. Thus began the mission to the New World of the Society of Jesus, carrying Catholic priests in league with Huguenot devils, carrying French patriots in unanimity with black-robed Spanish agents. Being winter, it was of course a stormy passage.

The landing in Acadia was stormy, also. Poutrincourt, on shore with his half-starved colony, clashed immediately with the Jesuits. Then a sullen peace ensued, until bitterness broke out again when the son of a trader, wintering his ship in a nearby inlet, took French leave with an unwilling Indian maiden. The savages were outraged and howled for justice. Being more numerous, their demands seemed reasonable. Poutrincourt agreed; punishment was in order. The Jesuits, however, urged forgiveness and soon carried the day. "Father," said

Poutrincourt in exasperation, "I know my duty, and I beg you will leave me to do it. With my sword I have hopes of Paradise, as you have with your breviary. You show me my path to Heaven. I'll show you yours on earth."

As Poutrincourt expected, the Indians soon found means for a subtle vengeance. Father Baird, in his desire to teach the Indians the Christian religion, had set out to learn their language. He had made considerable progress, he thought, when it occurred to him that all the Indian words he knew were words for the things of this world. He had words for snow, water, food, shelter, tree; but the Indians seemed to have no abstractions, such as God, Eucharist, Trinity, religion. He plied various savages with food and questions, seeking one who knew the words he needed. Finally, one day, came a willing subject who took the proferred biscuits and replied with a string of ready responses. What was the Indian word for God? The Indian offered a word. What for the Trinity? Again, the Indian grasped the meaning and presented a word. What for the Eucharist, redemption, penitence? More responses. So it went with the whole necessary language of religious training. Here was a clever Indian, mused the Father, scribbling furiously.

Armed with these, Father Baird began his preaching, and noted with pleasure the attentiveness and joy with which the Indians heard his words. Christianity had finally arrived in the New World, and at each session, the priest saw his audience grow steadily.

It was not until long after that Father Baird realized his garrulous Indian had substituted a string of scurrilous blasphemies for the holy words, and the glee of his savage listeners was not the joy of Christian discovery but the rattle of lurid humor.

On another occasion, Parkman relates, Father Baird was teaching Membertou the Lord's Prayer, which that ancient savage accepted with good grace until the phrase, "Give us this day our daily bread," was reached. Baird writes that the old Indian refused to go further, saying: "If I ask for nothing but bread, I shall get no fish or moosemeat."

But now this first New World mission fell on evil days. Fathers Baird and Massé had landed on May 22, 1611. They were joined on January 23, 1612, by Gilbert du Thet, a lay brother. He was sent out by Madame de Guercheville, the Jesuits' powerful patroness and close friend of the queen. Du Thet conferred with Fathers Baird and Massé, then hurriedly returned to France. Poutrincourt, meanwhile, had not been invited to join any of their discussions, but he knew something

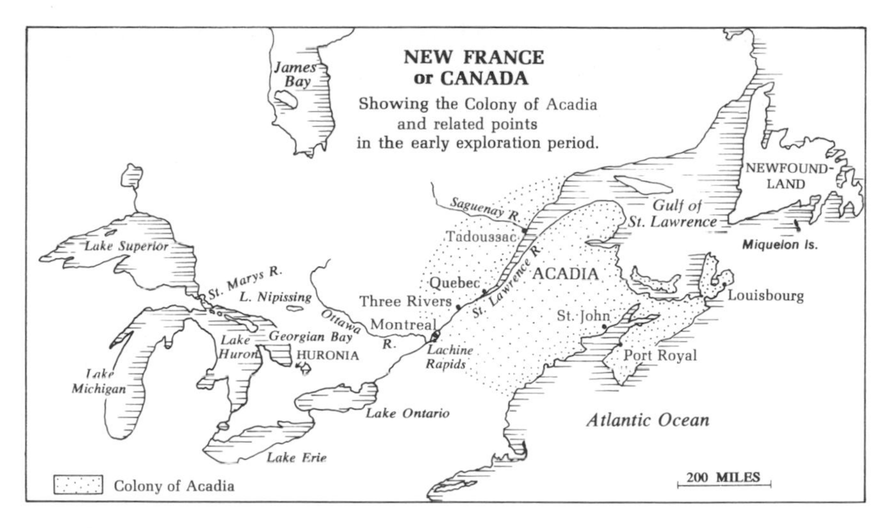

The first semipermanent French settlement in the New World was founded by Huguenots and adventurers in the winter of 1608. This map of Acadia shows Port Royal, where they landed.

was afoot. In May 1613 du Thet and another Jesuit, Father Quentin, returned aboard Madame de Guercheville's ship *Jonas*, arriving while Poutrincourt was absent hunting. Without even a farewell, Fathers Baird and Massé boarded the *Jonas* and sailed away to the north.

The plan was to establish a separate Jesuit colony along the northeastern headlands of our continent. Here the Jesuit work could flower without trouble from the commercial world. They soon found a likely spot and landed. The natives were friendly, but an argument over procedure soon ensued among the company itself. While this spat continued, a British man-of-war suddenly appeared on the horizon. It bore down on the group, bristling with guns, obviously guarding the whole New World for England. The warship opened fire from close range. The Jesuits attempted to fire back, but gunnery was not taught in the seminaries of Europe, so after a brief battle the company was captured. Du Thet, however, was killed, thereby becoming the first Jesuit to lose his life in the struggle for North America.

The captain of the British ship was Samuel Argall, who had sailed north on purpose from Virginia to disrupt French settlements. With his prize in tow, Argall proceeded south to Port Royal, the Acadian colony so recently deserted by the Jesuits. There he demolished Poutrincourt's fort. The French fled to the hills, so all the New World was once again secure for England. Argall then headed for Virginia, still towing the *Jonas*, but en route, a storm hit the Atlantic, driving the two ships off to the Azores. After obtaining fresh supplies, Argall decided to sail for England before returning to Virginia. There the priests in his charge were unceremoniously landed, ultimately finding their way back to France. Thus ended the first attempt of the Jesuit mission in France's New World colony.

The second attempt began in 1625. That spring, six Jesuits landed in Quebec to replace the sagging Recollect mission which Champlain had started in 1615. One priest from the ill-fated Acadian venture, Father Massé, was among them. But again war between France and Britain brought an end to the mission four years after it was founded, British gunboats capturing the entire colony on July 20, 1629. It was during this fighting that Brulé deserted to the British side. David Kirke, the freebooting British commander who took over the Quebec colony, transported the entire French force to England. There everyone learned that the war had ended the previous April, three months before Quebec was captured. Kirke freed his prisoners on English soil, and like their predecessors, they returned to France.

Despite a similar ending, however, the second Jesuit mission on these shores had accomplished far more than the first. During their four years at Quebec, the six Jesuits made considerable religious progress. They translated tracts, learned the Huron language, and gained an understanding of the work to be done. Father Le Jeune, the superior of the mission, soon realized that his best chance was to seek out the settled tribes in the Great Lakes area. If one Huron tribe was converted, others nearby might follow suit. The effect could snowball. Someday even the rapacious Iroquois Five Nations might be converted.

The nomadic northern Algonquians, on the other hand, were few in number and had little effect on other Indians. Their devotion to Christianity might be as fleeting as their attachment to the land. Believing that the greatest emphasis should be reserved for the greatest number, Le Jeune reached a political conclusion: the more northerly Algonquians would be bypassed, making the Huron mission the main target.

When under the terms of the peace treaty, Quebec was restored to France, two Jesuits returned on the first ship in July 1632. Others came with Champlain in 1633, when he was reinstated as governor. By 1634 six Jesuits were in residence, forming the nucleus of what later was to be the most determined group of missionaries ever seen on these shores. Their desire was the conversion of a continent. Their way of convincing the Indians was through acts of faith and piety. Their proofs were courage, self-denial, and martyrdom.

One of the sturdiest Jesuit leaders was Father Jean de Brébeuf, the priest who came with Champlain. Brébeuf was born in Calvados, France, in 1593. Entering the Jesuit order in 1617, he arrived in Quebec in 1625. He was taken by Kirke to England with the other Jesuits after the battle of 1629, but returned in 1633. In 1635 he journeyed to the land of the Hurons with Fathers Daniel and Davost and a small band of Frenchmen. Brébeuf wrote at length of the trip west, described the country, and provided such details as the following:

"I have kept count of the number of portages, and found that we carried our canoes thirty-five times, and dragged them at least fifty. I sometimes took a hand in helping my Savages; but the bottom of the river is full of stones, so sharp that I could not walk along, being barefooted.

"The second ordinary difficulty is in regard to provisions. Frequently one has to fast, if he misses the caches that were made when descending [from the Huron country to Quebec]; and, even if they are found, one does not fail to have a good appetite after indulging in them; for the ordinary food is only a little Indian corn coarsely broken between two stones, and sometimes taken whole in pure water; it is no great treat. Occasionally one has fish, but it is only a chance, unless one is passing some Tribe where they can be bought. Add to these difficulties that one must sleep on the bare earth, or on a hard rock, for lack of space ten or twelve feet square on which to place a wretched hut; that one must endure continually the stench of tired-out Savages; and must walk in water, in mud, in the obscurity and entanglement of the forest, where the stings of an infinite number of mosquitoes and gnats are a serious annoyance."

During the journey, Brébeuf was separated from his French companions and complained of the wearisome silence of his stoical Indian guides. Although he was unaccustomed to canoe travel, they forced him to paddle steadily. When they came to portages, the Indians hurried off with their baggage. Brébeuf had either to carry his own baggage or see them left behind. Some portages were several miles long, with each requiring several trips to transport all the luggage. Brébeuf's partners suffered even more, as his narrative continues:

"Father Davost, among others, was very badly treated. The Indians stole from him much of his little outfit. They compelled him to throw

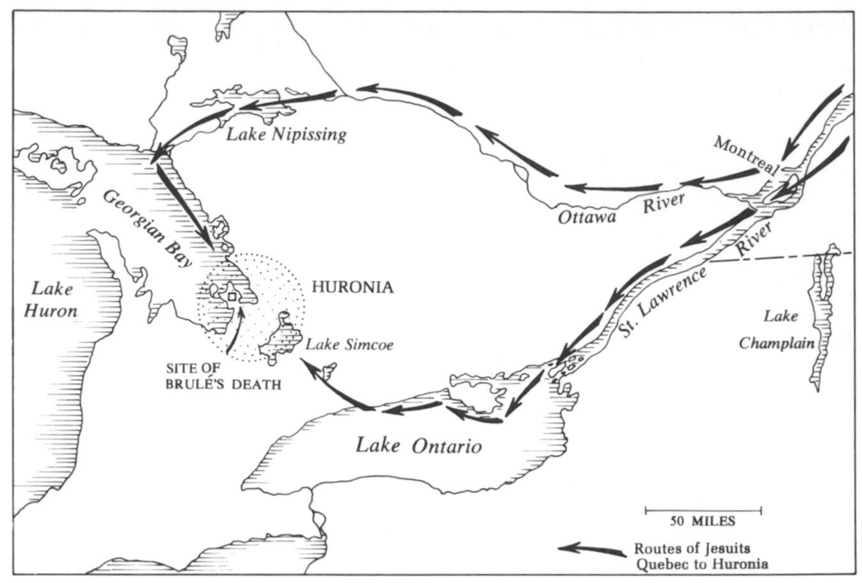

Jesuit missionaries traveled two different waterways to reach Huronia. Mainly they followed the northern route, up the Ottawa River to Lake Nipissing, then to Georgian Bay, and on to Huronia. The southern route followed the St. Lawrence to Lake Ontario, where a portage was made to Lake Simcoe, before continuing to Huronia.

away a little steel [grain] mill, and almost all our books, some linen, and a good part of the paper that we were taking, and of which we have great need. They deserted him at the Island, among the Algonquians, where he suffered in good earnest. When he reached the Hurons, he was so worn-out and dejected that for a long time he could not get over it.

"Father Daniel was abandoned, and compelled to seek another canoe, as also was Pierre, one of our men. Little Martin was very roughly treated, and at last was left behind with the Bissiriniens, where he remained so long that he was about two months on the road, and only arrived among the Hurons on the nineteenth of September. Baron was robbed by his savages on the very day he arrived in these regions; and he would have lost much more if he had not compelled them, through fear of his arms, to give him back a part of what they had taken. In short, all the Frenchmen suffered great hardships, incurred great expense, considering the few goods they had, and ran remarkable risks."

On arriving at the mission site, Brébeuf described the Huron dwellings:

"The cabins of this country are neither Louvres nor Palaces, nor anything like the buildings of our France, not even like the smallest cottages. They are, nevertheless, somewhat better and more commodious than the hovels of the Montagnais. I cannot better express the fashion of the Huron dwellings than to compare them to bowers or garden arbors—some of which, in place of branches and vegetation, are covered with cedar bark, some others with large pieces of ash, elm, fir, or spruce bark; and although the cedar bark is best, according to common opinion and usage, there is, nevertheless, this inconvenience, that they are almost as susceptible to fire as matches . . . There are cabins or arbors of various sizes, some two brasses in length, others of ten, others of twenty, of thirty, of forty; the usual width is about four brasses, their height is about the same. [A "brass" is six feet in length.] There are no different stories; there is no cellar, no chamber, no garret. It has neither window nor chimney, only a miserable hole in the top of the cabin, left to permit the smoke to escape."

The effect of such descriptions on luxury-loving seventeenth-century France can be imagined. After quartering with a few sympathetic natives for several weeks, a lodge was completed, and they moved in. Brébeuf describes the interior thus:

"As to the interior, we have suited ourselves; so that, even if it does not amount to much, the Savages never weary of coming to see it, and, seeing it, to admire it. We have divided it into three parts. The first compartment, nearest the door, serves as an ante-chamber, as a storm door, and as a storeroom for our provisions, in the fashion of the Savages. The second is that in which we live, and is our kitchen, our carpenter shop, our mill, or place for grinding the wheat, our Refectory, our parlor and our bedroom. On both sides, in the fashion of the Hurons, are two benches which they call Endicha, on which are boxes to hold our clothes and other little conveniences; but below, in the place where the Hurons keep their wood, we have contrived some little bunks to sleep in, and to store away some of our clothing from the thievish hands of the Hurons. They sleep beside the fire, but still they and we have only the earth for bedstead; for mattress and pillows, some bark or boughs covered with a rush mat; for sheets and coverings, our clothes and some skins do duty. The third part of our cabin is also divided into two parts by means of a bit of carpentry which gives it a fairly good appearance, and which is admired here for its novelty. In the one is our little Chapel, in which we celebrate every day Holy Mass, and we retire there daily to pray to God. It is true that the almost continual noise they make usually hinders us—except in the morning and evening, when everybody has gone away—and compels us to go outside to say our prayers. In the other part we put our utensils. The whole cabin is only six brasses long, and about three and a half wide. That is how we are lodged, doubtless not so well that we may not have in this abode a good share of rain, snow, and cold. However, as I have said, they never cease coming to visit us from admiration, especially since we have put on two doors, made by a carpenter, and since our mill and our clock have been set to work. It would be impossible to describe the astonishment of these good people, and how much they admire the intelligence of the French. But they have said all when they have said they are *ondaki*, that is, Demons; and indeed we make profitable use of this word when we talk to them: 'Now, my brothers, you have seen that and admired it, and you think you are right when you see something extraordinary, in saying *ondaki*, to declare that those who make so many marvels must be Demons . . .' "

And here, with the wondering Indians in their hands, the Jesuits began what they called a "steady harangue" on Christianity. When interest flagged, the Jesuits called on grain mill and clock for help, the latter being the marvel of all Huronia that year. Brébeuf writes of these two mechanisms:

"No one has come who has not wished to turn the mill; nevertheless we have not used it, inasmuch as we have learned by experience that our Sagamites [grains] are better pounded in a wooden mortar, in the fashion of the Savages, than ground within the mill. I believe it is because the mill makes the flour too fine. As to the clock, a thousand things are said of it. They all think it is some living thing, for they cannot imagine how it sounds of itself; and, when it is going to strike, they look to see if we are all there and if some one has not hidden, in order to shake it.

"They think it hears, especially when, for a joke, some one of our Frenchmen calls out at the last stroke of the hammer, 'That's enough,' and then it immediately becomes silent. They call it the Captain of the day. When it strikes they say it is speaking; and they ask when they come to see us how many times the Captain has already spoken. They ask us about its food; they remain a whole hour, and sometimes several, in order to be able to hear it speak. They used to ask at first what it said. We told them two things that they have remembered very well; one, that when it sounded four o'clock of the afternoon, during winter, it was saying, 'Go out, go away that we may close the door,' for immediately they arose, and went out. The other, that at midday it said 'Come, put on the kettle'; and this speech is better remembered than the other, for some of these spongers never fail to come at that hour, to get a share of our Sagamite. They eat at all hours, when they have the wherewithal, but usually they have only two meals a day, in the morning and in the evening; consequently they are very glad during the day to take a share with us."

Finally, Brébeuf plied the Indians with other wonders:

Father Isaac Jogues, shown here addressing the Mohawks, was one of several Jesuit missionaries who came to New France during the seventeenth century. Although they made some progress among the Hurons, the Jesuits were not trusted by the Iroquois. Father Jogues was tortured to death in western New York State in 1646.

Works of Parkman

"Speaking of their expressions of admiration, I might here set down several on the subject of the magnet, into which they looked to see if there was some paste; and of a glass with eleven facets, which represented a single object as many times; of a little phial in which a flea appears as large as a beetle; of the prism, of the joiner's tools; but above all of the writing, for they could not conceive how, what one of us, being in the village, had said to them, and put down at the same time in writing, another, who meanwhile was in a house far away, could say readily on seeing the writing. I believe they have made a hundred trials of it. All this serves to gain their affections, and to render them more docile when we introduce the admirable and incomprehensible mysteries of our Faith; for the belief they have in our intelligence and capacity causes them to accept without reply what we say to them."

But this use of "magic" led in a direction Brébeuf had not anticipated. The superstitious Hurons decided that Brébeuf's abilities with the clock portended other powers; they believed secrets of greater importance were locked under his skullcap. In succeeding years, when the weather worked well with crops, he and his Jesuit brothers were thanked. When a drought came, they were upbraided and asked to mend their ways. Suggestions that the Indians join in their prayer brought only rebuke; or when the Jesuits prayed without producing a downpour, the Hurons were sure the palefaces were summoning fiendish spirits to punish the Indians. Even worse, smallpox began to devastate the tribes in the region, and this led directly to serious trouble for the Jesuits.

Unknowingly, like their fellow colonizers farther south, the French had introduced smallpox to Canada early in the seventeenth century. The French had a measure of immunity to the disease, but it rapidly spread in epidemic proportions throughout the tribes of the Great Lakes region. The Indians soon saw that only they were dying, so the surviving natives placed the blame on the priests. The sickness was the result of evil spells. It came from the priests' incantations; it came from their praying. It came from the ribbon tied aloft on a tree by Jesuits to tell the wind's direction, which the Indians now interpreted as deadly spirits wafting over the land.

Indian persecution of the Jesuits began in the late 1640's, increasing as the epidemic continued. The Jesuits considered the persecution inspired by the devil to prevent their work. They had obtained a few converts; they were making progress. The devil became alarmed and sent his strongest forces against their work. They, in turn, responded by working even harder for Christianity—all of which only increased the Indians' wrath. And so passions rose.

The Indians, however, were awed by the Jesuits' remarkable abilities or cowed by their courage, thus refraining from outright slaughter. The Christians therefore persevered with reckless determination. When a pox-ridden infant was heard wailing through lodge walls, the passing Jesuit forced himself inside, spoke any commonplace, or offered gifts as bribes, or did anything else to reach the dying child. Then, as though suddenly seeing the infant, he would touch the fevered forehead with a wet handkerchief, murmur baptismal words without moving his lips, and thus rescue another soul from eternal fire.

The touch of the handkerchief and the moment's silence were not, however, lost on the watchful Indians. When death rapidly claimed the feverish child, they leapt to the obvious conclusion: the priest and his spell had killed the child.

Father Paul Le Jeune baptizes an infant dying of smallpox while the suspicious parents look on. The Jesuits, themselves somewhat immune to the disease, unwittingly spread it among the Indians. It quickly grew to epidemic proportions, and the Hurons accused the priests of using magic to kill their children.

Works of Parkman

So the storm grew, with the persecution increasing to stone-throwing, threats against the Jesuits' lives, destruction of their property. One Jesuit who entered a lodge during the smallpox epidemic was suddenly faced by a drawn bow, the arrow aimed directly at his chest. The priest stood his ground and stared the savage down, all the while "commending myself to God and expecting to leave this earth at any moment."

But Christianity had some effect on the Hurons for the martyrdom that came to Jean de Brébeuf, Isaac Jogues, Gabriel Lalemant, and many others did not come from the Hurons but mostly at the hands of the Iroquois. Father Jogues was captured by the Iroquois, tortured, then escaped to France aboard a Dutch vessel. Returning to Canada the same year, he went again to the Iroquois nation and was there killed by torture in 1646. Brébeuf and Lalemant, despite their harassment among the Hurons, were never physically harmed until they were captured and tortured to death by the rampaging Iroquois. Other French Jesuits were killed by the Yazoo, the Sioux, the Natchez, and the Chickasaw Indians. But only one died at the hands of a Huron. That slaying occurred in December 1649 at the height of the Iroquois attacks on Huronia. It later was considered merely an isolated incident. Nearly two dozen Jesuits died violent deaths in Canada during this period, while many others died of disease or natural causes. Most never returned to their native France.

Despite these losses, the Jesuits thrived in the New World, at least for a time. Their *Relations*, printed in France, inspired other Jesuits, nuns, and wealthy patrons to aid the Canadian missions, so that each year saw more and more Jesuit activity on these shores. Their star rose until about 1685 when the Society of Jesus began to lose ground in Europe, the Canadian missions feeling the pinch soon after. European political struggles also began to bear down upon the New France colony. The Treaty of Utrecht in 1713 stripped France of Newfoundland, Acadia, and Hudson Bay. Growing English power galvanized French and Jesuit forces in the eighteenth century, but by then it was too late. After several inconclusive wars, Quebec fell to the British in 1759, and the next year Montreal fell, completing the rout. In 1761, the French parliament forced Louis XV to suppress the influence of the Jesuits in France. By 1773, only eleven of them remained in Canada. That year, Pope Clement XIV suppressed the Society of Jesus throughout the world, excepting only Russia and parts of Poland. The order was restored in 1801 by Pius VII, and began to rebuild after that date.

About twelve hundred Jesuits are now in Canada, principally in the eastern provinces.

The dynamic activities of the Jesuits in the Great Lakes region were marred in later years by bickering and petty slanders. Their superiors quarreled endlessly with Governor Frontenac in the last decades of the seventeenth century, disputes over property or jurisdiction often replacing attempts to Christianize the Indians. Complaints of profiteering in the fur trade and self-aggrandizement hovered over some of the Jesuit leaders. Those living in the frontier wilderness found it hard to square their efforts with these inequities.

Despite all, however, the Jesuits were a powerful influence during the entire history of New France, and their writings have left a useful record for understanding a colorful chapter in the Great Lakes story.

Perhaps the most important animal in American history is the beaver, pictured here beside a woodland pond. The fur trade, which it largely inspired, led to the exploration of the Great Lakes region, caused war between France and Britain, and hastened the downfall of the American Indian.

Horace T. Martin, *History and Traditions of the Canadian Beaver*

8

Long Live Castor

THE GREAT LAKES COUNTRY developed many intrepid explorers, selfless missionaries, and national leaders in the early colonial period, but the magnet that drew all these men of history was a silky-furred industrious little creature interested only in popple sticks, dams, pond-lilies and mud. The attraction of this animal engulfed Europe in war, led to conquest of our continent, and brought both the animal and his Indian neighbors nearly to extinction.

The North American beaver, *Castor canadensis,* was found in 1600 all across our watery continent in large numbers. His habitat included all of Canada and the United States, excepting only small areas in the southwestern and southeastern states. Stretching from coast to coast and from the Arctic Ocean to Mexico, its range was sprinkled with rivers, lakes, marshes, ponds, creeks, and myriad other crannies where rain and meltwaters could gather. Castor lived here, built his dams and homes, and raised his young in profusion.

The beaver's adult life starts at about two years of age when he is forced out of the parental home after the birth of a new litter of kittens, or kits as they are generally known. He must then find a mate and build his own lodge, as his house is called. If his home pond is already crowded, he must travel until he finds a suitable patch of water. When he finds it, it is always where the water is flowing, and as though in terror at its loss, he starts constructing a dam immediately. With his sharp incisor teeth, he chews down trees and saplings, then drags them to his dam site to block the flow of water. His front paws are excellent for this work, almost like human hands. When grown, the beaver weighs between thirty-five and sixty pounds, and measures up to three feet in length from nose to flat tail tip. If his size prevents him from moving a large tree, he simply chews it into convenient lengths.

The beaver is a member of the rodent family distinguished by their prominent incisor teeth. In the beaver, these front teeth grow throughout his life. It is said that unless he keeps chewing steadily, they will grow until his jaws cannot move, and he will die of starvation. To be "busy as a beaver" thus is demanded by nature, and throughout their range in the sixteenth century, beavers were obviously busy. The first explorers found beaver dams in profusion. These formed the most perfect flood-control system ever devised, the network of small dams producing widespread and effective water conservation. Moisture was available for soil, ground water, forests, fish, and waterfowl. The destruction of these natural resources did not start until after 1600 when the beaver population was reduced by trapping. As the beaver was trapped out, the dams went unrepaired and soon washed away. Floods, soil loss, and other destruction of our natural resources soon followed. With the ponds went the waterfowl. Loggers and settlers completed the job in the 1800's by stripping away forest cover, further exposing the soil to water and flood erosion. Today the beaver has not vanished, but their number is but a mere fraction of its former total, primarily because so much of the beaver's natural habitat is gone.

Beaver lodges are built in ponds created by beaver dams. They are dome-shaped piles of sticks and branches, anchored to the bottom, usually six to eight feet in diameter. The construction is a dense tangle, difficult to tear apart. Inside there are upper and lower chambers, the lower provided with escape holes to the water below. There the beaver pair raises its young, usually two to six kits. Beaver mate for life, and when the lodge becomes too crowded, the parents drive away the grown kits who amble off to find their own patch of water and repeat, in turn, the activities of their parents.

So castor spread his kind and for centuries lived beside the Indian as both proliferated over the continent. The Indians trapped and hunted beaver to fit their needs, but these needs were limited and the number killed was never very high. Accordingly, the beaver prospered.

When the first explorers reached the Great Lakes region in the sixteenth century, they were deeply impressed by the beaver. Fur was already in short supply in Europe, having long been used for luxury clothing. Methods of wildlife conservation were unknown, and the European beaver population was dwindling. Under steady trapping, beaver were last noted in England in the 1520's. Supplies were also thin in Poland by that date, and the garment guilds of Europe were starved for good fur. When the first North American beaver pelts reached Europe in the mid-sixteenth century, the commercial world was electrified. The possibilities for large profits were apparent, and a lively trade in beaver was soon under way. No one has ever identified the first of these traders although it is known that ships from many nations probed our eastern seaboard during the 1500's. At first these ships came only to fish. Their captains, however, soon realized that the Indians would trade valuable furs for trinkets, axes, knives, and brandy. From this time on, the trade increased steadily, and many nations took part.

In 1600, Pierre Chauvin secured from Henry IV of France a ten-year monopoly on all fur trading along the Gulf of St. Lawrence. In turn, Chauvin agreed to found a settlement of five hundred persons along the river. Chauvin's monoply was the first of many in what became one of the most colorful commercial periods in history. The fur companies were without parallel as business ventures, leaving a trail of amazing activities, many of which were outside the realm of profit-making.

Chauvin's expedition in 1600 traded the Indians successfully out of a shipload of furs, including marten, otter, and fox, but primarily beaver. Chauvin died in 1602, perhaps from the shock of this success, but a partner returned in 1603 to continue the trade. Champlain was on that expedition, the sights he saw whetting his appetite. When he returned in 1608 it was as a founder of the Company of Associates, a group of St. Malo and Rouen merchants who now pushed the fur trade in earnest. With the backing of the French crown, these men controlled the colonial trade for nearly twenty years. In 1622 two Huguenots named William and Emery de Caën persuaded the French government to oust the earlier company, and though Champlain objected vigorously, the De Caëns held the monopoly until Richelieu came to power in France.

Richelieu was quite another story. The wan, slender Cardinal ruled France brilliantly but seemed to lack commercial acumen in his New World dealings. Ousting the De Caëns, he formed the Company of 100 Associates in 1627. Bravely, this group of powerful Frenchmen began to invest in the fur trade, but suffered one reverse after another until 1645. At that time, light seemed to penetrate, and the eight principal

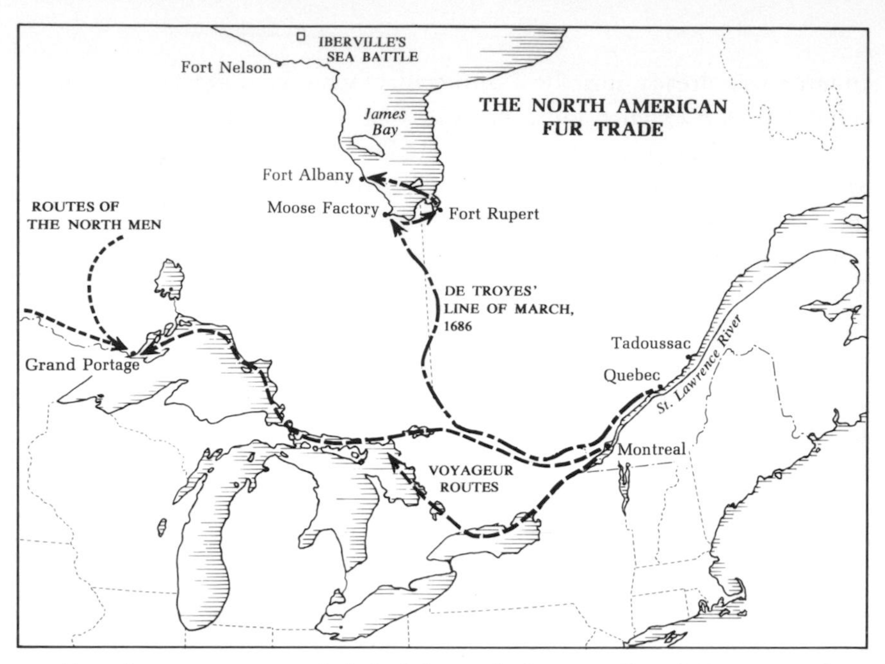

French voyageurs traveled the lakes and rivers to Grand Portage and other gathering places, bringing trade goods from Quebec. There at annual rendezvous they traded their goods for the furs that the so-called North men brought in from the wilderness.

traders took over. The old organization was leased to the Compagnie des Habitants, sometimes called the New Company. Different trade policies were then placed in force; profits began to accumulate, and jealousies to grow. By 1664 the company was accused of using brandy in trade with the Indians. It was dissolved, to be replaced the same year by the Company of the West Indies, or the West as it was familiarly called. The same year Canada became a royal colony under a governor general, with the king's "intendant" being added a year later. The governor was the king's military, political, and administrative agent in Canada, while the intendant controlled legal and financial matters. These two ruled with a bishop, backed by five councilors, an attorney general, and a secretary. The group judged all civil and criminal matters, controlling of course the fur trade as well, the one business of New France. The fur trade was closely restricted under this new system, with licenses issued to the twenty-five leading traders. Such a limitation was designed to keep fur prices high, but the Great Lakes country was already sprinkled with traders who were increasingly discontented with Quebec and Montreal. This new restriction to twenty-five legal traders only meant new difficulties for the coureurs de bois. Many began to trade illegally with the English and Dutch colonies to the south, placing new strains on English-French relations.

These strains took concrete form when two coureurs de bois, Médard Chouart, Sieur des Groseilliers, and his brother-in-law, Pierre Esprit Radisson, were fined for trading without a license. They had been in the bush, they said, when the rule was established; they did not know about it. They also tried to suggest that Hudson Bay offered an easier route for the collection of furs. Their complaints and their suggestions were ignored; the fines were enforced.

But these two men would not be put off so easily. They had reckoned correctly that by 1670 the fur trade was already moving beyond the Great Lakes region. They had seen what was happening, and their observations meant a new and vigorous era was to open on the Great Lakes.

The Great Lakes by this time had become a water highway for the fur trade, useful as a transport route, but long and dangerous. The voyageurs had created their own way of life, using large Montreal canoes to make the thousand-mile voyage from tidewater to Grand Portage, Minnesota, on the northwestern shore of Lake Superior, the jumping-off point for fur-trade activities in the watery northwest interior. The French voyageurs were hardy and tough. An inkling of their brand can be gleaned from the comment of one of them, which prefaces Grace Lee Nute's book *The Voyageur*: "I could carry, paddle, walk, and sing with any man I ever saw. I have been twenty-four years a canoe man, and forty-one years in service; no portage was ever too long for me. Fifty songs could I sing. I have saved the lives of ten voyageurs. Have had twelve wives and six running dogs. I spent all my money in pleasure. Were I young again, I should spend my life the same way over. There is no life so happy as a voyageur's life."

On their journeys, these men paddled steadily hour after hour, day after day. The cargo was made into packs weighing some ninety pounds each. When heavy rapids forced them to portage overland, each voyageur normally carried two such packs at a jog trot. Some were said to carry three and even four packs.

Passengers often went west from Montreal on these journeys, sometimes writing about their experiences. One has described the scene as follows: "These canoes were exceedingly strong and capacious, they were about thirty-six feet in length by six feet wide near the middle; and although the birch bark which formed a thin external coating for their ribs of white cedar, and their longitudinal laths of the same wood appeared to compose but a flimsy vessel, yet they usually carried a weight of five tons. It may be as well to state that this cargo was very carefully stored, in order to remove any unequal pressure, which would have been fatal to such a vessel. Four poles, three or four inches at their thickest ends, denominated by the Canadians *grand perch*, were laid side by side in the middle of the bottom of the canoe. On these poles, the cargo was carefully arranged so that all the weight rested on them, and none allowed to press against the bare and unprotected sides of the canoe. Every package was made up of the weight of ninety pounds and none heavier.

"The five tons included the provisions of ten men, sufficient to support them about twenty to twenty-two days. Each canoe was provided with a mast and lug-sail, and also each man had a ten-foot setting pole, of good ash, shod with an iron ferrule at each end, for assisting the men towing with a strong line in ascending the rapids. The paddles were supplied by the canoe-men, each bringing his own. Each canoe had also a camp-kettle, provided by the owners, as also a few Hambro lines, a bundle of *watap*, roots of the pine tree, for stitching up any seam that might burst, a parcel of gum of a resinous nature, for paying over the seams when leaky, a piece of birch bark for repairs, hatchet, crooked knife, and a few other indispensable articles."

Every ax, knife, and copper kettle had to be carried west in these canoes for many weeks before a beaver hide was ever seen. Grand Portage, Minnesota, on the northwest shore of Lake Superior was the gathering place. Now a National Monument, that post saw the trappers from the forest meet the voyageur canoes each spring. These "North men" brought their furs, collected over the winter, to exchange for the voyageurs' trade goods. The furs were loaded into the Montreal canoes and the trade goods went into the trappers' canoes. After a good rousing drunken brawl, everyone returned whence they came.

The canoes of the trappers were somewhat smaller than those of the voyageurs, averaging twenty-five feet in length. They normally carried three thousand pounds of cargo and an eight-man crew. A helmsman stood in the stern. Such a boat probably weighed not more than three hundred or four hundred pounds, so with cargo and crew it was transporting at least ten times its own weight. The smaller size was required on the more restrictive waterways north and west of Lake

Superior. The trappers, of course, claimed their canoes required more skill in the rugged Canadian interior, while the Montrealers said their larger canoes called for greater strength. Such differences of opinion were generally expressed at Grand Portage, and the resultant scenes of carnage may be imagined.

While under way, the voyageurs ate about as follows, morning and evening, day after day, as reported by a company clerk who accompanied them on one nineteenth-century trip:

"The tin kettle in which they cooked their food, would hold eight or ten gallons. It was hung over the fire, nearly full of water, then nine quarts of peas—one quart per man, the daily allowance—were put in; and when they were well bursted, two or three pounds of pork, cut into strips, for seasoning, were added, and all allowed to boil or simmer till daylight when the cook added four bisquits [sic], broken up, to the mess, and invited all hands to breakfast. The swelling of the peas and bisquit had now filled the kettle to the brim, so thick that a stick would stand upright in it. . . . The men now squatted in a circle, the kettle in their midst, and each one plying his wooden spoon or ladle from kettle to mouth, with almost electric speed, soon filled every cavity."

The long voyageur journeys from Montreal to the interior emphasized the peculiar geography of North America. Sixty-five per cent of Canada drains north to the Arctic Ocean or Hudson Bay. Another large portion lies west of the Rocky Mountains, draining to the Pacific. Likewise, the United States drains mainly south to the Gulf of Mexico or west off the Pacific slope. The Great Lakes chain, although it reaches nearly the middle of the continent, drains east along the St. Lawrence River valley and involves only a relatively small portion of the whole continental land area. The Great Lakes offered easy access to the interior of our continent in the early days, but by the 1670's, exploration was ended, settlement had not yet begun, and the number of beaver was declining. Clearly the fur trade, the only commerce in the area, had to move west. Groseilliers and Radisson were correct in maintaining that the shortest, easiest route to the wealth of furs in western Canada was no longer through the Great Lakes but through Hudson Bay. But the French fined the two trappers heavily and ignored their suggestion.

With their trade stopped at Montreal, and smarting under their punishment, Groseilliers and Radisson took their case to the English, who listened more sympathetically. A plan was hatched, and on May 2,

1670, the English crown provided a charter for the enterprise which was issued to "The Governor and Company of Adventurers of England trading into Hudson's Bay." This group was composed of wealthy London merchants and members of the aristocracy who signed Groseilliers and Radisson to lead a few gentlemanly adventures on Hudson Bay—so long as these carried high profits. The group was not disappointed. It became known as the Hudson's Bay Company, providing its owners large measures of both adventure and profit.

From the founding of the Hudson's Bay Company to 1763, the fur trade of North America was marked by constant clashes between the French, the British, and their Indian allies. The Hudson's Bay Company was one of the major bones of contention throughout this century of conflict. In the early years, it quickly presented the French traders with tough-minded competition in the Canadian interior. For a time after Hudson's Bay Company was founded, the Indians so liked English bargains that they carried their finest furs to Moose Factory, Fort Albany, and York Factory, all located on Hudson Bay. Factories, or the factory system, involved a central trading post where goods were stored for any Indian who cared to exchange furs for trinkets,

William Del'Isle map, Paris, 1703. Del'Isle, a cartographer, drew together information from many sources to produce this early, surprisingly accurate map of Canada. It is the first map to include Detroit, which was founded in 1701.

Michigan Department of Conservation

axes, knives, guns, or whisky. The post was run by a factor, an employee of the Hudson's Bay Company. This was a low-cost system compared to the earlier method of the one-man traveling trader, who went from tribe to tribe, collecting furs and dealing with Indians on an individual basis. The problem of the factory system was to obtain cooperation from the Indians. On Hudson Bay, the English for a time had only to unload their wares from ships, make their trades, and load the furs aboard the waiting British vessels. They could afford to give bargains. To meet this low-overhead competition, French merchants had to trim profits sharply. The pinch was felt as far as Paris.

In the wilderness, the struggle for the fur trade resulted in virtually uninterrupted warfare between French and British for almost one hundred years. In Europe, the two nations remained nominally at peace for long intervals, although on four occasions war was declared officially, with ownership of the North American fur trade counted as one of the main prizes of victory.

During the several clashes in that century-long conflict, the fur trade rose and fell depending on the course of the struggle between France and Britain. Most of the fighting occurred on Hudson Bay and

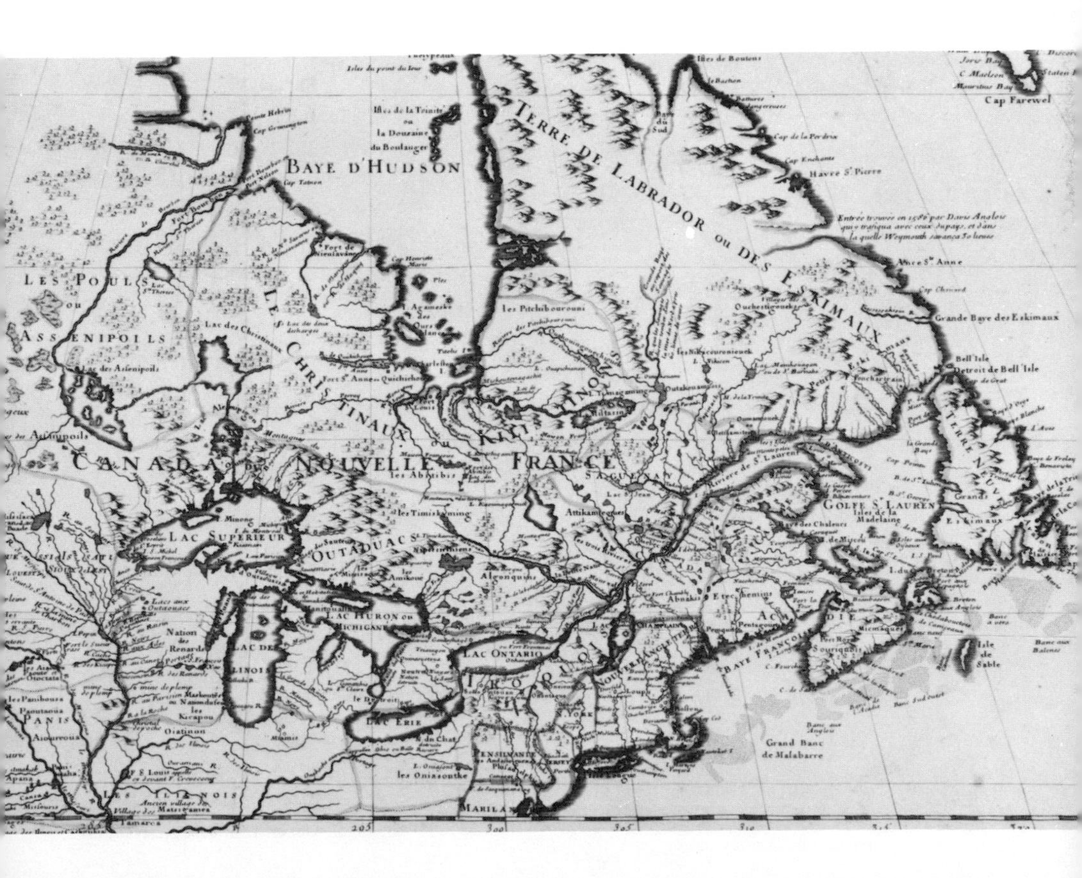

in the Great Lakes region, even though the furs now were coming from Northwest Canada. Some years, the English incited the Iroquois to kill the French fur trade by raids along the Ottawa and St. Lawrence Rivers. But occasionally, the supply of furs was so great that prices dropped sharply. Merchants sometimes even destroyed furs to restore the price—a frightful waste of resources. In 1700, for example, three fourths of all the furs collected in Montreal were burned, the smoke and stench hanging over the city for days.

Trapping methods varied. The Indians often hunted during the night or at twilight when they could glide down lakes or ponds in canoes and catch the beaver unaware with an arrow or bullet. Heavy log deadfalls were used, too, supported so that the beaver would be crushed when he tugged a piece of bait from under a log. Spears, snares, and pits also were employed. Iron traps, roughly similar to present-day traps, were used after 1700, mostly by white trappers. But Indians also obtained some traps, usually on condition that they trade only with the owner. The iron in these traps was of poor quality, frequently breaking when operated in icebound beaver ponds. This caused the Indians to inspect and criticize traps before accepting them, ultimately leading to improvement in trap design. Traps were constructed in blacksmith shops at key points throughout the fur country, such as at the Straits of Mackinac, where one shop produced 347 beaver traps and 600 muskrat traps during the winter of 1734–35.

Three methods of fur collection developed. One group of individual traders went among the Indians, lived with them, took wives in various tribal areas, and traded goods for furs. The Indians trapped the beaver and prepared the pelt. The trader passed from tribe to tribe, collecting as he went; among other things, his numerous wives were a practical answer to the question of Indian loyalty; the trader could count on friendly relations in any tribe where he kept a wife. A second group of whites went into Indian territory and trapped on their own, competing directly with the Indians without offering trade goods in exchange. The Indians sometimes grew testy about this approach, but it was commonly used. Then there were trappers who worked for the large fur companies, being paid fixed wages for their winter's work.

Out of these three methods grew others as the fur trade moved into the Northwest. The factory system, first used by the Hudson's Bay Company, was prevalent in the American Northwest from 1796 to 1822. The rendezvous system requiring a prearranged meeting place where the year's trade goods were exchanged for the winter's furs, grew up somewhat later. Grand Portage on Lake Superior was in effect such a rendezvous point, although it was never so designated. The Rocky Mountain rendezvous system really lasted only about a decade, from the 1820's into the 1830's, with rendezvous points at Pierre's Hole under the shadow of the three Tetons, in the valley of the Green beside the Wind River Mountains, in Cache Valley north of the Great Salt Lake, at South Pass, and at a few other points.

The men who first developed the fur trade in the Great Lakes wilderness seldom won any hold on large fortunes. Daniel Greysolon Duluth is a case in point. He became the uncrowned king of the voyageurs, developing the fur trade extensively around the west end of Lake Superior. He explored the headwaters of the Mississippi for the government of France. He rescued La Salle's vain and unappreciative Recollect priest Father Louis Hennepin from the Sioux. But for all his trouble his furs were confiscated, and he was thrown into prison in Montreal. A change in French colonial policies had made his long-established trapping efforts illegal. He was later released and returned

French voyageurs carried on the fur trade in sturdy birchbark canoes. In these canoes they traveled a thousand miles to Grand Portage on the northwest shore of Lake Superior. There their cargoes were traded for beaver pelts brought in by the coureurs de bois, or woods rangers.

Michigan Historical Commission

to his trade, thanks to Frontenac, but his activities thereafter lay under a cloud, and he died a lame, penniless old man. La Salle, as seen earlier, met his end in a Texas swamp, having never realized any real profits from his fur-trade enterprises.

Pierre Verendrye was another who suffered from his ambitions. He was authorized to push the fur trade west from Lake Superior, setting out from Montreal in 1731 with a large flotilla of canoes and with his hopes high for success. By 1744, he had nine battle wounds; one son and a favorite nephew were dead; his property at Montreal had been seized. He was also obliged to pay his fur-trade successor three thousand livres a year out of his supposed profits. Supposed profits were all he ever made. He died penniless.

Hundreds of unknown coureurs de bois and voyageurs lived similar financially unrewarded lives, suffered similar unrewarded ends. They advanced the cause of New France more than any other group, but their efforts passed largely unrecognized by the colonial government. This was the period when merchants along the St. Lawrence, known as the *bourgeous*, reaped the profits and managed the colony to their general advantage. Even some Jesuits were tempted to deal in fur,

This map, published in 1744, helped early fur traders find their way in the Great Lakes region. It appeared in Charlevoix's book, Journal of a Voyage, *and was prepared by N. Bellin, a Paris cartographer. Note the fictitious islands in Lake Superior and the mountain range down the center of Michigan's Lower Peninsula. Both of these false features continued to appear on maps for about a century.*

Michigan Department of Conservation

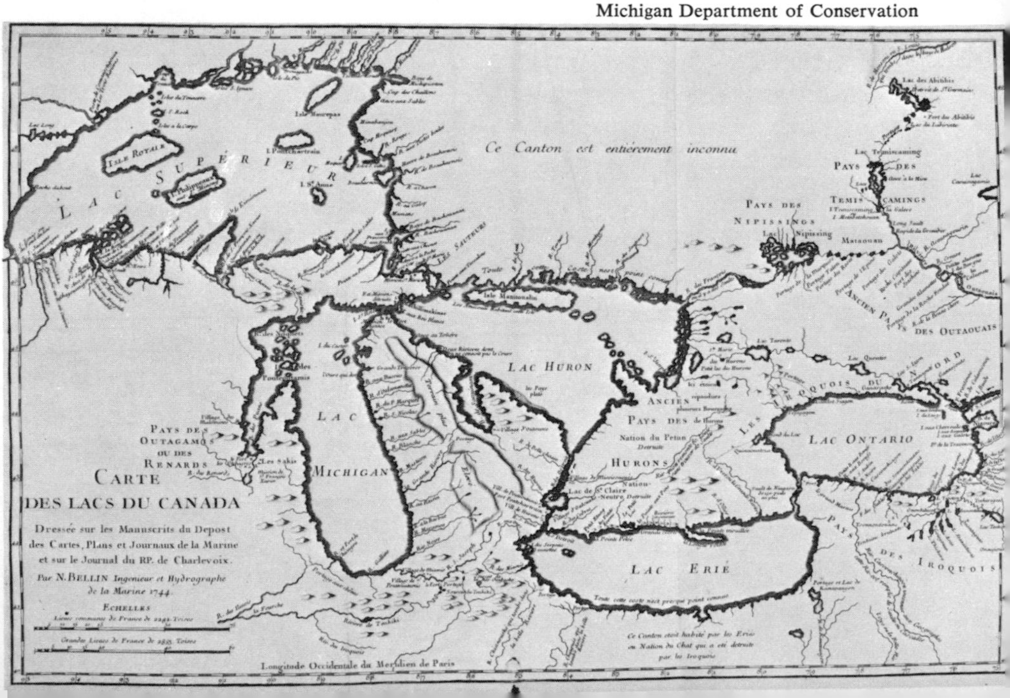

CARTE
DES LACS DU CANADA
Dressée sur les Manuscrits du Depost des Cartes, Plans et Journaux de la Marine et sur le Journal du RP. de Charlevoix.
Par N. BELLIN Ingenieur et Hydrographe de la Marine 1744.

Lac Superieur
Isle Royale
Ce Canton est entierement inconnu
Lac Huron
Lac Michigan
Lac Erié
Lac Ontario
Pays des Outagamis ou des Renards
Pays des Nipissings
Lac Nipissing
Ancien Pays des Hurons
Les Iroquois du Nord
Pays des Iroquois
Ancien Pays des Outaouais
Lac Temiscaming
Longitude Occidentale du Meridien de Paris

causing comments such as that of Frontenac, who accused the Black Robes, as he termed them, of being more concerned with conversion of Canadian beaver than of Indian souls. Being free of all trade restrictions, the Jesuits were not hampered in their activities. Their fur trading could be carried out secretly. Priests ordinarily did not engage directly in the fur trade, hiring secular *donnés*, or *engagés*, to increase the wealth of the order—all for the advancement of the Jesuit cause. One Ursuline nun even stored two hundred and sixty pounds of beaver pelts in her room as evidence of her piety.

With the fall of New France in 1763, one era of the fur industry ended, and another began. France had pioneered in the fur trade, but her colonial empire did not survive to see the peak of that commerce. The French are thus not remembered so much for their commercial success as for their exploration. Champlain, Jolliet, La Salle, Duluth, and many others were primarily interested in the profit to be made from furs. But they saw more of the continent than they did of beaver, leaving a knowledge of the country that after 1763 was to be turned into profit by Scotch and English businessmen. No private monopoly during French rule ever produced high profits, but their methods of dealing with the Indians, their transportation routes, and even their trapping procedures were adopted by British and American traders to make their fortunes in the fur trade.

The French really lost in two ways. They suffered commercial losses in colonial days, and the fur trade itself finally incited English jealousy, bringing on war, which led to the collapse of the entire colony of New France. Through the Hudson's Bay Company, Britain found a way to make the fur trade pay, and the profits were too tempting to ignore. In 1676, for example, the company transported 650 pounds sterling worth of trade goods into the Hudson Bay area, carting home in exchange 19,000 pounds worth of furs. By 1700, English traders were probing the lower Great Lakes, then crossing the Mississippi into Missouri and Iowa. In the north, they were firmly entrenched in Hudson Bay. From these two pincer points, they kept steady pressure on French trade in the center. While stirring the Iroquois tribes to cause trouble in the south, their shorter transportation route and factory system in the north established a favorable climate for trade, thus luring furs away from the French. Such free-booting frontier trade policies kept scratching at the sore until the so-called French and Indian War finally brought on the collapse of New France and placed Great Britain in full control.

Under British rule after Quebec fell in 1763, the fur trade was no longer a state-controlled monopoly. The Hudson's Bay Company was the oldest and strongest British enterprise but after the effects of the war receded, a group of Scottish merchants settled in Montreal, ready for business. By 1766, many individuals were trading furs in a limited but growing way. By 1780, competition was widespread and fierce. Ruthless and wasteful practices prevailed. Even young beaver were trapped, producing only small, relatively useless pelts. Trapping was carried on in summer and fall when the fur is in its worst condition. Brandy seduced Indians into such trapping or drew them away from loyalties to other traders.

In 1783 the glut of furs at Montreal had dropped profits to a disastrous level. A severe smallpox epidemic among the Indians aggravated the problem, thinning the number of available trappers. Driven to the wall, a group of Scottish traders formed the Northwest Company, their canoe flotilla leaving Montreal in the spring of 1784 as a small navy. This was the first unified effort to overcome the growing power of the Hudson's Bay Company.

For nearly forty years these two companies vied with each other on the frontier as well as on the auction blocks of Europe. No more varied companies ever existed, carrying on trade in a variety of Indian dialects, as well as in French, English, Dutch, and the brogue of the Scottish Highlands. The company ranks included bewigged merchants, red-sashed voyageurs, grizzled frontier traders, and naked savages. Fleets of weathered sailors and unweathered tailors were added, all being jumbled together to produce beaver garments for the fashionable in Europe and North America.

The advantage, however, remained with the Hudson's Bay Company, both because of its location and its single-minded beginnings. The Northwest Company, formed as a compromise out of necessity, had rancor built into its charter. Twice after its founding, splinter groups sheered off on their own. These splits occurred in 1785, a year after the company was formed, and again in 1801 when Alexander Mackenzie led a group of dissident Northwesters to start the XY Company. Both offshoot groups had brief lives, but they helped sap the strength of the Northwest Company. Its existence ended in 1821, when the Hudson's Bay Company bought it out. The combined companies, which retained the name of the older one, then formed a solid front in the rich fur lands of the west.

But before this happened, while the Northwest Company and the

Hudson's Bay Company were battling to gain control of the continental trade, a third giant was coming to life in the recently formed United States. This was John Jacob Astor's American Fur Company, based in New York. Astor was born in Waldorf, Germany, on July 17, 1763, just a few months after the Treaty of Paris gave Canada to Great Britain. He immigrated to New York in 1783, where he started his career as a musical-instrument dealer. Falling in with a fur trader almost by accident, the young drum salesman quickly saw the business possibilities in furs, soon after selling his music business for beaver pelts. To avoid the high British tariffs against American furs, he moved to Montreal, becoming a power in that city by 1800. When the tariff restrictions lessened, he returned to New York, founding the American Fur Company in 1808.

An old French trapper of the nineteenth century. Details in construction of the steel traps places the time as mid-century or later, well after all real activity in the North American fur trade had ended.

Horace T. Martin, *History and Traditions of the Canadian Beaver*

Astor was a brilliant tactician as well as a shrewd businessman. He early saw that divisive competition could ruin the fur trade for all concerned—himself most of all. He suggested to President Jefferson that his American Fur Company should incorporate all elements of United States trade against those of the Hudson's Bay Company. Jefferson's patriotism was properly aroused by his proposals. Since the Northwesters were trading in the Great Lakes region, Jefferson urged Astor to seek an alliance with the Montreal group. The Northwesters refused, but Astor got what he wanted—a split in the Northwest ranks. Several of their leading traders now joined the American Fur Company, and with great energy, Astor pushed his plans for a commercial fur empire stretching from coast to coast. In 1810 he founded the Pacific Fur Company, a subsidiary of the American Fur Company, sending two expeditions to establish trade in Oregon. One pushed up the Missouri River from St. Louis, armed with the knowledge Lewis and Clark had brought down that river a few years earlier. The other expedition went by sea, around Cape Horn, headed for the mouth of the Columbia River. This group arrived first and established the trading post of Astoria in March 1811, on the site of Fort Clatsop, the old Lewis and Clark wintering post.

By that time fur trading in the Great Lakes region was becoming an echo of the larger Western trade. Several British merchants had formed a small group named the Michilimackinac Company in 1783 with headquarters at Detroit and the Straits of Mackinac. The company grew to control much of the Michigan fur trade, but by 1796 competition from Astor's traders squeezed it without mercy. In 1811 the Mackinac Company, as it was called, finally sold out to Astor, who renamed it the South-West Company. It survived only until 1814 when it was absorbed by the parent American Fur Company.

With the fur trade moving ever more steadily toward the American Northwest, trapping declined elsewhere, and the Great Lakes became mainly a highway for east-west traffic. Several trade vessels regularly sailed the Lakes, and cities were growing on their shores, including Chicago, Detroit, Cleveland, Buffalo, and "York," which later changed its name to Toronto. Astor, with his usual acumen, foresaw the approaching end of the fur trade and in 1834 sold out his interests. By 1843 the company was in bankruptcy. It was reorganized as a commission house for furs in 1847, but North America was settling down to other commercial pursuits, and the fur trade was practically at an end.

Those who have started this journey with great fondness for the silky, industrious beaver and who have seen him and his world systematically destroyed, can now take heart. All is not lost. The beaver, under modern conservation laws, is once again prospering throughout large sections of North America. Like most vegetarian animals, his numbers are directly dependent on the amount of habitat available, and modern trapping laws allow the harvest of only those beavers surplus to that habitat. In many parts of the continent, the loud slap of castor's tail on still pond waters may yet be heard. The cautious canoeist can glide in close on a misty morning to observe a furry fellow here and there, popple stick in paw and glint in beady eye. The beaver was the first owner and prime protector of all North American natural resources, and it is cheering to know that he plans to remain at least awhile longer.

This drawing shows Indian and Northwest Company traders at Fort Thompson on Grand Island, near the south shore of Lake Superior. This post was used during the early nineteenth century.

The Great Lakes Historical Society

In the battle of Quebec, the British gained control of Canada, but they lost their leader, General James Wolfe. The above painting of his death is by Benjamin West.

National Gallery of Canada, Ottawa

9

To the Plains of Abraham

THE FIRST KNOWN CASUALTY in the struggle for the control of Canada was a luckless seaman killed by Basque fur traders at Tadoussac in 1608. The last was a gallant military commander who fell at Quebec a century and a half later, but little more than a hundred miles away. Both died beside the waters of the St. Lawrence, the only drainway of the Great Lakes, and both were Frenchmen.

That century and a half was marked by repeated war between France and Great Britain in both Europe and North America. In North America, there were four main periods of conflict: King William's War from 1689 to 1697; Queen Anne's War from 1702 to 1713; King George's War from 1744 to 1748; and the French and Indian War from 1754 to 1763, with final victory in the struggle going to the British, thus ending the long battle for the control of Canada.

Certainly it was fitting that these wars should begin and end on waters that had flowed through the Great Lakes, for the main focus of Canada's early history was centered around the Lakes. The early settlements, the first Jesuit missions, the exploration, the early fur trade were all located around the Lakes. The dreams of Champlain and La Salle were shaped by the Lakes, and the main cities and industries of present-day Canada are still found beside these waters.

The first skirmish in the battle for Canada occurred in 1608 when one of Champlain's ships arrived on the St. Lawrence to proclaim Tadoussac a French possession. The only ones who heard the announcement were aboard a Basque trader standing in the bay, and they objected strenuously, pointing out that they were first on the scene. In the ensuing debate, a French seaman was killed; three others were wounded; and the French were persuaded of the justice of the Basque argument. But when Champlain's larger, more heavily armed vessel arrived a few days later, a more reasonable solution became apparent to the French: Canada was not large enough for both Basques and Frenchmen. The Basques, suddenly appreciating the forcefulness of the French logic, agreed to go elsewhere. The unfortunate seaman, meanwhile, was buried at Tadoussac.

While the Basques happened to be involved in this first incident, the two prime contenders over the years were always France and Britain. North America, for all its vast wilderness, was not big enough for both. The French colony of New France, settled mainly at Quebec and Montreal, strengthened its hold over the Great Lakes and the Ohio and Mississippi Rivers. To slow the French advance, the British gave the Iroquois rifles and brandy, then reminded them of French military invasions and bad French goods. The result was continuing frontier clashes between the two nations.

When the Hudson's Bay Company successfully established its first factories in 1670, the scale of the conflict increased. Despite the nominal peace then prevailing, the French decided to mount an overland expedition in March 1686 against the British company. Chevalier de Troyes, the French commander, led a troop of a hundred men north-

west from Quebec in hopes of striking secretly at each British post in turn. These posts—Moose Factory, Fort Rupert, and Fort Albany—were located at the mouths of the principal rivers flowing into James Bay. It took three months for the expedition to make the journey, traveling overland and by canoe, but the French carried it off without arousing the British. When their scouts came in sight of Moose Factory on the Moose River, they crept up to watch through willow thickets, then drew back behind a slope to wait for nightfall. Puffing pipes and slapping blackflies, the French planned their attack.

Although called a factory, this post was actually a fort, forts being built at strategic locations throughout the North American wilderness in the seventeenth and eighteenth centuries. A good fort might be built on an elevation or at a river mouth. Heavily timbered palisades surrounded the perimeter; a snug redoubt was built in the center. A poor fort had, at least, a palisade, if not a redoubt. The basic principle was drawn from the medieval use of fortified feudal castles, and it worked with fair success in the wilderness. A small force could successfully defend a good fort against a large force. A small force could also raid travel routes in the wilderness, then retreat to the fort where it would be secure. A small force, in short, could control a large territory from a fortified central location. Anyone who desired continued use

The city of Quebec as it appeared in the nineteenth century, looking across the St. Lawrence from Beauport. During the siege of the city in 1759, the British attackers surprised the French by scaling the bluff beyond the fort on the left. The French then were forced to fight on the Plains of Abraham, where the control of Canada was won by the British in a single decisive battle lasting less than half an hour.

The Great Lakes Historical Society

of such territory had first to neutralize the fort that controlled it.

The French lay on their packs, watched the sun drop through the afternoon, and when darkness claimed the horizon, stole forth to reconnoiter. No one at the fort was on guard; no one raised the alarm; the cannon atop the redoubt stood untended. When all the lights in the fort were out, the French eased up to the palisade. Using a long pole as platform, two raiders shinnied up to the top of the wall, dropped inside on moccasined feet, and swung open the gate. The troop poured into the fort yard, howling the Iroquois war cry, "*Sassa Koues! Sassa Koues!*"

Till that point in their service, the company clerks in the fort had heard only the honking of geese along the Moose River and the daily squawks of the whiskey-jack. Now out of deference to those Indian howls, and to end the musket fire and grenades pouring in their windows, the fifteen clerks agreed to surrender. With Moose Factory secure, the French pushed on to Fort Rupert, where a ship and the fort were captured in a similar midnight raid. The French then used the ship to sail to Fort Albany, where the outnumbered clerks of that post also surrendered after a brief fight.

James Bay, the south lobe of Hudson Bay, was now securely in French hands, but in England, the Hudson's Bay Company howled for retribution. The dispute was settled in the courts of Europe, and the Bay posts soon returned to English control.

One of the men who went on this expedition was Pierre Le Moyne, Sieur d'Iberville. Born in Montreal, he was then in his twenties, and this was but the first of many battles for Iberville, who was to take part in a number of campaigns against the British and achieve permanent fame in the annals of French naval history. In the spring of 1697, Iberville was placed in charge of five French men-of-war with orders to evict the British once again from Hudson Bay. Sailing from Quebec, he passed through Hudson Strait where storms promptly separated the ships. When Iberville arrived before Fort Nelson, the planned rendezvous for his fleet, he found himself alone. A few days later, three ships appeared on the horizon, and thinking it the remainder of his fleet, he sailed out to greet them. But the three ships refused his welcoming salute and bore on steadily. They were three British men-of-war, and the scene on the French decks now changed from one of welcome to a scramble for arms. Iberville, with characteristic determination, wrote simply, "Seeing they were English, I prepared to fight them."

He was hopelessly outclassed. The British flagship *Hampshire* had 52 guns and 150 men; the *Dering* had 30 guns and 100 men; and the *Hudson's Bay* had 32 guns and 100 men—a total of 114 guns and 350 men. Against this, Iberville's ship, the *Pelican*, had 50 guns and 150 men.

Being so heavily outgunned, Iberville knew the British would try to box him in to train all their guns upon him at once. He decided to board the *Hampshire*, for a good rousing deck fight would keep the other English ships from effective battle. The *Hampshire*, however, saw his scheme and kept her distance—enough distance to make her guns ineffective. Iberville then turned between the two smaller ships and raked them both with broadsides. Immediately the *Hampshire* tried to close in, but adroit sailing kept Iberville to windward. As the running fight kept up, the *Hampshire* edged closer, and Iberville realized the English were planning to board. He held his broadside, and they held theirs. At the crucial moment, when the two ships were nearly locked together, the *Hampshire* let fly. The broadside whistled over the *Pelican's* deck to fall harmlessly in the sea beyond. A wave had lifted the ship at the instant of firing, saving the French from destruction. A moment later, Iberville fired his broadside with exactly the opposite effect. His ship was plunging into a wave's trough, and all his shots struck the *Hampshire* at the waterline. The British ship went down like a stone, the flag still flying, the surprised crewmen struggling in the icy water.

The loss of the *Hampshire* stunned the British. Iberville saw their hesitation and pressed his advantage, despite the fact that he was still outgunned. Bearing down full tilt on the Dering, he attempted to get into range, but the English fired only a single broadside before fleeing. The *Hudson's Bay*, suddenly alone and outgunned, then struck her colors. The battle was over. The fight had lasted three and a half hours, but British gunnery was so poor that only one French sailor was killed and seventeen wounded. This storybook battle gave the French undisputed control of the waters of Hudson Bay. They soon captured several British forts ringing the shore by land actions directed from the *Pelican*. A few days later the remainder of the French fleet arrived to seal the victory.

But again the terms of peace, signed in Europe in 1698, returned Hudson Bay to the English. The Hudson's Bay Company went back to work; trade between Indians and British continued to grow, and the French fur industry in Canada continued to suffer. Wars broke out again in 1702 and 1744, but, like the 1689–97 war, produced little change in land ownership.

In 1756, however, the final campaign for the control of Canada got under way. The British had suffered many setbacks during the eighty-year struggle. By the summer of 1758, their morale was at a low ebb. Their colonies along the eastern seaboard had a total population of two million; the French in Canada numbered no more than sixty thousand. Despite this, the French had ambushed, attacked, harassed, and hampered British expansion. British attacks had hardly bothered the French colony, and French control in the Great Lakes and throughout all of Canada seemed as strong as ever, excepting only in Hudson Bay.

But French strength was mostly an illusion. British control of the entrance to the St. Lawrence made it almost impossible to supply Quebec and Montreal, and the French colonial government was nearly exhausted. Years of war had taken their toll. Crop failures and brutal winters had demoralized the colonists. Corrupt officials had further sapped the colony's resources.

Marquis de Montcalm, the experienced and sage French military leader, knew by midsummer of 1758, when Louisbourg was captured by the British, that the decisive battle for Canada would be fought at Quebec. He realized that the English must also be aware of this, and that the battle for the city would not be long in coming. So long as Quebec stayed in French hands, New France could continue, despite English raids and frontier actions. And, if handled properly, the siege of Quebec could become a drain and burden on the British, and might well turn into French victory. By the fall of that year, Montcalm was withdrawing his forces toward Quebec; delaying here, raiding there, but steadily moving toward the city. Already he was beginning his plan for Quebec's fortification and laying his strategy for the final great fight for Canada.

Montcalm's apprehension, however, was not shared by the French governor, Pierre de Rigaud, Marquis de Vaudreuil-Cavagna, who overruled his general on the matter of fortifications, on the mobilization of reserves, on the use of food stores. He refused to fight corruption or quell the black market draining supplies away from the military forces. The two men were soon quarreling in private. Vaudreuil wrote letters to Paris, criticizing Montcalm's actions, saying that he was too cautious, that he lacked leadership. Their differences grew steadily until the winter's night when Montcalm exploded at a social evening in Vaudreuil's house. The occasion began with a military discussion in which Vaudreuil was openly critical of Montcalm's abilities. The general returned the fire, writing later of the evening: "I cut him short by saying as modestly as I could that I made war to the best of my ability, in accordance with such experience as I had, and told him that if he was not satisfied he must take charge of the campaign in person and carry out his own plans. His teeth ground at this and his face filled with rage. 'I would be honored and would serve willingly under your command,' I told him."

When Madame de Vaudreuil attempted to smooth over the matter, Montcalm turned on her.

"Madame," he wrote that he addressed her, "without departing from the respect due you, I should be honored to comment that ladies should not enter a discussion on matters of war."

She attempted to continue.

"Madame," he said, "without departing from all due respect, permit me to say that if Madame de Montcalm was here, and she heard me discussing military matters with Monsieur le Marquis de Vaudreuil, she would keep silent."

This exchange took place before other officers and leading members of the colony. It quickly became the talk of the city, and helped undermine French morale.

In April 1759, Montcalm sent a coded message to the minister of war in Paris: "Canada will be taken this campaign, or certainly in the next, unless there be some unforeseen good luck or some gross blunders by the enemy. The English have 60,000 men, we only 10–11,000. Our government is worthless; money and provisions are failing. . . . Everybody appears to be in a hurry to make his fortune before the colony is lost, which event many, perhaps, hope for to draw an impenetrable veil over their conduct."

At the end of the same month, Vaudreuil still failing to see the need for the preparations that Montcalm was making, wrote in turn to the minister: "I doubt very much if the English will undertake to descend on Quebec."

But the English were already making plans. A young brigadier general, James Wolfe, had returned to England in the fall of 1758 as hero of the Louisbourg campaign. He had led the successful assault on that Acadian stronghold; the victory gave the British new hope after many defeats. The loss of Louisbourg opened the St. Lawrence to invasion by the British fleet. Prime Minister William Pitt now overrode army seniority, and named the young brigadier to lead the

The two opposing generals were both killed on the Plains of Abraham. Mortally wounded, British General James Wolfe (left) gave the order to fire with his last breath. Marquis de Montcalm (right), the French gen-

expedition against Quebec. Wolfe was promised twelve thousand men and told to take Quebec in the coming year, 1759. The nation, but not the army, applauded Pitt's choice.

Wolfe, a commoner, had his work cut out for him. Piqued by Pitt's selection, Britain's military leaders set roadblocks in his path. The promise of twelve thousand men was cut to eight thousand, and even the power of Pitt failed to budge it above that figure. As consolation, Pitt told Wolfe he could choose his own commanders. Monckton, Murray, and Burton, said Wolfe, without hesitation, naming the three who had fought with him at Louisbourg. Again Pitt agreed, but again he failed to keep his pledge. Monckton and Murray were assigned, but Burton was replaced by George Townshend, a haughty aristocrat who cordially despised Wolfe's plebeian background. Townshend was a source of discontent, his sharp tongue nettling Wolfe steadily throughout the campaign.

The expedition sailed from Portsmouth and Spithead in February, and during the two-month voyage, Wolfe was able to cement relations with his naval commanders. In these men he was fortunate. A spirit of friendship and cooperation developed on the voyage that paid important dividends in the coming battle.

Montcalm had completed his defenses at Quebec by the time Wolfe arrived and was waiting behind heavy fortifications with seven thousand French regulars, fifteen hundred marines, and fourteen thousand colonial militiamen. Against this army the English were sending six to

eral, was hit at almost the same moment as Wolfe. But he lived long enough to know that Quebec had fallen.

A. Doughty, *The Siege of Quebec and The Battle of the Plains of Abraham*

eight thousand men, mostly English regulars and Scottish Highlanders, with some American rangers and militia from the English colonies. Montcalm's main protection was the city's fort and walls, crowning the three hundred-foot high bluffs above the upper city. Seemingly the fort would have to be leveled or neutralized before any force could scale those abrupt cliffs, and in all of North America there were not, Montcalm knew, enough cannons to do that. He also spread his defenses east along the north shore of the river to control the land approach to his redoubt.

The plan was simple and solid. The guns in the fort overlooked the river and could force British ships toward the south shore, thereby keeping the river between the British and the city. The shore force east of the city was placed on ridges along the river and could fight a devastating small arms battle against any force landed at that point. Unless the English came with an overwhelming army, an attack at that point would be suicidal.

Montcalm had reasoned well. The British fleet appeared as he expected off the south shore of the Island of Orleans on June 26, 1759, a few miles east of Quebec. It was in full view of the city but out of range of French guns. The city turned into bedlam at sight of the British, and despite all the preparations seemed only then to realize the peril. By the next morning, the British had occupied the island and scattered the local residents. Then British troops landed on the south shore of the river, where they captured Point Levis and set up siege guns aimed at Quebec. These began to bombard the lower city, built on the flood plain below the fort, but were unable to reach the fort itself.

Montcalm had expected all this. The British had occupied the obvious positions, none of which were overly dangerous to the French. But these positions could not be improved without dangerous exposure. And while the British force was well trained, it was far smaller than the French army. Montcalm knew Wolfe would have to take the initiative to win, and if he did, all odds lay with the French. Montcalm held his fire and waited.

Surveying with his glass from a picket boat, Wolfe quickly saw the formidable task that lay ahead. Montcalm's play was obvious. He would remain in his fort until Wolfe attacked. If Wolfe failed to attack, winter would drive the British back to the sea and the colony of New France would be saved. For Wolfe, a frontal assault was out of the question; the French would annihilate British troops if they tried to scale those cliffs. Wolfe saw only one solution. Somehow, he must draw Montcalm out. Then his experienced regulars, backed by artillery, could cut the French to pieces.

But even here Montcalm correctly gauged his opponent. He steadfastly stayed in his fort despite all the feints Wolfe designed. The days dragged on. Indians and settlers started guerrilla tactics, and in response, Wolfe began a systematic campaign to level all the French property in the area. This failed to budge Montcalm. Wolfe then pushed his troops farther along the south shore. Still Montcalm waited. Then Wolfe decided to try an assault on the east end of the French defenses along the north shore, a move that nearly proved disastrous.

The French lines stretched east from the city to the Montmorency River, which tumbled down from a high bluff before reaching a few hundred yards of level ground. There it flowed into the St. Lawrence. At low tide, this flat section of the Montmorency River looked as though men could wade across. Wolfe elected to attempt it.

He had stationed a small holding force on the east bank of the river, and now he proceeded to strengthen this with more men and supplies and stronger fortifications. To mask his movements and to test the fort's guns, he sent two frigates and several sloops upstream. Surprisingly, they scampered past unscathed and were then west of the fort. Their guns were too small to reach the fort, but if they could squeeze past, perhaps bigger vessels might also be able to do so. The first chink in Montcalm's armor had appeared.

Setting his Montmorency River plan aside, Wolfe sent one of his commanders with six hundred men to drag longboats overland on the south shore. Soon they, too, were west of the French defenses, and made a landing at Pointe aux Trembles on the north shore, eighteen miles west of Quebec. They captured supplies and threatened communications between Montreal and Quebec. This drew Montcalm out but not very far. He sent a small force west of the city, and it quickly ended British harassment at that point. The bluffs along the river were simply too high for the invaders to scale.

Wolfe now returned to his earlier plan east of the city. He hoped to cross the Montmorency, capture two outposts guarding that river, and then move along the shore to draw the French forces into a general fight. Despite French superiority in numbers, Wolfe believed his regulars could outfight the French militia. His men were also eager for a fight, having now waited more than a month.

As it turned out, they were too eager. At low tide on July 30, Wolfe sent his first brigade wading across the Montmorency. It quickly captured the outposts and their defenders. With good timing, another British force landed in small boats from naval units. The plan was now to move west along the shore, but the taste of action was too heady for the British regulars. They broke ranks, and instead of following the shore, stormed up the bluffs in pursuit of the French. Halfway up, French musket fire began to pour down upon them in a steady barrage. The British troops were slaughtered. The attack ground to a bloody halt, and the British were forced to back off from their foothold under steady fire from French muskets. Wolfe dressed down his haughty brigadier Townshend for failing to control his men during the attack, and the incident added to the smoldering differences between the two men.

The fact that trained British regulars would break ranks to mount an attack indicates the kind of stalemate that had developed. Only a few simple ground assaults had been carried out in the first full month of operations, and now this attack on the north shore was quelled with heavy British losses. The British were stumped, and both Wolfe and Montcalm knew it. Both sides now returned to their drilling and waiting, while Wolfe and his brigadiers searched for an opening.

To pass the time, a stiff military courtesy developed between officers of the opposing armies. The British sent to their French counterparts kegs of ale, and the French returned bottles of champagne. The British sent haunches of mutton; quarters of venison came in return. Each side attempted to outdo the other. Flags of truce were used to carry the gifts through the lines. With these gifts went the most polite messages of military diplomacy. Rank for rank, officers exchanged courtesies with each other, and many began to know their opponents on a personal level. Wolfe and Montcalm even exchanged gifts on several occasions, and as the days passed, Montcalm's simple, exasperating, and brilliant game began to tell. The summer days dragged on. Somehow Wolfe must make an assault, yet Montcalm offered no opening. The days lengthened into weeks. By August the siege force had been before Quebec nearly two months. The French, with their numerically larger force, still gave no hint they ever planned to come out and fight. Wolfe's brigadiers, and particularly the aristocratic Townshend, began to snipe steadily at their commander. More and more comments were made about inaction and the need for decision.

Despite all the outward clamor, the main struggle was still centered in the minds of the two commanders. Wolfe was gradually becoming more silent and brooding, often not even telling his associates what he thought. Both sides suffered from informers, and Wolfe lashed out several times over leaks in information. As he began to keep his own counsel, Wolfe must have known that he was now totally alone. And perhaps this was what he wanted. He began slowly but steadily to mount what can only be called a confusion of orders. His officers who were accustomed to far more orderly procedures tried to follow as best they could, but the daily snarl of troop and ship movements now became a regular joke among the ranks. Sometimes two countervailing orders would arrive at company level at almost the same time. Tempers flared in the confusion, and the strain began to tell on everyone. A fever put Wolfe to bed. Still the flow of confused orders issued from his headquarters. His fellow commanders were vexed, and on occasion openly hostile. But if Wolfe's army was confused, French intelligence was likewise. Every scrap of information in those last weeks of August must have proved false. The British continued to change plans, to feint or parry, then to pull back before any action resulted. But in the meantime, Wolfe was steadily increasing his force upriver, and here lay the key to his entire strategy.

On the twenty-fifth of August he called his commanding officers together and asked them to consult with him about a frontal assault on the city. Long before Wolfe ascended the St. Lawrence, he had said the city could only be taken by assault from beyond the fort, upriver from the main defenses. What he now suggested has therefore provided military experts two hundred years of inconclusive speculation. His plan, he said, was to attack from the east where there were three possibilities. The British could again cross the Montmorency and push toward the fort from along the northeast shore. Or they could move inland from the east, circle through the forests and come round on Quebec from the north. Or third, they might attempt a frontal assault directly against the entrenched French lines east of the city.

One of these suggestions, that of crossing the Montmorency where it joins the St. Lawrence, had already been tried with near fatal results. The second, to circle east of Quebec and come down from the north, had been dismissed at the outset as too dangerous. A small force could ambush the main British column in the woods where it would not know the terrain and systematically mow the redcoats down. Wolfe's third suggestion, a frontal assault on the French lines, had been ruled out automatically as far too dangerous. It was just the sort of attack the French must hope for. Guns in the fort could tear the British apart.

To the British officers it now seemed apparent that this waiting game had addled their commander's reason. They rejected all three proposals out of hand. Singly and collectively, they reasoned that the best chance was an assault at some point west of the town, beyond the fort, and soon they presented this plan to Wolfe. The British leader accepted readily, so readily in fact that the officers began to formulate field orders immediately. Perhaps this was Wolfe's scheme all along. His growing force west of the city fitted into the plan. His commanders were working in unison on the plan they had suggested. All approaches from the east had been explored and ruled out by his advisers. It all fitted in with his earliest statement, that the only hope to take the city was from the west.

It is also possible to view Wolfe as an excellent leader on the brigade level but as a poor tactician and as a man without the military seasoning needed to dislodge wily Montcalm. That would explain Wolfe's confusion of orders and make understandable the three foolish proposals he offered his brigadiers. It would also explain his eager acceptance of their plan. The events that now followed, however, indicate that Wolfe was still very much in command.

Agreeing to the plan suggested by his fellow commanders, all four men set to work on their task with an unusual unity of spirit. They agreed to continue the naval feints east of the city, the reconnoitering, the general activity on the Island of Orleans and at Point Levis. The encampments at these locations would be sustained; the tents would remain in place; the campfires tended. But the bulk of the British force would quickly move upriver, at night, in small contingents. The boats and men already on the upper river would continue their harassment to veil the operations. Meanwhile, the British commanders would scout the north shore for a landing place and then bide their time for a chance to strike. Both the landing place and the chance to use it presented themselves even sooner than the British leader hoped, and he was quick to seize the opportunity.

Disguised as British regulars, Wolfe and his three brigadier generals stumped along the south shore on the tenth of September, looking through telescopes for a landing site opposite. Everywhere on the north shore, the bluffs looked formidable. Finally, however, they noticed a narrow path angling up the cliffs a short distance west of the Quebec citadel. It was nearly covered by vegetation. Through the glass, they also saw sentry tents hidden by trees at the top. Now the brigadiers were doubtful. The spot was guarded. Townshend, in particular, pointed out reasons why the location was bad. Wolfe heard them out and agreed it was dangerous. Every place was dangerous. He appeared to leave the matter hanging, but his own decision was made. This was the place.

That night Wolfe learned from a French deserter that several small supply boats would pass his landing spot on the night of September twelfth. That was two nights away. If Wolfe could capture the supply boats, he could replace them with British assault boats. French guards along the river would think the boats their own, and the British could land unchallenged.

So the plot took form. To keep the French off his trail, Wolfe sent several small ships upriver, embarked and re-embarked his troops, and on the evening of September twelfth, selected twenty-four volunteers for what he termed his "forlorn hope." They were to be his assault force; they were to scale the bluffs and secure the pathway at the top. Depending on how well they carried out their work, the full British force might be able to reach the plateau above. He crowded the men into his flagship's cabin and explained their mission.

At two o'clock on the morning of September thirteenth, a signal light was hoisted aboard Wolfe's flagship *Sutherland*. Up and down the river, the assault force and its support, all in longboats, pushed away from mother ships and headed across the St. Lawrence River. It was a journey into history, and one that changed the destiny of our continent. Wolfe, with only eight hours left to live, was in the

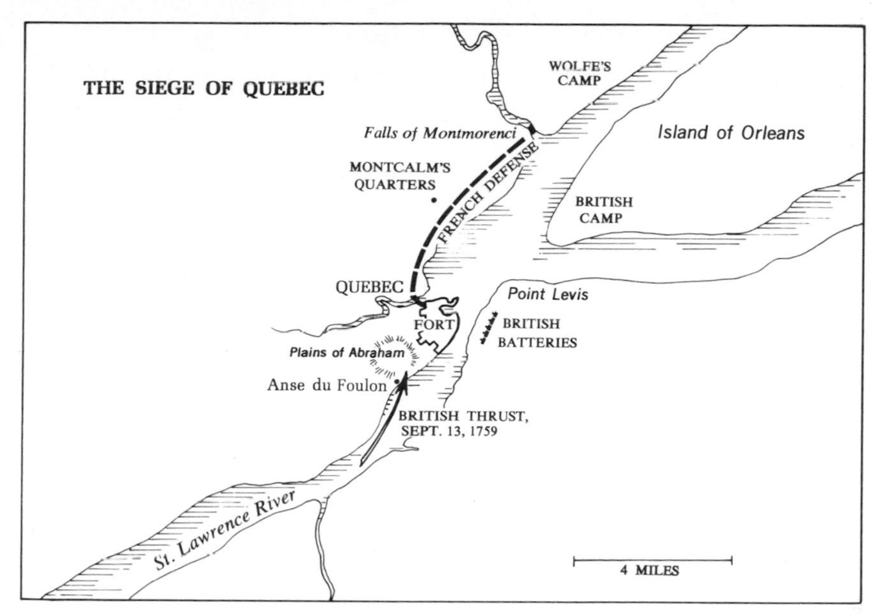

On the Plains of Abraham, the British won final control of Canada in September 1759, defeating a superior French force. The British gathered upstream from Quebec beyond the French line of defense, then scaled a steep bluff to reach the Plains on the unprotected side of the citadel. This forced the French to come out and fight on the Plains, where the decisive battle lasting less than half an hour took place.

first boat, and legend has it that he recited poetry to his men in a quiet voice while they pulled steadily toward the north shore.

Halfway over, disaster nearly ended the expedition. A British sloop, anchored on picket duty in the river, had not been told of the assault, and Wolfe heard the ominous roll of cannon wheels and running feet aboard the ship. As quietly as he could, he called to the ship in English, but raised no answer. Pulling closer he called again, just as sparks from the cannon torch were seen. The British gunners heard his call just as they were ready to touch off the charge. Within seconds, the whole expedition might have been wrecked.

Meanwhile Montcalm slept but not peacefully. He had again been feuding with the French governor, this time about protection for a point of land overlooking the river. The point was called L'Anse au

Foulon. Governor Vaudreuil had ordered that the company of his friend Duchambon de Vergor be placed on the point. But, Montcalm told the governor, Vergor had been court-martialled for failing to defend a fort in Acadia only four years earlier. And the British were along the river. L'Anse au Foulon could be a trouble spot.

Vaudreuil said the 180-foot cliffs were unscalable; Montcalm countered by offering to place a company of regulars on the point. Then Vaudreuil insisted, and Montcalm finally gave in wearily to the governor's demands. Ironically, it was to Anse au Foulon that Wolfe now directed his thin line of assault boats.

Approaching shore in the darkness, the boats were hailed by a French sentry. One of Wolfe's captains reassured him in flawless French. "Provision boats," he called in a low voice. "Be quiet." The sentry let them pass. Farther on, another hailed them, and again the captain quieted the man. Rounding a projecting point, the British boats were suddenly at their destination. They turned in and bumped against the rocky shore. No sentries were in sight. The bluff above was outlined against the night. It looked ominous and almost perpendicular. Without a word, the twenty-four chosen men found the narrow pathway and began their ascent, led by the French-speaking captain. It was four in the morning. The sky was still almost totally dark, and looking back across the water, Wolfe could barely see his other assault boats as they in turn made their way into the cove.

The picked force of twenty-four men eased up the hill, favoring silence over speed. The path was narrow and crowded by shrubs and rocky outcrops. The ascent took almost fifteen minutes, but they reached the top without incident. On the bluff above they found themselves near a patch of tents, and they waited quietly among the trees until the last man was up. Then they moved. Almost immediately they were hailed in French. Again the French-speaking captain misled the sentry. It was a relief force from the fort, he said; they had come from Quebec. The unsuspecting sentry let them come closer, then fell like an ox under one blow from a British rifle butt. The British swarmed over the little cluster of tents. Vergor, the weak-willed French commander, was shot in the foot, trying to escape. Most of his men were taken in their beds. None of the twenty-four volunteers was even scratched. They immediately sent a signal down to shore, and struggling British regulars were soon puffing up the path in a steady stream. Darkness was just giving way to a dull gray dawn, covered by threatening clouds. Engineers were already clearing fallen trees from a second pathway and soon the troops were streaming up the hillside in a double column. More men splashed ashore, inched their way up the slope, and disappeared at the top. Daylight was increasing steadily. Still no sounds of gunfire from above. Wolfe watched for a time, directing operations on the river bank, then pulled his tall frame up the slope to take command. Pushing ahead with a small patrol, he reconnoitered his battleground. To his right lay the river; that flank was secure. To his left, across a rolling plain, a line of trees marked the edge of the wilderness. In the distance, the fort of Quebec itself was dark and low on the horizon. The best ground for a fight was here, on this open rolling plain. What did the map call it? The Plains of Abraham; it was named for an early resident of the colony. Very well, draw the battle line here. When Montcalm saw what had happened, he would be obliged to come out and fight. He had to protect the back door of his fort.

So Wolfe drew up his force, gradually strengthening it through the morning hours. By eight o'clock, he had 3100 men on the plain. There, at right angles to the river, he spread them out across the mile width of the plain, two riflemen deep, in what must have been one of the thinnest red lines in British military history. With loaded muskets, they waited quietly for the coming of the French.

Montcalm, meanwhile, was unaware of Wolfe's threat to his position. He was having a morning cup of tea while he mulled over his problems and cleared sleep from his head. His position was far from strong. He was wracked by a failure of supplies and troops at every point. Of late, the governor, too, had been particularly intrusive Yet Montcalm's thoughts that morning continued to center on Wolfe. The French general knew his opponent would have to move soon. Indian summer was coming, and that would quickly harden into fall, and the British would then have to get their ships downriver. When ice begins to form on the St. Lawrence, he thought, we will have won. The siege will have to lift. He sipped his tea and waited. He was forty-seven years old, and he had served France as a soldier all his life, from early youth to his present generalcy. If he could hold on another month, Quebec would be safe. Then he could go home for a long rest.

But unfortunately Montcalm, like Wolfe, had seen his last dawn. He had but a few hours more to live, and his long rest was closer than he knew.

When the first runner brought news of the British invasion, he refused to believe it. Wolfe's army could not have scaled the bluffs.

They might attack at Pointe aux Trembles, eighteen miles upstream, but they could not be on the Plains of Abraham.

Close behind this message came others, giving details of the British strength; with dread on his face, the French general mounted and put spurs to his horse. Across the city bridge he rattled and up the other side. Beyond the fort he came around a turn and clattered to a stop. The sight that confronted him sealed his worst fears. There a mile away across the plain stood the British regulars, waiting quietly, drawn up in line for battle. Montcalm wheeled his horse and rode for his troops. By this time it was full daylight, and the French general must have known the end had come. What he dreaded most of all now faced him. His indifferent and undisciplined local militia, backed by a small force of French regulars, would have to face the seasoned British redcoats.

By ten o'clock that morning, Montcalm had five thousand troops drawn up in battle line facing the British. The French military superiority was now obvious to everyone—everyone but Montcalm, that is, who knew from experience what that thin red line of British regulars could do. The French home guard, however, saw only its own impressive numbers and soon became unruly. Small units began to push forward, eager for the fight, and soon the whole line was charging toward the British, firing wildly. Montcalm rode ahead of them, trying to halt the charge. French infantry officers cursed, struggling to keep the men in some sort of line.

The British troops continued to wait, and when a man dropped, his comrades stepped to the right or left to fill up the gap. With unflinching courage, they stood their ground, and a few minutes after ten, when only forty yards separated the two lines, Wolfe gave the command to fire. The great volley rang out, and when the smoke cleared, the French front line had been decimated. The remainder of the French stumbled and stopped, and in the space of a moment, turned into a panicky mob. The British line took two steps forward, reloaded, and fired again.

The swift turn of fortune was now complete. The French turned and fled, followed closely by redcoats with fixed bayonets and Highlanders wielding claymores. Within ten minutes it was all over.

Wolfe, as though determined to die on this rolling plain, had walked up and down before his troops while the French were advancing. He was first wounded in the wrist. When this happened, he stood quietly before his men, wrapping his handkerchief around the shattered arm.

A moment later, he was hit in the groin, but he still kept his feet. Finally, a moment before he gave the order to fire, he was hit full in the chest—a mortal wound. He clutched his two aides, and they carried him upright back of the lines, where the men could not see him fall. With his last breath he gave the order to fire. And there he died.

At almost the same moment as Wolfe, Montcalm at the head of his troops was also mortally wounded. But he lived a few hours, long enough to know the French had lost and that Quebec had fallen. It was a bitter way for a gallant soldier to end such long years of service to his country.

British losses in the battle included nine officers and forty-nine men dead and about six hundred wounded. Ten times as many French were slain, and three hundred and fifty were taken prisoner. Five days later, the garrison at Quebec capitulated. Within a year the garrison at Montreal was starved out, and all of French Canada fell to the British. Scattered fighting continued along the Great Lakes and the Canadian Northwest, but the main fight was over, and in 1763 when the peace was signed, Canada was given to England. It never again returned to French control.

About the time of the Revolution, pioneers from the east floated down the Ohio in large rafts such as these. High bullet-proof sides protected them from Indian snipers who lurked along the river banks. Farther downstream, in safer territory, the rafts were dismantled and the planks used for building wilderness homes.

Grace Vollintine, *The Making of America*

10

War on Western Waters

THE BATTLE for Canada was over. The battle for the Great Lakes was about to begin.

After the fall of Quebec, British rule and British influence blanketed the entire eastern seaboard, the Great Lakes, and all the known lands of Canada. As in the years of exploration, the main travel route into this vast empire was still along the Great Lakes waterway. The British used the French-established outpost of Detroit as center of their important Indian Department. From there great annual disbursements of supplies, trading goods, and munitions were made to Indian tribes in the region, a practice that maintained British strength north, south, and west of the Great Lakes.

Three periods of outright warfare were needed to shake the Lakes region free from the grasp of Britain. The first was the Revolutionary War, when Detroit was the British base for raids on Pennsylvania, Virginia, Ohio, and Kentucky. The Americans sent raiders to retaliate, and a number of wilderness clashes resulted. The second period came in the 1790's, ending with Britain's withdrawal from Detroit and the Straits of Mackinac in 1796. The last period of struggle was the War of 1812, when the British finally recognized United States' demands and withdrew permanently to Canada.

In April 1775, the month that in Massachusetts "the shot heard round the world" was fired, Henry Hamilton, a young British officer, was selected as the first lieutenant governor of Detroit. Born in Ireland, Hamilton had come to this continent in 1758. He fought at Louisbourg and was on General Wolfe's staff at Quebec. In Canada at the time of his appointment, he prepared to take up his new post at Detroit. Before he could proceed there, however, the Revolution had broken out, and American lines formed near Montreal. There the young officer was forced to wait. In late fall, he found his chance to slip through the lines, and disguised as a French peasant, he made his perilous way to Detroit. His new post, known at that time as Fort Pontchartrain, consisted of a stockaded village of eighty buildings. The entire white population, including the garrison of 120 British regulars, stood at about fifteen hundred, most of it settled on farms within a ten-mile radius of the fort. Mainly, these settlers were French, their loyalty to Britain doubtful and divided.

Hamilton immediately began to mobilize and train the local tribes for action against the rebel Americans. In 1777 he sent thirty British rangers and nearly three hundred Indian warriors to raid frontier settlements. Lonely farmhouses in the wilderness were attacked and settlers murdered. Scalps were taken and exhibited at Detroit. Hamilton tried to curb such Indian atrocities without much success, and because of the scalps, he soon gained the nickname "Hairbuyer."

These raids shocked the colonists and hardened their opposition to the British. In retaliation Lieutenant Colonel George Rogers Clark led a small band of men overland through British territory and captured the forts at Kaskaskia, Cahokia, and Vincennes, in Illinois and Indiana. On word of this, Detroit was in a panic, but Hamilton immediately mobilized about two hundred British and Indian troops and set out for Vincennes. He left Detroit in charge of Captain Richard Berringer Lernoult, a British career officer, who quickly began construction of a new and stronger fort, which later was known as Fort Lernoult. Hamilton, meanwhile, advanced on Vincennes and easily recaptured it. For the moment, British fortunes looked brighter, and Hamilton decided that all he needed to hold the fort was a small force of regulars. Dismissing his Indians and militia, he settled down at Vincennes for the winter.

It was a disastrous decision for the British commander. Clark was soon at his throat, after a daring forced march across the winter-drenched countryside. He recaptured Vincennes in February 1779, taking Hamilton and his entire force prisoner. Hamilton was shipped to Virginia where he remained in prison until exchanged in 1781.

At Vincennes, Clark found a letter from Captain Lernoult to Hamilton, telling of the fort under construction at Detroit. As a taunt,

Clark wrote Lernoult: "I learn by your letter to Governor Hamilton that you were very busy making new works. I am glad to hear it, as it saves the Americans some expenses in building."

But Clark was unable to mount his attack. He did not have enough men for the expedition, and it was never carried out. For the remainder of the war, United States and British forces in the Great Lakes region traded raids on settlements and wilderness forts. Such fighting continued long after Cornwallis surrendered at Yorktown.

Clark's victories, however, were probably the determining factor that gave the present Great Lakes states to the United States. The treaty negotiations signed in 1783 in Paris recognized the new nation's claims, and the area was awarded to the United States. But Clark's efforts were largely unrecognized at the time, and he was forced to pay his troops out of personal funds, an act which left him penniless. Years later, when Thomas Jefferson, then President, asked Clark to explore the land beyond the Mississippi River, he refused, leaving the task to his younger brother William, who thus became the Clark of the famous Lewis and Clark expedition of 1804.

The region given to the United States under the Treaty of Paris became known as the Old Northwest. It was a huge area, stretching north from the Ohio River to the southern shores of the Great Lakes, and from the Allegheny Mountains in the east to the Mississippi in the west and northwest. The British agreed to the terms of the treaty, but not to the fact, and British forts and fur traders continued to dominate the region. They were not to be dislodged without a fight by the American settlers now streaming into the region.

Even before the Revolution, trickles of settlers had moved out of the Piedmont, over the spine of the Appalachians. They were the advance guard in America's great westward expansion, a movement that ultimately became one of the greatest migrations in all human history. In Kentucky, Daniel Boone led the way. He took a wagon train of neighbors over Cumberland Gap in the 1770's, settling them in the Blue Grass country near what is now Lexington. That route, known as the Wilderness Road, was to be trod into a broad pathway after the Revolution. Hundreds and then thousands of settlers from Virginia and the Carolinas joined the march.

Colonists from more northerly Pennsylvania and Maryland chose a different route. Those who contracted the westering itch traveled down the Ohio River from Pittsburgh on specially constructed rafts. This meant they had to do less walking but more worrying. Both banks of the Ohio were infested by British-oriented Indians who considered every boat a legal target on that watery shooting gallery. Settlers had to construct large, unwieldy rafts with thick bulletproof sides of heavy timbers. Frequently these rafts were built of lumber sawed by hand in "mills" at Pittsburgh. Downriver, they were dismantled, and the planks used to build new homes in the wilderness. Afterward, on wintry nights, small boys would pry out the musket slugs embedded in the planks and later pot squirrels with the lead, melted and reformed into new musket balls.

Most of western New York and northern Ohio was settled by emigrants from the northeastern colonies. Massachusetts land speculators, for example, formed the Ohio Company and in 1788 sent out its first group of settlers to what is now Marietta. Soon after, a New

As settlers moved west, they displaced Indians who soon rebelled and attacked frontier settlements. In 1794 General "Mad" Anthony Wayne defeated the Indian forces at the Battle of Fallen Timbers, near the present site of Toledo. Wayne's victory opened eastern and southern Ohio to settlement.

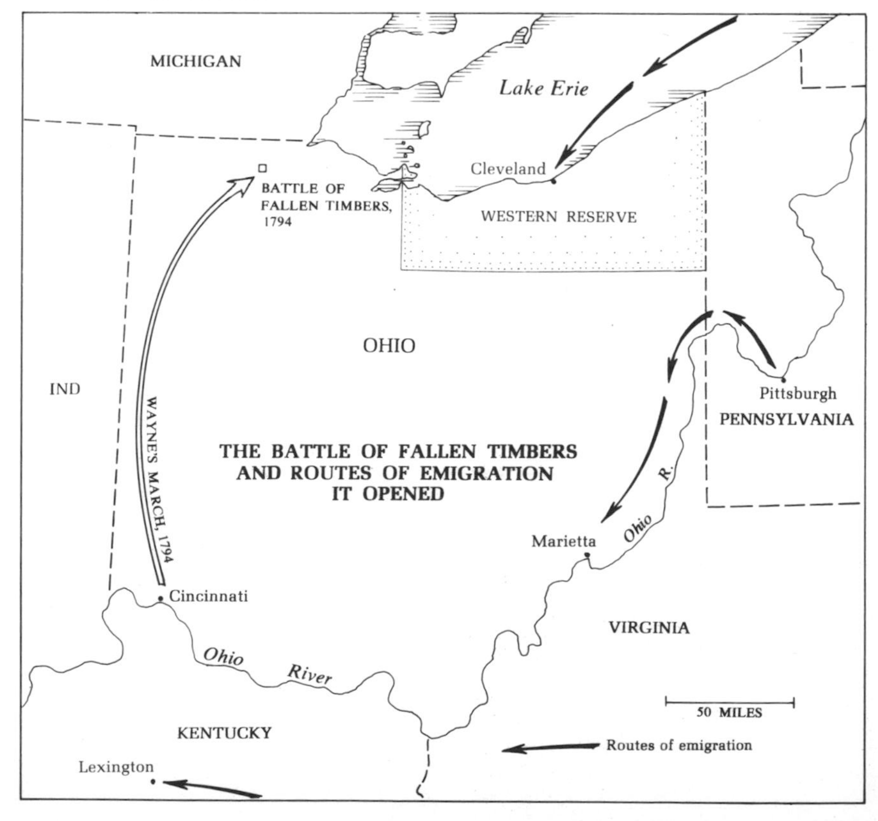

Hero of the Battle of Fallen Timbers, General "Mad" Anthony Wayne. On the morning of August 20, 1794, he led a frontier army against the Indians who were terrorizing northern and western Ohio.

Harry Emerson Wildes, *Anthony Wayne*

Jersey group settled at Cincinnati. Others drifted west in small bands or as individuals so that the settlement of Ohio was well under way by 1790. The Western Reserve, centered around the present site of Cleveland, was a tract of 3,500,000 acres of land reserved for Connecticut as a result of Revolutionary War claims. The Western Reserve was parceled out piecemeal to land companies and individuals who disposed of it to settlers for fat profits.

These settlers, unlike the earliest traders, trappers, and hunters who came and went with the seasons, were seeking land for permanent settlements, and they soon alarmed the Indians. As a tribe was displaced, it was forced onto the territory of other nearby Indians so that the shock of waves of displaced tribesmen quickly reverberated through the entire region. No outpost settlement was safe from Indian uprisings. In response, the settlers mounted abortive military campaigns, first under General Josiah Harmar, then under Arthur St. Clair, governor of the Ohio Territory. The failures of these men strengthened Indian determination to resist.

President Washington sent General "Mad" Anthony Wayne to deal with the Indians. Wayne, dubbed "Mad" during the Revolution because of his impulsive courage, took command of his so-called army at Pittsburgh. It was a collection of misfits and castoffs. But Wayne knew his business and Washington knew his commander. The President held the general in check for nearly two years while Indian negotiations were underway. Wayne chafed at the delay, but spent the time turning his rabble into a tough frontier army. When the Indian peace talks collapsed, late in 1793, Washington gave him permission to move. In the spring and summer of 1794, Wayne pushed west, probing here and there, but not coming to grips with Indian forces until August 20 when the fight came, in the fog of morning. It was a brief, pitched battle at a place called Fallen Timbers, near the present site of Toledo. After forty minutes, the Indians withdrew to a nearby woods to lick their wounds. The Indians were not completely defeated, but the action had been enough to blunt their desire to fight, and most of them soon drifted away to join their tribes.

This action freed southern and eastern Ohio to the invading whites and put the British on notice that their days there were numbered. The British had encouraged the Indian attacks in Ohio and provided most of the weapons from their post at Detroit. Now, as settlers in Ohio grew in numbers, it became apparent the Indians were no longer effective mercenaries. As United States strength increased, control of the area also became less attractive to the British for other reasons. Fur trade on the Great Lakes was already declining, having been milked dry by steady pressure from the Montreal companies. And with Great Britain embroiled in war in Europe, the English were becoming wary of further entanglements in North America.

The result of these pressures was a new treaty, negotiated in 1796, under which the British ceded to the United States all their posts on what is now American soil, thus opening up to settlement a vast tract of Great Lakes land. General Wayne took command of the garrison at Detroit, and for the moment the threat of British and Indians was removed. But peace did not last for long.

As new groups of emigrants moved west, across Ohio, Indiana, and Illinois, they clashed with remnants of British authority. The fur trade still recognized no boundaries, and Indians of the region were constantly angered by the invading whites. The British fed this anger at every chance. Finally, the great Indian leader Tecumseh and his dynamic brother, the Prophet, forced a show of strength at Tippecanoe Creek, Indiana, in 1811. The number of British guns recovered from Indians killed in that battle raised the frontier to a flame of anger. The incident added to strains caused by the British impressment of American seamen and by British interference with overseas trade. War was declared on June 18, 1812.

As a military operation, the War of 1812 was a failure. It was ineffectual and inconclusive. Almost nothing went as planned. The United States suffered embarrassing military defeats; no territory changed ownership; and the biggest battle was fought after peace had been signed. The issues that caused the war had dissolved before the war even started, and when the peace was signed, those same issues were not mentioned in the treaty. Ironically, however, this bumbling bit of military strife ended two centuries of frontier conflict and produced a peace that has lasted ever since.

During the first summer and fall of the war, the United States made three forays into Canada. The first expedition bravely crossed the border at Detroit, then hurried back across the river with British units following like angry hornets. They surrounded Detroit and captured the city and the garrison, throwing the whole region into a panic.

The second force crossed into Canada at Niagara, captured Queenston Heights, and waited for the militia from New York to bring up support. The New Yorkers refused to cross the border. When counterattacked, the American units on the heights were quickly defeated and captured.

The third attempt was similarly unsuccessful. The American forces advanced from Plattsburgh, New York, to the Canadian border, but the New York militia again refused to go farther. The whole troop simply turned and went home, without firing a single shot.

The next year proved a mixture of successes and failures, but the major success probably saved the Old Northwest for the United States. The year started with an angry, vicious battle south of Detroit. The American troops advancing toward the town were not only stopped, but crushingly defeated by British forces in January 1813. This battle occurred on the Raisin River at a place called Frenchtown—now Monroe, Michigan. The British led off all the able-bodied men as prisoners, but their Indian allies slaughtered those Americans lying wounded on the battlefield.

News of this atrocity reached a shipyard at Erie, Pennsylvania, where a fleet of American ships was under construction. Both Britain and the United States had realized as soon as war started that control of the Great Lakes region depended on effective naval mastery. Both sides, therefore, began to build warships: the Americans at Erie; the British at two points near Detroit. The British, who already had the nucleus of a fleet, were adding only one large ship and a pair of gunboats. The Americans, however, had to build their entire fleet from timber cut from the forests near Erie. With British forces controlling Detroit and threatening Niagara, there was precious little time to get the job completed. In the fall of 1812 a young naval lieutenant named Oliver Hazard Perry was sent to command the entire operation. President Madison had little hope of success on the Lakes, as his choice of

Perry, then only twenty-eight years old, indicates. Perry's opponent was Captain Robert H. Barclay, a veteran of several naval engagements including the battle of Trafalgar, where he had suffered the loss of an arm.

Perry worked his men furiously during the fall and early winter of 1812, and when word of the Frenchtown massacre arrived, he impressed upon them the need for even greater speed. An attack from land might come at any time, and an attack from sea could come as soon as the weather warmed into spring. His small band of shipwrights, he realized, would be no match for the British regulars; his only hope was to get his force afloat. All winter long he and the men labored. When spring came, a few hulls were launched, but not one ship was ready for service. Perry's shortage in supplies was slow to be filled—too slow, he thought. He needed ordnance, shipfittings, capable seamen, all hard to obtain. He began training sessions, using his few experienced seamen as cadre. He wrote to Washington again and again, asking for fittings, guns, and men. And he waited daily for the British attack, which miraculously still did not come, each day that passed making the American fleet stronger and more prepared.

Meanwhile, the British commander was having his own troubles. Captain Barclay realized his chance for easy victory was slipping away, but his calls for trained seamen also produced little response. The British garrison at Detroit was short of provisions, and available British ships were being held for convoy work on Lake Erie.

By mid-July the last of Perry's fleet was ready to sail on Lake Erie, and a sea battle was now certain. Criusing slowly and training his men, Perry watched for the British fleet. He knew that the British had but six ships to his eight; but the British had more guns, and their armament included some long-range cannon that the Americans lacked.

Perry waited at Put-in-Bay, knowing Barclay would have to fight if he hoped to relieve the British garrison at Detroit, then running short of supplies. July passed, and August came. More weeks passed, and then it was September. The hero of Tippecanoe, General William Henry Harrison, the man who was to be the ninth President of the United States, commanded a growing army in Ohio. He was planning to move against Detroit during the coming winter, and he now visited Perry's fleet. Together, the two men planned strategy. Perry thought that he might challenge and beat Barclay on the Detroit River in case the British failed to come out and fight. Harrison counseled patience. He thought a battle on the wider waters of Lake Erie would give

Commodore Oliver Hazard Perry, winner of the Battle of Lake Erie on September 10, 1813. The American fleet, built at Erie, Pennsylvania, defeated and captured the British fleet.

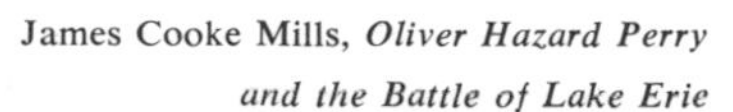

James Cooke Mills, *Oliver Hazard Perry and the Battle of Lake Erie*

a better chance for complete victory. If Perry could triumph on the lake, taking Detroit should prove a simple matter, and all the British posts on the upper Lakes should fall once Detroit was taken. Heeding this counsel, Perry waited.

At daybreak on September tenth, Barclay's fleet was sighted, sailing from Detroit, on Lake Erie. A light breeze pushed the British along. Perry's ships, waiting at Put-in-Bay, clamored to get under way and by eleven o'clock, both commanders had their fleets drawn up in battle line.

Both fleets moved slowly in the light air; both held their fire. It was shortly before noon when the leading British ship began to fire. But almost at the same time, the wind shifted from the southwest to the southeast, favoring the Americans and working a sudden disadvantage against the British. Perry's vessels could now move in close where their short-range, heavy guns would be more effective than the British long-range weapons. Perry was aboard his flagship the *Lawrence*, and at the yardarm flew his standard bearing James Lawrence's dying words, "Don't give up the ship."

British long-range fire, however, began to tell on some of Perry's smaller vessels. They had closed to the battle ahead of the *Lawrence* and were soon in trouble. Fortunately the British shifted their fire when Perry's flagship approached, giving the smaller American ships a chance to recover. It took twenty minutes for the *Lawrence* to close with Barclay's flagship, the *Detroit*, but by twelve thirty the two ships were side by side, hammering at each other steadily. At close range, losses on both sides began to mount. Perry had placed some Kentucky riflemen in his rigging, and they sniped so effectively that all the

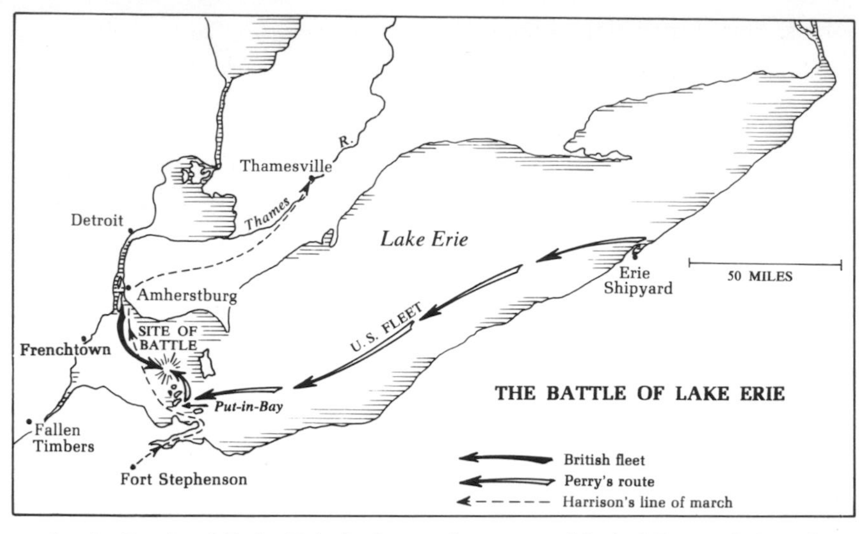

In the Battle of Lake Erie in September 1813, Admiral Perry defeated the British fleet, which had sailed to the battle from the Detroit River. The British abandoned Detroit and fled into Ontario. General Harrison pursued them to Thamesville, where they surrendered after a short battle.

chief British officers were killed or wounded in the first hour of fighting.

Perry's second large ship, the *Niagara*, was in charge of Lieutenant Jesse D. Elliott who showed no enthusiasm for the battle. He had his ship placed a safe distance from the battle, and there it remained. When the *Lawrence* became disabled, Perry pulled down his colors, took four seamen in a long boat, and rowed for the still unscathed *Niagara*. Once aboard, he placed Elliott in the lifeboat and ordered him to lend a hand on whatever American ship he could find. Then Perry hoisted his colors and turned the *Niagara* toward the British line. He sailed right into their center, placing three enemy ships on his port and three on his starboard. In this position, he wrote later, he was able to rake their decks with broadsides. He was preparing to close with the *Detroit* when through a fluke, the rigging of the two largest British ships became entangled, virtually disabling them. The American fleet, meanwhile, kept hammering away from all sides, and soon Barclay was forced to strike his colors. Perry then sent his famous message to General Harrison: "We have met the enemy and they are ours; two ships, two brigs, one schooner, and one sloop." Barclay had been seriously wounded but survived. British losses were forty men killed and a hundred wounded; the American losses were thirty killed and a hundred wounded.

The battle lasted three hours. It was decided by a lucky shift of the wind, by a mishap that rendered two British ships useless, and by Perry's determination to fight to the finish. Contrary to his motto, he had given up his ship, the *Lawrence*, in the heat of battle, but the *Niagara* proved a worthy substitute and carried the United States fleet to the victory. After the fight, the *Lawrence* was rehabilitated and continued in service.

Perry's sea victory made Harrison's capture of Detroit almost a certainty, and the British, realizing this, abandoned it without a struggle and retreated toward York on Lake Ontario. Perry ferried Harrison's army across Lake Erie where the troops set off up the Thames River in pursuit. On October fifth they caught the British just east of what is now Thamesville. A short, sharp fight ensued, but the British were hopelessly outnumbered and soon surrendered. Nearby on a rise of ground the Indian Tecumseh, leading about eight hundred warriors

Detroit, long a base for British raids in the Midwest, was captured by U.S. forces during the War of 1812. The British launched attacks on Niagara, Buffalo, and Plattsburgh. In 1814 they sailed into Chesapeake Bay, occupied Washington briefly, and burned the capital.

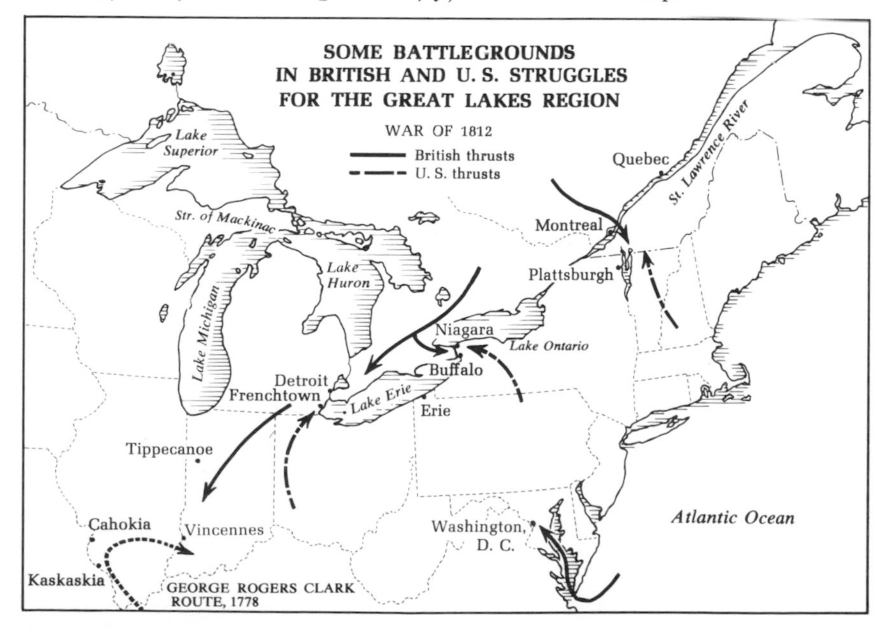

James Cooke Mills, *Oliver Hazard Perry and the Battle of Lake Erie*

During the Battle of Lake Erie, the wind changed, favoring American ships. In this painting Perry's flagship Niagara *is breaking through the British line. From here Perry sent his message to General Harrison: "We have met the enemy and they are ours; two ships, two brigs, one schooner, and one sloop."*

fought on stubbornly until he was killed and his men forced to surrender.

In December, however, there was a turn in fortune. The British captured Buffalo and Fort Niagara, burning those towns and taking prisoners, supplies, and munitions. By 1814, the British were steadily reinforcing their Canadian army with 18,000 troops released from duty in Europe after Napoleon's defeat. This destroyed any American hope of conquering Canada. In several scattered campaigns, the British pushed American troops across the border and then took the offensive, launching a three-pronged attack.

In the spring of 1814 one British force drove down the west shore of Lake Champlain, supported by a British fleet of four large ships and a dozen galleys. As they approached Plattsburgh Bay, they saw the American fleet anchored across the mouth of the bay. If their army was to continue, the British ships could not avoid a battle.

The fight was a disaster for the British. The American ships were deployed to simulate a land fort, and their combined firepower proved highly effective. The American flagship *Saratoga* was anchored and cabled so it could turn end for end to throw fresh broadsides against the British. The entire British fleet was destroyed or captured. The British land column fled up the shore, harassed from the lake by the victorious American fleet.

The second attacking column proved considerably more effective, but this force too was severely mauled. Sailing into Chesapeake Bay, the British landed a strong force and occupied Washington, D.C. The Capitol and other buildings were burned before they were routed.

The third force of eight thousand British regulars landed at New Orleans, where General Andrew Jackson had forged a sizable army out of regulars, local sharpshooters, pirates, and tough inhabitants of the bayou. The British, true to the military tradition of the time, marched in regimental line against this murderous force on January 8, 1815. About a fourth of the entire British army was wiped out before the attack fell apart.

It was unfortunate no one knew that the war had already ended two weeks earlier. The Treaty of Ghent had been signed on Christmas Eve, 1814, but like everything else in that confused war, it hardly resolved anything at all. All territory captured by either side was returned to its former owners. The treaty did not even mention blockades, impressment of seamen, or interference with trade. And finally, the location of the United States-Canadian border was left to a boundary commission of representatives from both governments.

With the war over, new floods of pioneers pushed west. The Congressional Ordinance of 1787 had decreed that the Old Northwest Territory should be divided into half a dozen states. A state could apply for admission to the Union when it had sixty thousand free adult male inhabitants. The states in the Old Northwest included Ohio, Indiana, Illinois, Michigan, Wisconsin, and Minnesota. But the streams of westward migration can be discerned from the dates on which these and other states entered the Union. Kentucky became the fifteenth member of the Union in 1792; Tennessee was admitted in 1796; Ohio in 1803. After the war, Indiana became a state in 1816, Illinois in 1818, and Missouri in 1821. The line of settlement was traveling down the Ohio River. Michigan did not enter until 1837 nor Wisconsin until 1848. Minnesota was admitted in 1858. These last three states lay north of the main stream west. They were not settled until the Erie Canal opened the Great Lakes eastward in 1825.

The settlers moved west by almost every means imaginable; the cavalry pony and "shank's mare" were drafted for the migration. Those who could afford to often traveled in wagons pulled by oxen that were fitted out with the essentials needed for life. The limited size of wagons was the great leveler. Loadings and unloadings continued until each small company of travelers had winnowed its belongings down to what the wagon could carry. And for all, the wagon never seemed able to carry enough.

Consider the circumstances of crowding all the belongings of a family into a buckboard three and a half feet wide by eight feet long. Of absolute necessity were the following: rifle, powder, and ball; ax, hammer, and other tools; seed for planting; food for the journey; sufficient clothing for each person; pots, pans, kitchenware; bedding. To this heap add spare wagon parts and harness, a plow, rope, a bucket or two, a spinning wheel, candle and shot moulds and ladles, extra lead for shot, a small tub of nails, spare pieces of iron, a hand flour mill, a clock, a Bible, and a Jew's-harp, and readers and primers for the children.

For northern emigrants after 1815, the way west lay along two main routes. They could go overland to Pittsburgh and raft down the Ohio River, or they could book passage at Buffalo and travel on a Great Lakes packet to Detroit, Cleveland, or even Chicago. This latter route soon proved most popular.

The first steamboat on the Great Lakes, *Walk-In-The-Water,* was launched at Buffalo in 1818, and began irregular service to Detroit. Each summer, it carried as many travelers and as much freight westward as its decks would hold. *Walk-In-The-Water* was wrecked in 1821, but the engine was salvaged and installed in another vessel. By that time a sizable squadron of other sailing vessels and steamboats was carrying passengers west on the Lakes.

Apart from the Ohio River and the Great Lakes, travel routes to new lands were limited. Roads overland were seldom more than narrow ruts winding through the forest. Creeks were forded, and rivers ferried—when a ferryboat happened to be available and the traveler could pay the price of operation. Swamps, likewise, were negotiated on their own terms, being reasonable in dry weather and outrageous in wet. Thus any water transportation was attractive, and the Great Lakes packet fleet prospered accordingly. Besides, all the easily available land along the Ohio River had been claimed by 1820. This influenced later emigrants to take the Great Lakes route. Governor Clinton of New York was swift to recognize this shift and pressed feverishly for the construction of the Erie Canal, connecting the Hudson River and Lake Erie to provide an all-water route west. The whole nation hailed this project with noisy enthusiasm. Eastern merchants wanted

Burton Historical Collection

The first steamer on the Great Lakes, Walk-In-The-Water, *was launched in 1818 and carried emigrants from Buffalo to Detroit. In the background is the city of Detroit as it appeared in 1820.*

the canal so that they could send goods west. Mid-western farmers wanted the canal so that they could send farm products east. Emigrants and land companies also favored the canal for obvious reasons. The builders lacked both funds and labor. Ague, fevers, and other illnesses plagued the workers, but still the canal went forward.

Governor Clinton's 364-mile "ditch" was started at Rome, New York, in 1817. When the completed canal was opened to traffic in 1825, a barrel of Lake Erie water was brought by canal boat from Buffalo to New York and dumped in the ocean, attended by ringing phrases and proper festivities. It had, as they say, a good press, and the Erie Canal soon began to make money. It was an absolute top-notch marvel of the day and became the main factor in the development of the northern Great Lakes states.

Rates on the canal were considered low: a penny per mile, or twice that amount if food was provided. Fast canal packets that traveled night and day charged five cents per mile. They provided better quarters and food, and carried passengers up to a hundred miles a day, a really surprising feat for the time. All the boats were beamy, squarish, and shallow, and were pulled along the canal by horses or mules. Most of the boats were brightly painted. The cabin extended nearly the full length of the boat and was divided into the crew's quarters at the bow, followed by a small dressing room for women passengers, a sitting room for women, and a large main cabin where food was served. Men also slept in this main cabin, which was converted at night by means of bunks stacked like shelves around the walls. At the rear was a kitchen and a bar. Ventilation was nonexistent. Most passengers stayed on the deck, above the cabin area, where baggage was stored. Regardless of weather, this was preferred to the close, dirty, suffocating cabin below. But the top deck also had its hazards. Numerous low bridges along the way required a passenger's close attention and his head to be regularly ducked. When corn whiskey from the bar below had drowned all reason or a whist game claimed too much attention, duckings turned to dunkings. Then the quiet rustic countryside was enlivened by shouts, threats of legal action, and loud guffaws from the more prudent, drier passengers. Since the average depth of the canal was four feet, it was difficult to create a serious tragedy out of such a mishap, and a trip along the canal was less dangerous than sportive.

Buffalo grew rapidly once the canal opened, attaining a population of eighteen thousand by 1840. It became a stopover point between lake traffic and canal traffic. In 1833 sixty thousand persons passed through Buffalo on their way to faraway settlements, and the following year, eighty thousand went west through Buffalo. Each year thereafter, except for the depression years of 1837 and 1839, the number of those moving west mounted. Settlers kept filling up northern Ohio, southern Michigan, the northern Indiana-Chicago area, and southern Wisconsin. Detroit still had only nine thousand inhabitants by 1840, but many inland towns were developing, and these soon favored Detroit with commerce and growth. Sectional rivalries were bitter.

Michigan held a census in 1834 and discovered a population of nearly a hundred thousand. This was well above the sixty thousand required for statehood, and territorial leaders quickly applied for admission to the Union. The application requested that the new state's southern boundary should run from the southern tip of Lake Michigan due east

The Great Lakes Historical Society

After the Erie Canal opened in 1825, Detroit grew rapidly, as shown by this picture of the city in 1836. Steamers such as the Michigan *continued to bring new arrivals from the East.*

to Lake Erie. This line had already been established by Congress in the Ordinance of 1787 as the proposed southern boundary for Michigan when it became a state. But Ohio, a state since 1803 and already claiming a population of nearly a million, had long used a boundary that lay north of the 1787 line. For a decade before 1834, the dispute had been smoldering. At stake was a narrow strip of land along the present southern boundary of Michigan. Toledo, then called Port Lawrence, lay in the disputed strip and was a bustling commercial center. It was also the starting point of a canal under construction between Lake Erie and the Ohio River. The Michigan request for statehood now brought this dispute to a head. Thirty years of political temporizing had to be quickly settled, but maneuvers in Congress and on the frontier failed to produce a settlement.

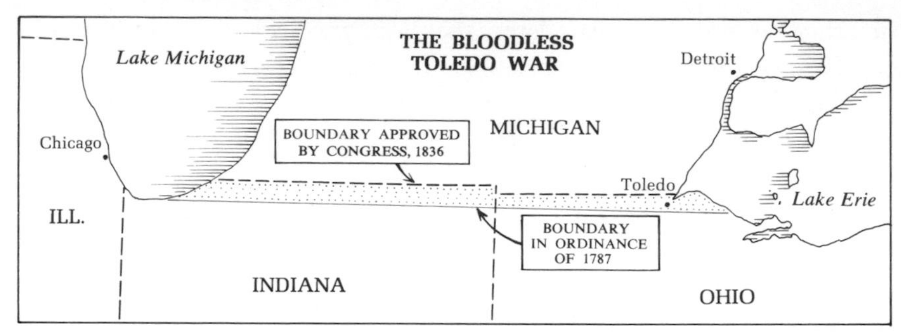

In 1835 Michigan and Ohio raised armies in a border dispute over a narrow strip of land across what is now northern Ohio and Indiana. The armies shuffled about in the field but avoided pitched battle. A year later Congress approved a compromise: the northern boundary was chosen, and Michigan was given the Upper Peninsula as consolation.

In the spring of 1835, both sides raised armies and marched against one another. Michigan had about a thousand men under arms, Ohio six hundred. Each army was under the command of a local military leader. For several weeks, ferocious maneuvering went on as these forces attempted to find each other in the border wilderness. Fortunately, they never did make contact. There is something to be said for the argument that neither side really wanted to find the other as opposed to the reverse that neither was able to. In any case, the so-called bloodless Toledo War continued through the fall of 1835 and, as the adjective implies, almost passed without bloodshed.

Two encounters, however, did take place. The first occurred at a place called Phillips Field near Toledo. There, thirty Michigan militiamen were aroused at their encampment one evening by sounds of carousing. The sounds came from a nearby tavern. Outraged, the militiamen stole up to the saloon in the dark and burst in, capturing four rosy-nosed Ohio colonels, one major, two captains, three privates, and an important quantity of corn liquor. The whole job lot of Ohioans were taken off to suffer hangovers in a Michigan stockade.

The other encounter, in the same locale, was more desperate. It also took place at night and featured a swoop by Michigan militia to capture an Ohio man appropriately named B. F. Stickney. While being captured, Mr. Stickney stuck his penknife in a Michigan sergeant's arm and thus drew the only human blood of the war. Soon after, however, a white mule who had the misfortune to shamble onto this field of battle was shot by someone, probably from boredom over the lack of other targets. Ten years later, the Michigan legislature authorized reparations amounting to fifty dollars be paid to the mule's owner.

Soon after the mule met his end, President Jackson and Congress stepped in to prevent either military commander from taking himself too seriously. They decreed that the Toledo strip was part of the state of Ohio. As consolation for its loss, Michigan received the Upper Peninsula. This decision was extremely unpopular in Michigan, until immense deposits of iron and copper were located in the Upper Peninsula a few years later. Then the decision was extremely unpopular in Wisconsin, which originally owned the Upper Peninsula. Wisconsin, however, did not become a state until 1848 and thus was in no position to claim the territory until too late.

The Erie Canal had opened Michigan to settlement, but large portions of the area were scarcely known, even as it became a state. Henry R. Schoolcraft, Indian authority, geologist, and explorer, wrote in the *Democratic Free Press* in 1836: "It should not be forgotten in this era of emigrating fervour that scarcely eighteen years have elapsed since Lower Michigan was officially reported to the government as unfit to be patented in donations to the soldiers who had served in the War of 1812. A few enterprising individuals from Detroit penetrated the interior in 1819. Public opinion was, however, slow in receiving their reports of the soil and forest growth. The first surveyor who was employed in running out the western townships told me that even in 1822 and 1823, he deemed it a project of very questionable expedience; so much so, that he had reason to doubt whether the land sales would ever justify it.

"A hundred thousand inhabitants in that portion of the peninsula have now given their united testimony in favor of its exceeding fertility, bland climate and high advantages."

The same newspaper noted that a wagon left Detroit that summer every five minutes during daylight hours. Covered wagons of settlers were also approaching Detroit through "dismal stretches of upper Canada, with 318 passing through Chatham in ten days." On a single day in May 1837, seven hundred passengers reportedly disembarked from packets and river ferries in Detroit, and most headed off for the interior as quickly as possible.

The soil outside Detroit was surprisingly good, but the newcomer had to work hard to clear his land and get a crop planted. One settler named John Nowlin led his family to a wilderness area near the present city of Dearborn in 1834. In the manner of the day, he received hos-

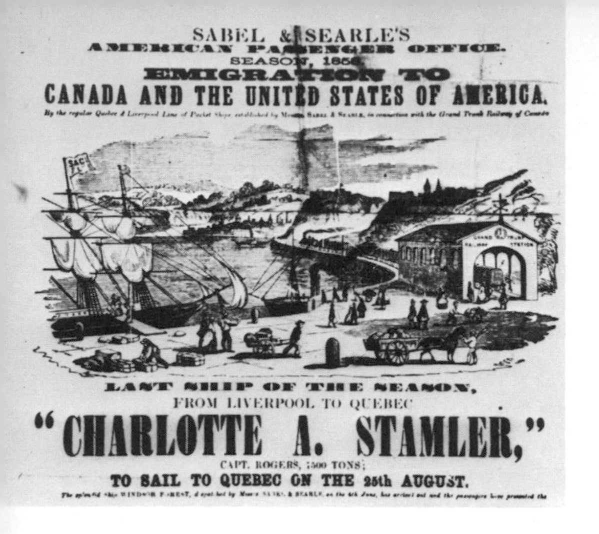

SABEL & SEARLE'S
AMERICAN PASSENGER OFFICE.
EMIGRATION TO
CANADA AND THE UNITED STATES OF AMERICA.
LAST SHIP OF THE SEASON,
FROM LIVERPOOL TO QUEBEC
"CHARLOTTE A. STAMLER,"
CAPT. ROGERS,
TO SAIL TO QUEBEC ON THE 25th AUGUST.

Settlers to the Great Lakes came not only from the eastern seaboard, but from Europe as well. This 1858 poster lured emigrants from Liverpool, England.

Michigan Historical Commission

pitality from another settler until his house could be erected. Nowlin's son William, writing in later life, described the circumstances of settlement on arriving at the neighbor's house:

"Father immediately commenced cutting logs for a house. In one week he had them ready, and men came from Dearbornville to help him raise them. He then cut black ash trees, peeled off the bark to roof his house, and after having passed two weeks under Mr. Pardee's hospitable roof, we moved into a house of our own, had a farm of our own, and owed no one.

"Father brought his axe from York State; it weighed seven pounds; he gave me a smaller one. He laid the trees left and right until we could see the sun from ten o'clock in the morning till between one and two in the afternoon, when it mostly disappeared back of Mr. Pardee's woods.

"Father found it necessary for him to have a team, so he went to Detroit and bought a yoke of oxen; also, at the same time, a cow. He paid eighty dollars for the oxen and twenty-five for the cow. These cattle were driven in from Ohio. The cow proved to be a great help toward the support of the family for a number of years. The oxen were the first owned in the south part of the town of Dearborn. They helped to clear the logs from the piece father had cut over, and we planted late corn, potatoes and garden stuff. The corn grew very high but didn't ear well. The land was indeed very rich, but shaded too much."

This family had traveled west on the Erie Canal to Buffalo, there taking passage for Detroit aboard the new steamer *Michigan.* Some earlier steamers have already been mentioned, and in 1826, the year after the Erie Canal opened, four more joined the lake traffic. These were the *Henry Clay*, *William Penn*, *Niagara*, and *Enterprise*. The *Sheldon Thompson*, big for its day at 242 tons, was launched in 1830, and after that date, more steamers were added rapidly, the *Michigan* being launched in 1833.

The wilderness road that the Nowlin family followed from Detroit to Dearborn was the Old Northwest's most notable highway. Originally it had been an Indian trail from southern Lake Michigan to the Detroit River. With the coming of settlers it became known as the Chicago road, and was the most used highway west from Detroit. Many emigrants continued west on this road, after completing the Erie Canal and Lake Erie portions. Over this road ran the first stagecoach to enter Chicago, making the run from Detroit in September 1833. The route gradually became more popular, and stage travel followed schedules. The Western Stage Company, for example, advertised in 1837 a daily coach from Detroit to Chicago that ran "through in four and a half days." That is a direct-line distance of over 250 miles, or more than 50 miles traveled per day.

In the first half of the nineteenth century, the Old Northwest began to grow rapidly. Settlers poured into the territory in canal boats and covered wagons. Later, as roads improved, stagecoaches made the trip from Detroit to Chicago in four and a half days—covering more than fifty miles per day!

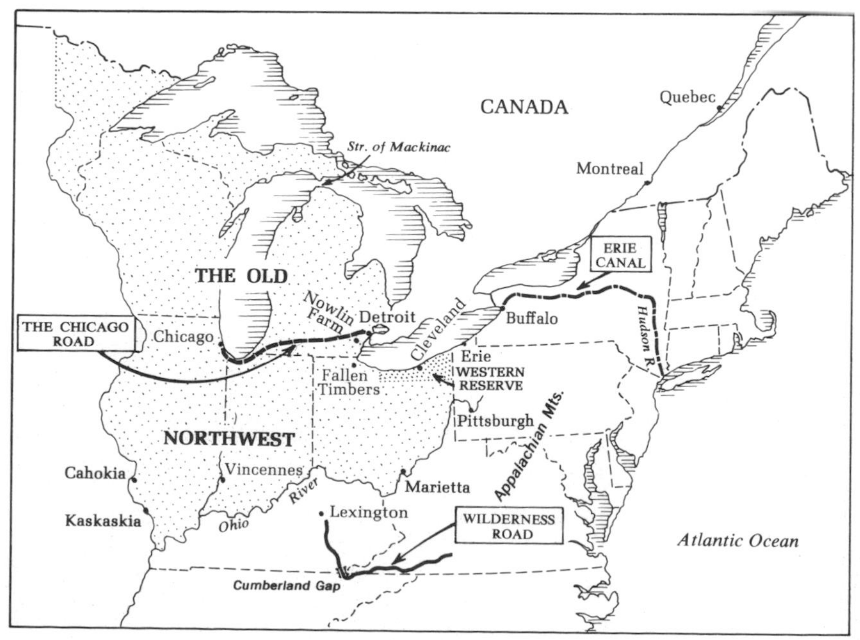

A sled load of white-pine logs in northern Michigan in 1880. Sleds were sometimes piled two stories high, and loggers hit the runners with mallets to get the load moving. It was a dangerous job for horses. On icy, downhill roads, they were sometimes run down by the heavy sleds.

Michigan Department of Conservation

11

The Wealthy Land

DURING THE MIDDLE of the nineteenth century, the people of the Great Lakes area more and more settled down to use their lands. In the 1840's and 1850's, the Lake Ontario, Lake Erie, and Lake St. Clair regions were widely settled, and cities, canals, railroads, farms, and Great Lakes fisheries were becoming established. The frontier was northern Michigan and Wisconsin. Tales of lands farther west, with possibilities for investment, now stirred European speculators.

For centuries, rumors of vast copper deposits in the Lake Superior region had captured the imagination of Europeans. Strange stories were told of ancient mines on Isle Royale, of prehistoric diggings, of the awe the Indians showed toward Lake Superior. Supposedly, somewhere "up there" huge copper boulders lay exposed on the surface. Early explorers, traders, trappers, and Jesuits were infected by speculator's fever. Champlain had received a lump of copper from the Indians when he founded Quebec in 1608, and was told it came from a mysterious land far to the west. In the 1630's, 1640's, and 1650's, such tales grew as the French penetrated deeper into the interior. Father Allouez, sent to Lake Superior in 1665, was told to look for copper. He did not learn much from the Indians, who were reluctant to talk of the sacred metal and spoke only of a floating island of copper far out in the lake. They warned it was surrounded by spirits who struck intruders dead. This challenged the Christian's conscience. He urged disbelief, but the Indians were obdurate. The father tried sweet reason. No, the Indians held firmly to their belief: the island was guarded by spirits, and they would not take him there. Many Indians had gone to look for that island—it was in the legends—but few ever returned. There were those who did know where the sacred metal was to be found, but they would not talk about it.

Disconsolate but determined, Father Allouez began a search of the Keweenaw and Ontonagon areas. He soon found what he sought—some small chunks and jagged pieces of pure copper. The purity must have amazed Allouez, and it certainly interested his superiors in Quebec. Attempts were made to find more, but again the Indians demurred. Their reluctance and the natural barriers of wilderness, distances, and lack of facilities combined to put the French off the trail once again. Further fruitless attempts were made in 1667, in 1687, and in 1710.

In 1727, however, Louis Denis, Sieur de la Ronde, was named commandant of the trading post on Madeline Island, then known to the Indians as Chequamegon, the Island of The Golden-Breasted Woodpecker. Here La Ronde held sway for many years, and he too heard the stories of copper treasure. In 1738, he formed a partnership, built a twenty-five-ton vessel, imported two miners, and began operations near the mouth of the Ontonagon River. The miners, a father and son, wrote of the place that, "one could never see a finer mine, apparently, and it is certain that if one wished to start in the business and invest money there, a great return of copper might be hoped for." La Ronde removed a modest quantity of copper before a Sioux uprising against the resident Chippeways ended his efforts.

In the 1770's, after the fall of Quebec, the English tried their hand. They were more systematic but no more successful. They built a forty-ton vessel at the Sault, again imported miners, and constructed an assay furnace. But the miners were so dismayed by the winter's ferocity that they came close to open revolt and were soon transported home to gentler climes.

In the 1820's, Henry R. Schoolcraft, the explorer and Indian authority, puffed new life into the search with one of his reports. This was followed by a report from Major Stephen Long, a government surveyor, returning from a field trip to Minnesota. These reports inspired the Michigan legislature, as one of its first acts, to hire Douglass Houghton as state geologist. The legislature sent him to the area in the late 1830's, soon after Michigan became a state. The report of his trip appeared in 1841.

Houghton correctly foresaw that reports of copper in the district might mislead prospective investors, and he couched his comments in heavily guarded phrases. Each optimistic statement was followed by a dash of cold water. In summary, he wrote: "While I am fully satisfied that the mineral district of our state will prove a source of eventual and steadily increasing wealth to our people, I cannot fail to have before me the fear that it may prove the ruin of hundreds of adventurers, who will visit it with expectations never to be realized. The true resources have as yet been but little examined or developed, and even under the most favorable circumstances, we cannot expect to see this done but by the most judicious and economical expenditure of capital, at those points where the prospects of success are most favorable."

Nevertheless, those who read the report immediately packed up their belongings and headed north, thereby inaugurating America's first mining rush.

One who went to the copper country was Julius Eldred, a businessman from Detroit, who planned to capture the Ontonagon Boulder, a huge mass of copper which Houghton in his report had described and located. Eldred planned to move it to Detroit, place it on display, charge admission, and make a fortune. It was a grand scheme. Houghton's report stated that the boulder was pure copper, and that it probably weighed three to four tons. Such an object would certainly attract great attention. The state was still fuming over loss of the Toledo strip and this valuable nugget from the Upper Peninsula would give Michigan the last laugh. At the going price for copper, the boulder probably was worth about $1500. As a curiosity, it was worth far more. The mineral region would prove a far more valuable prize than anyone ever imagined.

Eldred reached the Ontonagon River in the summer of 1841 and easily located the boulder. However, a modest difficulty now arose. An Indian claimed the nugget, and as the Ontonagon River was in Indian territory, Eldred was obliged to pay him $150 for the boulder.

Eldred felt that his property was unwieldy enough to be safe from theft and left for Detroit to plan for its removal. The following summer he returned with block and tackle, some men, a sturdy flatcar, and two short sections of railroad track. He found the boulder guarded by tough-looking miners and, despite his protests, Eldred saw that he was outnumbered and outmaneuvered. He bought the boulder a second time, now paying $1365.

With their money in their pockets, the miners now suggested that it might be well for Eldred to look up the local government agent, just to ask him about the boulder. They were all still in Indian territory, and the government might have to give its approval. It sounded as though these men knew trouble was afoot.

The agent was General Walter Cunningham, located at Ontonagon, and after tracking him down, Eldred received a permit to remove the boulder. Work began. The mass of metal was heavier than expected. Cables snapped. Hoists broke. The men sweated and fumed. Finally the boulder was hoisted far enough to plop it aboard the flatcar standing on one section of the track. The second section of track was laid ahead, and the car was rolled forward. Then the back section was moved to the front, and again the car rolled forward. In this leapfrog fashion the boulder was moved four miles to the main stream of the Ontonagon River, where it was placed aboard a raft and floated downstream to Lake Superior. Here it was seized by the government agent, General Cunningham.

Eldred stormed and raged. He pulled out his permit, signed by Cunningham. He showed his bill of sale from the miners. He recounted his purchase from the Indian the year before. He waved wildly at his expensive crew of men and his pile of equipment.

But Cunningham had his orders, new orders, received soon after issuing Eldred his permit. He was to seize the boulder and hold it until an Indian treaty was settled. With Eldred in a fury, Cunningham found a solution. He suggested that Eldred take the boulder to Detroit, where the whole matter could be thrashed out in court. Eldred agreed, thereby lifting three tons of dead weight off the agent's shoulders, solving the government's transportation problem, and pacifying the fuming promoter.

Eldred took the boulder by ship to Detroit, and it gained fame as it went. By the time it arrived, there was no need to advertise, and he displayed his prize, charging a quarter for admission. After a few days, in which several hundreds viewed the curiosity, the federal government again seized the huge mass of copper and shipped it to Washington—with a raging Eldred riding on top.

In the capital the government agreed, after a long legal struggle, to repay Eldred $5665 for his expenses. The boulder then was placed on display in the capital, free of charge, where it attracted attention for awhile before fading from public interest. Today it lies in the Natural History building in Washington after years of hiding in a remote hallway of the Smithsonian Institution.

The fame of the Ontonagon Boulder spurred new mining activity, and in the spring of 1843, the first boats north were loaded with a new kind of emigrant. These men shouldered picks and shovels; their rucksacks were filled with salt pork and dry beans. The schooner *Swallow* beat the rest of the pack, cracking through shell ice to land twenty miners at Copper Harbor as soon as navigation opened.

That ship was followed by the *Algonquin* and the *Astor*, both carrying men whose one interest was copper. They had been farmers, clerks, livery hands, sailors, mechanics, storekeepers—and virtually not one of them had any previous mining experience. No trained geologist came with them, and no one had troubled to bring other forms of enlightenment. Their total geological knowledge lay in the vague surmise that copper was red. Their mining methods showed the result of this lack of preparation.

The Keweenaw Peninsula was an impenetrable tangle of boggy swamp, bluffs, cedar and tamarack thickets, outcrops of rock. The miners, driven by visions of quickly-found wealth, stumbled into this wilderness totally unprepared. They did not know how to look for copper, how to remove it from the rock once it was found, or what it was actually worth. Working as individuals or in small companies, the men hunted over the peninsula without plan or pattern. Most found only bits of "float" copper—chunks torn from bedrock by glacial action or erosion and deposited later, perhaps miles away, on stream banks or rocky outcrops. To these unwitting prospectors, however, such a find called for digging, blasting, and mining at the site in the belief that more copper lay directly beneath. That was one method of mining. Another was to search out prehistoric Indian pits and enlarge them first with dynamite, then with picks and shovels and chisels. The Indians, using only stone tools in their mining, often left behind metal they were unable to remove. The boomers now sought out every hollow that might have been an Indian site. In some they found copper; in most they found only vast quantities of disappointment.

The third mining method, employed by those of relatively greater common sense, was to search along springs, freshets, creeks, and streams. There they watched for telltale signs of green or copper coloration; the green indicating cuprous lodes nearby, the copper indicating either chunks of float copper or, more hopefully, veins of native metal. The rich Copper Falls mine was found when a sharp-eyed prospector saw glints of metal in a small creek.

Out of all this activity, some men gathered a little copper but most left the Keweenaw much poorer than when they arrived. And most of the riches that were obtained quickly found their way from the pants pockets of the prospectors into the coffers of camp hangers-on. All the more common forms of these appeared, with dealers in "land per-

The first commercial mine in the world to extract native copper as its sole product was the Cliff Mine, on the Keweenaw Peninsula, Lake Superior. For three years after it opened in 1845, the mine was a costly disappointment. Then rich new shoots were found, and the mine prospered. The drawing shows Cliff Mine as it appeared in 1850.

Foster and Whitney Reports

mits" being especially numerous. The land permit was an early form of claim ticket required to validate a stake. Prospectors with soft hands and sharp heads stuffed their pockets with blank permits and followed the boomers north, mining the miners' wealth with eminent success. The miners, after all, had no choice. When a chunk of land looked highly cuprous, a miner felt obliged to file a claim. Mail to the nearest land office took weeks. In the meantime he had to camp on his claim to protect it. If he left for a new supply of grub, another claimant could take over. Just when provisions ran lowest and anxiety highest, the land shark appeared with a plan. The plan was to sell the prospector a blank permit with which his claim could be quickly and properly filed. Permit forms were available free in Washington, but the miner did not know that and had no choice anyway. Washington was a long

way off. So hands were joined and then money was exchanged for the permit. The prospector was left with mining risks and empty pockets, and the permit holder went to look for more customers.

Meanwhile, in the delusion that the miners needed protection from the Indians, the War Department sent two companies of infantry to the copper country in 1844. These troops immediately constructed barracks and a stockade. The local Indians, watching this activity, concluded that the stockade was meant to keep drunken miners away from the soldiers. The soldiers, in turn, looked meanly at the Indians. The place was named Fort Wilkins, after the then Secretary of War, and for two years the contingent cut bread with bayonets while they sat about hoping for an Indian uprising. The Chippeways were disappointing in this respect. However, in 1846, the War Department was lucky enough to have the Mexican War begin, and the two companies trooped off to fight it, leaving their quarters in charge of caretakers. Even these were withdrawn twenty-five years later, when the place was formally abandoned—as it might well have been years earlier. The buildings and stockade have since been rebuilt as a museum, now besieged by thousands of tourists annually. The place makes a marvelous State Park, and is well worth a visit.

Out of all this confusion a thriving copper industry slowly developed. By 1845, most of the original prospectors had scrubbed out or gone to work for the few organized mine companies then emerging. But general malaise lay over the region; the shattered hopes of early prospectors ruled out further local investment. From a distance, however, the copper country still looked profitable, and Eastern dollars began to flow with steady confidence into the Keweenaw. That confidence was soon rewarded.

In August 1845 a prospecting crew of the Pittsburgh and Boston Mining Company stumbled onto a pinch of copper south of Eagle River. According to legend, one prospector tripped on a rock, bumped downhill, and bruised his backside on a projecting bit of copper. Following his lead, the entire crew slithered down to the cliff's bottom. The company geologist was uncertain. It looked promising, but so had many other places. After some discussion an adit, or tunnel, was driven into the hill. After desultory chipping and hauling, at a depth of seventy feet, the miners suddenly came on a mass of pure copper. It was the first such vein to be uncovered, proving that far greater riches were still locked in this craggy land. The location was named Cliff Mine and was the first commercial mine in the world to extract native copper as its sole product.

For nearly three years, however, the new mine was a costly disappointment and more than once was nearly abandoned. Two years after the first discovery, all the available cash was spent, and the company's directors refused to make a further investment. Then Dr. Charles Avery of Pittsburgh decided to gamble his entire personal fortune on the mine; he put up $80,000. In a mining venture of such proportions, $80,000 could not last very long,, and when $60,000 had been spent, the company was ready to quit. The remaining $20,000 would pay off the miners, remove the equipment, and settle the debts.

But almost as closing orders were being prepared, rich new veins of copper were found, angling off from the main shaft, and owners and miners alike took heart. The veins proved sizable and held their strength, soon leading to others. Within a year and a half, the Cliff Mine repaid all its debts and became the first in the district to declare a dividend. This fabulous property continued to pay dividends for thirty-five years, producing 38,000,000 pounds of copper and repaying investors twenty times their capital.

Another rich mine was the Minesota, in Ontonagon County. Apart from producing a large amount of copper, this mine gained fame because of its misspelled name. According to local legend, the name was penned late one night by a weary mining engineer soon after the lode was discovered. Filing the claim form, he mistakenly wrote "Minesota," and this spelling was later entered in the government records, hence becoming the official name of the mine.

The Minesota and Cliff mines found their copper in cross fissures—cracks in the main rock formations of the peninsula. These openings were generally small, and the amount of copper they contained was limited; nevertheless, work in the fissures claimed nearly all mining attention until 1856 when the great Pewabic lode was discovered in a main lava flow. This lode was not so rich as the veins of the Cliff Mine, but its extent was far greater. The Quincy Company soon began mining the Pewabic, and by 1862 it paid its first dividend. During the Civil War, the Quincy produced all the copper needed by federal arsenals, becoming a key factor in the Union victory.

The Quincy kept right on producing after the Civil War, and its copper helped to wire the nation's streets and homes after Edison invented the electric light bulb. It helped to carry the nation through the Spanish-American War and the First World War, and during all that time, it paid at least one dividend a year as a steady stream of copper poured out of its shafts.

Other veins were discovered in the Keweenaw's lavas and conglomerates, and from 1845 to 1890, the peninsula led the nation in copper production. From 1850 to 1877, Michigan mines produced from three fourths to four fifths of all the copper mined in the United States. After 1877, production gradually declined until in the 1890's the Butte district of Montana began to surpass it.

Copper was more popular than other minerals as a mining venture, and for several years detracted from the potentially more important iron-ore deposits in the Lake Superior region. Iron, however, is found as a ferrous compound, not in a pure state; its value per pound was less than that of copper, and it required a costly process to make it useful. While copper melts at a fairly low temperature, iron calls for a very high temperature, and the nation at that date was not geared to blast-furnace production. So, Lake Superior iron reserves were developed more slowly.

The discovery of iron was an unexpected part of the copper-mining story. William A. Burt came to Michigan Territory from New York in 1924. He was a self-taught surveyor, and invented the solar compass, having been too often frustrated in using magnetic compasses. In 1833, he was named United States deputy surveyor for the Michigan Territory. When the copper country was opened up in 1841, Douglass Houghton realized that linear and geological surveys were needed throughout the region. Soon after Houghton returned, a conference took place, with the result that Burt and a survey team were sent to the Upper Peninsula.

September 19, 1844, dawned overcast, and Burt was unable to use his solar compass. While running lines that morning near the present city of Negaunee, progress was brought to a halt because the magnetic compasses seemingly "went crazy." Burt's journal for that day is simply a prosaic listing of the compass readings obtained. But fortunately Jacob Houghton, Douglass Houghton's younger brother and the barometer man on the expedition, described the event more vividly. He

Philo M. Everett, a merchant with no mining experience, founded the Jackson Pit Mine near Negaunee, Michigan. In 1847 his company mined and smelted the first iron ore in the Lake Superior region.

The Great Lakes Historical Society

Everett's Jackson Mining Company wanted to mine copper or silver, but were uncertain where to look. After a vain search, Chippeway Chief Marji Gesick (back row, center) led them to a large iron lode near the present site of Negaunee.

The Great Lakes Historical Society

wrote of the day as follows: "So soon as we reached the hill to the south of Teal Lake, the compass man began to notice the fluctuation of the magnetic needle. At length, the compass man called for all to 'come and see a variation that will beat them all.' "

The needle had turned more than a quarter circle from true. With the sun now appearing, Burt began to exclaim proudly over the triumph this meant for his solar compass. Houghton quotes him as saying: "How would they survey this country without my compass?" After wondering about the magnetic variations, Burt added, "Boys, look around and see what you can find."

What they found, scattered everywhere at their feet, were lumps of heavy gray stone. These were from a very rich iron-ore outcropping, each lump being about half iron, half unusable stone. It was of course this iron that had deflected the compass; and the discovery of the ore being duly recorded in the survey, the party continued with its work.

But while Burt thought of the discovery as little more than vindication for his solar compass, others soon became interested in the ore itself. Among these was Philo M. Everett, a storekeeper from Jackson, Michigan, who formed the Jackson Mining Company in July

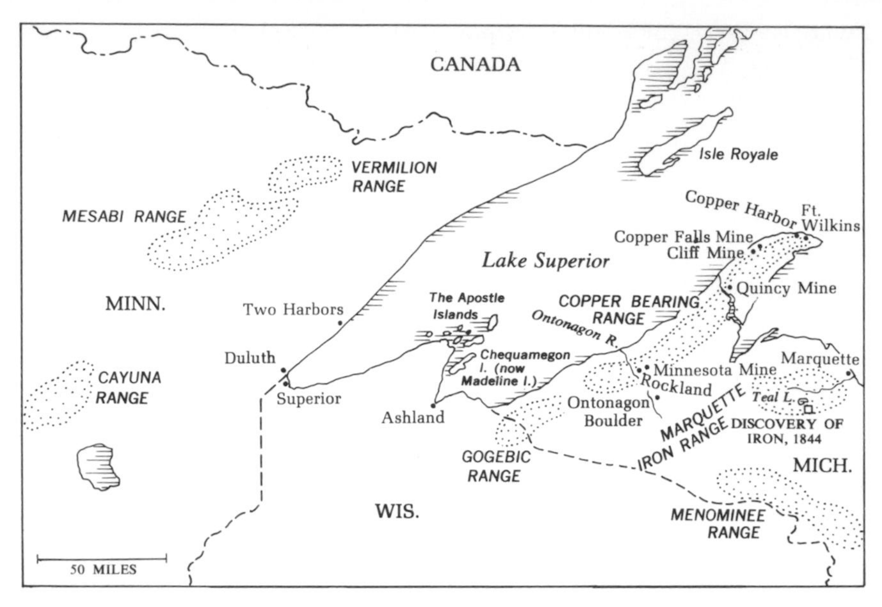

The iron and copper region of Lake Superior includes three states—Michigan, Wisconsin, and Minnesota.

1845. He and his fellow businessmen wanted to find copper or silver, but they had no knowledge of mining and apparently knew nothing of Burt's discovery at the time of their incorporation. That summer, Everett headed an expedition north, ostensibly to look for copper. At the Sault portage, they heard about Burt's mountain of ore. Hoping the ore might be copper, they bought a boat and hired a local pilot to sail them to the Carp River in Marquette County. There they found nothing. The pilot then suggested they sail on to L'Anse to find a Chippeway chief who, he thought, might lead them to the ore deposit. The idea sounded flimsy, but Everett had nothing else to go on. At L'Anse, hopes were renewed. The Chippeway chief, Marji Gesick, told them, Yes, he knew where heavy stones were located on the Carp River. The Carp drains Teal Lake through a creek, and when the party arrived at the river, the Indian led them directly to a hill overlooking the lake. There, under an upturned pine stump, they found a solid mass of iron ore. They had hoped for copper or silver, but it was to be their fate to mine the first iron in the district, a quirk of fate that disappointed several members of the Jackson Company.

On November 10, 1845, Everett wrote to a friend of his adventures that summer: "There are no white men on Lake Superior except those who go there for mining purposes. We incurred many dangers and hardships. We made several locations, one of which we called Iron at the time. It is a mountain of solid iron ore, 150 feet high. The ore looks as bright as a bar of iron just broken. Since coming home we have had some of it smelted and find it produced iron and something resembling gold—some say it is gold and copper. Our location is one mile square, and we shall send a company of men up in the spring to begin operations."

But 1846 had nearly passed before Everett could proceed with his venture, and the work crew sent to the scene was caught by the severe winter of 1846–47. Still they pushed ahead, and on February 10, 1847, the company blacksmith worked the first iron made in the Lake Superior district. In his tiny forge, he mixed the ore with limestone and charcoal, and soon pulled a white-hot spongy mass from the bright heat. After hammering it a short time, he pronounced it excellent iron, and success now seemed assured.

City of Marquette, as it appeared about 1850. As the iron industry grew, the city evolved from this smelting settlement at the mouth of the Carp River, Lake Superior. The ore was mined in the hills a few miles inland.

The Great Lakes Historical Society

Costly obstacles, however, soon forced the company to abandon the entire project. All food and equipment had to be packed into the location. Supplies of charcoal and limestone were uncertain. A flood washed the forge away. Teams had to cart the blooms ten miles to Marquette over rough roads. Worst of all, the market for iron was very uncertain; expenses kept mounting and income lagged. In March 1849 the Marquette Iron Company was organized from leases obtained from the Jackson Company, and for all practical purposes, the Jackson venture had come to an unprofitable end. Nevertheless, the little group of Jackson merchants had opened the way and the long, profitable history of Lake Superior iron mining was now underway. The Marquette Range claimed all attention until the Menominee Range opened in the 1870's, followed by the Gogebic Range about 1880. Then in 1884, the rich Vermilion Range on the northwest shore of the lake was opened, followed by the Mesabi Range, largest of the lot, in 1892. Finally, in 1905, the small but productive Cuyuna Range was opened. These six ranges became the heart and core of United States iron mining, and the region continues to be to this day one of North America's most extensive and ambitious industries.

Hard on the heels of the copper and iron came the development of the noisy, boisterous Great Lakes logging industry. If all the rest of its history were stripped away, this one era alone would fill the Great Lakes region with interest and anecdotes for years to come. It was a time when the whole of northern Michigan, Wisconsin, and Minnesota was held together with haywire, Silver-Star galluses, and team harness. Starting as a mild-mannered infant in the 1840's, the logging industry grew into a squalling brat during the Civil War, pulled on hobnailed boots and fought all comers by 1880, and had practically run out of forests to conquer by 1900. Old before its time, it gasped loudly over the tricks of fate, and went off to die in peace after 1920.

During the eighty years this roughneck roamed the land, most of the forest in the upper Great Lakes region was chopped down and hauled away. It was said that the forests of the region were so dense a squirrel could journey from Detroit to Duluth without ever touching ground—if he could jump the Straits of Mackinac—yet Paul Bunyan's boys had hardly drawn a second breath before they ran out of trees to cut.

Early settlers around the Great Lakes cut or burned the forest mainly to get rid of it, to clear the land so it could be used for crops. Farmers kept some wood for buildings and fuel, but most of the trees were simply cut down and burned. As mining, fishing, and farming villages around the Lakes grew first to towns and then to cities, the demand for logs and lumber increased. A whipsaw was developed to reduce the logs to lumber, but it was plainly the most pernicious contraption that ever plagued a working man. The log to be cut was placed on a cradle over a pit, and one man climbed on the log while the other entered the pit below. From these awkward positions, the two men pushed and pulled the whipsaw up and down until the log was sliced into lumber. This work provided first-hand proof of something long suspected—that men's arms are mainly designed for work below shoulder level. The discovery was interesting, if academic, to the man on top. Out of sheer physical necessity, however, the man in the pit finally dug himself out of the insults and sawdust raining down just long enough to invent a frame to hold *his* end of the saw while it operated by water power. The interest of the man on top now quickened. He had a choice; he could invent a similar frame for his end or have his arms wrenched off by the waterwheel below. The capabilities of water power were thus driven home to the top members of the logging industry, and by the 1840's several small mills were operating near Lake Huron in Michigan's Saginaw River valley. Some used waterwheels, then converted to steam when it became available. Single saws were replaced by gangs of saws that cut several boards at once. This contraption soon fell of its own weight, however, when the circular saw came into play. Circular saws were much faster and simpler to operate. By the beginning of the Civil War, the logging industry had already passed these early hurdles, and it burgeoned rapidly as that conflict advanced. By 1865, a whole new way of life had opened in the northern pine forests of the Great Lakes.

The white pine in its mature form often stands a hundred and fifty feet tall in forest groves, with a base diameter of up to five feet. It grows straight upward with its long branches spreading at right angles, presenting a somewhat pagodalike outline. The needles are long and fine, and from a slight distance give the tree a misty, pale-blue cast mixing and blending with the greens of the surrounding forest. To the logger, the vast stands of these trees were beautiful to behold, even though such men were not particularly interested in aesthetics. They were mainly uprooted farmers and settlers, immigrants from northern Europe, and young toughs from various callings. Unlike the nonresident owners of the copper and iron mines, however, the men who became lumber barons generally started life as loggers. The camps set up in the Saginaw Valley soon advanced to "the Thumb," the peninsula that juts out like a thumb between Saginaw Bay and lower Lake Huron. As these areas were cut over, the camps turned northward, moving deeper into the Lower Peninsula along the river systems. The rivers of the Lower Peninsula drain east to Lake Huron and west to Lake Michigan, and these streams quickly became the prime avenue for transporting the logs to the sawmill. At the mouths of rivers, sawmills set up business as convenient middle points between the logging camps and the Great Lakes. Sailboats called "lumber hookers," then hauled the acres of pine lumber off to Chicago, Detroit, Milwaukee, and other Midwestern cities.

As the cutting advanced and crews worked farther and farther from base camps, an occupation called "landlooking" grew up. The landlooker's task was to walk off across the stump-cluttered countryside to find tracts of suitable forest where the lumber camp might relocate. Many of these men worked as individuals, laying claim to tracts of timber, then selling it for any profit they could make. The landlooker bore a family resemblance to the roving gambler, both professions working independently, both shifting their scene of operation quite often, and both being always just on the verge of making a really big haul. Like the gambler, the landlooker dealt with huge values, and the tools he used were a pair of sharp eyes and a knowledge of his surroundings. On any stand of trees, he had to measure out the available timber by eye, and if that instrument was keen and calculating, he could make fair wages. If his eye was dull or misled him, he could lose everything. This other tool, his knowledge of the country, was an even more exceptional belonging. To gain this, he tramped mile upon mile, and what he learned he kept to himself. Like the guildsman of old, he had secret knowledge of his trade. In the woods, these men lived on coffee, beans, and muskrat haunches—with visions of tall timber for dessert.

After the landlooker came the logging camps themselves—a wondrous tangle of peaveys and double-bitted axes, of horse harness and steamy wool socks. For housing, tents were often used, although ramshackle frame shacks were also constructed. These communities included teams of oxen and horses, a blacksmith shop, and a massive cooking establishment. Last and by all means least came the loggers themselves, most of whom were considered by the camp bosses as less important than the horses, blacksmiths, grub, or cooks, all of these in turn being less important than the timber. Timber was the essence of the logging camp. The very smell and sight of it permeated deep into the pores of every member of the camp. Men were killed and maimed by timber; they complained of sawdust in their griddlecakes; they were bought or sold by the way they worked with timber. Timber was and had been king a long time before the first logging camp drew breath. The stands of native white pine that made the forest had been seedlings when Shakespeare was scrawling his first verse. They were fuzzy-bearded poles at the time of Plymouth Rock, maturing giants when Lexington and Bunker Hill were fought and won. Before the lumber camps, the northern forests had paid allegiance to four nations: the United States, England, France, and earlier than any of these, the Chippeway. It was more than sheer circumstance that the loggers were merely incidental in the forest's domain.

During the last half of the nineteenth century, the logging industry flourished in the upper Great Lakes region. After the trees were cut, "drivers" ushered the logs downstream to the sawmill towns along the Lakes. In the above picture, taken in 1886, logs are being driven on the Muskegon River toward Lake Michigan. Tented rafts in the background are cookshacks called "wanigans."

Michigan Department of Conservation

The men of the logging camps had a unique society of their own, organized into a strict hierarchy. The upper classes were composed of camp superintendents and foremen, scalers and cruisers, barn bosses, clerks, and cooks—more or less in that order of descending importance. The great lower class was developed and reserved for those who showed as little regard for their own skins as possible. There were the top loaders, for example, the men who nudged the ton-weight logs into place on the sled loads—and suffered severe disarray when these logs developed sudden fits of gravity. To this category also belonged the teamsters. While the sled was being loaded, these men stood by expectantly, sometimes getting caught in a tangle of falling logs. However, the teamster's basic lack of interest in living could be clearly seen only when the loaders finished their work. Then the teamster climbed aboard the loaded sled and grabbed the lines, while men with mallets stood at each sled runner. At a signal, the horses strained forward, and the men with the mallets walloped the runners to free them from the ice. Then everyone stood back and bet, with the odds working pretty steadily against the teamster. With the sled sometimes piled two stories high, the teamster and his load went wobbling off down the road, headed for the river. The roadways were so iced during the winter that a single team could pull an impossibly large load if the course ran downhill, as it usually did. An impossibly large load could also push a small team, or overrun it, with expected consequences if the downhill run continued for a short distance, as it usually also did. Some said the horses were attached to the sled only by the force of habit; others said only for decoration. It is true, however, that they started the sled forward and offered some sense of direction, even if downhill losses were heavy. In any case, horses and teamster alike were clearly part of the great lower class—for as long as they could hang on.

Another member of this select group was the cutter. A good cutter bragged that he could set a small stake in the ground and then fell the tree squarely on top of it. That is what a good cutter could do. The ability to drop a tree exactly where desired offered a measure of reassurance to other cutters nearby, who preferred the idea of stakes, rather than they themselves, being driven into the ground. The woods was not always full of expert cutters, however. Hence the inclusion in this class of those cutters who survived.

The drive gangs that took the logs downriver each spring were also part of the great lower class. These crews were generally recruited from the younger, tougher members of the camp. River driving was somewhat like top loading. To stay alive, the driver had to know which way and when to jump. The basic task of the river driver was to see that the logs got downstream each spring to the sawmill towns on the Great Lakes. During the winter, the logs were collected in huge piles at river banks. When spring floods boosted the streams to high levels, logs and men tumbled into the river and roared downstream pell mell. So long as the logs kept moving and the men stayed out of their way, no trouble ensued. But if even a few logs snagged on a shoal, the entire stream would quickly jam, and the river driver would face the murderous task of freeing the obstacle. River driving paid well, but drivers were wet to the armpits all day, and consumption and rheumatism could be counted on as retirement pay—if a river driver wasn't already crushed or drowned before that time.

The vocabulary that came to life in the logging camps consisted mainly of words that first, were colorful, second, could be said without exercising the tongue too violently, and third, had a clear enough ring to carry easily. *Redhorse* was used for corned beef; *morning glories* were the inevitable breakfast flapjacks; *traveling dandruff* was lice; *chickadees* were the roadmen who kept the logging roads free of horse manure so the loaded sleds could move more safely. A *muzzle-*

Lumber schooner Day Spring *enters a mill town off Lake Michigan in the days of heavy logging. Log bays lie in the foreground.*

Michigan Historical Commission

loader was a kind of sleeping bunk designed, certainly, by the same fiend who invented the iron maiden. A muzzle-loader was usually three tiers high, and the men entered at one end only, hence the name. A *go-devil* or *come-along* was the travois used in skidding logs out of the woods. A *jobber's sun* was the kerosene torch that enabled crews to work after dark and into the night—at no extra pay. A *brier* was a saw, and a *wanigan* the floating cookshack that followed a river drive. Loggers, of course, had many other words of an unprintable nature, and they developed a whole technical jargon to ease the strain on their fund of profanity. Included in this technical group were such colorful terms as *parbuckle, cross haul, ross a log, key log, hot logging, bear traps, pig iron, jethro,* and many others. Most of these words and terms died with the times that brought them to birth. Others scrubbed clean were carried over to enjoy a more or less comfortable old age in respectable society.

But words were not the only things that needed to be scrubbed clean. The business methods used by some old rascally timber barons still bring *tsk-tsks* from the general public. For example, they logged off "round forties;" that is, a man cut both his own forty-acre tract and all the others surrounding it. Should the owners of the other tracts complain, they might win a modest judgment in court months later, long after timber and camp had disappeared. Sometimes squatters were hired to "homestead" a piece of land, obtaining it free from the government; then the owner took over and logged the timber.

When clerks from the lumber companies went on buying trips, they struck the ends of the logs with a marking hammer. Such a log mark was similar to the brand used on cattle, each company having its own design. After each log was marked, it was pushed into the river for the trip downstream. Around the first bend, however, sweating crews often snaked the marked logs out of the water, sawed off the ends, and soon had another pile ready for the unsuspecting clerk to mark.

By 1900 the great days of logging were numbered, and after another ten years the Great Lakes forest was essentially gone. Scattered cutting continued up to 1920. One study of Michigan's original stand of 380 billion board feet of saw timber shows that only 244 billion feet were turned to profitable use, while the remaining 136 billion feet—more than a third of the total—were burned in clearing the land or in the forest fires that followed logging operations or were wasted at the lumber mill.

The forest fires that followed logging were as destructive as the logging and highly spectacular. The first of these catastrophic fires occurred in the summer and fall of 1871. Logging had by that time advanced deep into both Wisconsin and Michigan, and large areas were littered with slashings—the dried tops and limbs of trees—left behind by the loggers. Fires started easily in such tinder and burned without anyone making a serious effort to control them. The summer of 1871 was very hot; the roads were powder dry. Wells failed; streams dropped to mere trickles; and crops were seared beyond use. No rain fell after early August, and by October the smell of smoke filled the air. Hundreds of fires burned over the lake states that fall, and soon were linked together in huge draft systems. These raced across the land at astonishing speeds. On October fifth, a dispatch in the *Detroit Free Press* spoke vaguely of intense fires burning in northeastern Wisconsin. Michigan suffered no less than other states, and on October seventh, the *Free Press* reported that ". . . navigation at Detroit has been suspended owing to the dense smoke and fog unparalleled within the memory of the oldest navigators."

These fires, however, were only a prelude to disaster. On October eight the great Chicago fire started, a spectacle of such proportion that it overshadowed all other losses. On that same day, however, the village of Peshtigo, Wisconsin, was overrun by fire and one thousand five hundred lives were lost. The same week, forest fires in Michigan destroyed half a dozen communities, burned an estimated two million acres and claimed two hundred lives.

Similar great fires scorched the northern states at periodic intervals thereafter, with little done to control them. The Thumb region of Michigan burned in 1881, costing nearly 300 lives and turning a million acres to ashes. In 1894, the village of Hinckley, Minnesota, was wiped out with a loss of 418 lives. In 1896, about a hundred square miles of Michigan's Upper Peninsula burned in one fire, a fact which seemed so unimportant that it nearly passed unreported. In 1908, a fire in northeastern Michigan destroyed the village of Metz with a loss of 29 lives. Seventeen of those deaths occurred when a train tried to race through the fire to safety. The rails were so hot they parted, and the train became stranded in the heat. Some who sought safety in the water compartment of the engine's tender were boiled to death.

Such fires generally raged until sufficient rain or snow fell to put them out, and it was not until the 1930's that effective measures to control forest fires began to take effect. In that decade, the terrible fires of the Great Lakes region came to an end—hopefully for all time.

The rapids that once obstructed the passageway between Lakes Huron and Superior are now skirted by the Soo locks. On the left is Sault Ste Marie, Michigan; Sault Ste Marie, Ontario, is out of the photo to the right. Lake Superior is in the background.

Michigan Department of Conservation

12

Blue-Water Tales

THE NEED FOR GREAT LAKES SHIPPING was growing. By 1850 the age of exploration had closed and the exploitation of the iron, copper, timber, and agricultural resources had begun. To help the new industries, ships, sailors, shipyards, ports, and channels were needed. The Great Lakes had been an important pathway for the early explorers. Now the Lakes were to become the main commercial waterway of the new nation.

The first, most obvious need was a canal at Sault Ste Marie. The failure of the Jackson Iron Mining Company was caused largely by supply problems, and the grumbles of powerful investors made it increasingly clear that the falls on the St. Marys River would have to be overcome.

At first, Congress was reluctant; in the Senate Daniel Webster roared that he would "never vote a penny to bring the rocky, bleak, uninhabitable shores of California one step nearer Boston." Webster spoke for Eastern commercial interests, which saw the proposed canal as a threat. Henry Clay likewise complained that the proposal was a work "beyond the remotest settlement in the United States, if not in the moon." But as more and more Eastern money was invested in the copper and iron lands of Lake Superior, the sentiment of these leaders changed. In 1852 Congress authorized a 400-foot canal strip through Fort Brady lands at the Sault. Michigan also received 750,000 acres of federal lands to sell, the money to be used for construction of the canal and its locks.

That same summer, the E. T. Fairbanks Company sent a young agent named Charles T. Harvey to sell scales, the company's main product, at Sault Ste Marie. A man selling scales naturally has an eye out for heavy objects to weigh, and Harvey soon discovered that the streets of Sault Ste Marie were frequently full of some quite remarkable heavy objects: ships on rollers being moved overland, up from Lake Huron or down from Lake Superior. As it often took several weeks to transport a ship from lake to lake in this way, no one much cared for the arrangement, excepting dray companies then thriving on the attendant business in freight. Harvey accordingly soon wrote to his company directors that a canal was needed. He suggested that they back the venture, and they agreed to the idea, providing it was not too costly.

Early in 1853 Harvey told the Michigan legislature his plan. He would construct a canal and lock 350 feet long by 70 feet wide, and 11½ feet deep over the sills. The plan received quick approval, and Harvey was chosen as a special state agent for disposal of the federal lands granted by Congress. It was hoped that some of the land might sell for as much as a dollar an acre.

Contractors were invited to bid for the work, and the state accepted the $1,000,000 price submitted by Harvey's company. But the agreement called for the canal's completion in two years, rather than ten, as originally planned, and this radically changed the prospect for success.

Work started immediately. Harvey was named agent in charge of the Saint Marys Falls Ship Canal Company, a Fairbanks subsidiary. In Detroit, he hired five hundred men from the lines of immigrants headed west. He chartered the steamship *Illinois* to freight this crew north, along with quantities of horses, mules, food, and tools. They landed at the Soo on June 1, 1853, and at once set to work, building a camp with kitchen and sleeping quarters. The immensity of their task soon showed itself, however, and by fall Harvey was frantic. A detailed survey showed the canal had to be a foot deeper than expected, a huge task over its whole length and breadth. Also, the cofferdam built to hold back Lake Superior simply would not hold back the water. In desperation Harvey had a tremendous piece of canvas placed as a seal on the outer face of the dam. Incredibly this did the trick and allowed the work to go forward.

But construction was painfully slow. All the earth and rock had to be removed by hand and trundled away by wheelbarrows and wagons. Five hundred men, Harvey soon realized, were only half the number needed, and he sent agents to New York, Cleveland, and Detroit to hire another five hundred. Weeks passed before the agents returned. They had barely unloaded their crews when Harvey told them more men were needed. "Get all you can," he said, "and get them back here as fast as you can."

When winter came, Harvey had sixteen hundred men at work in the widening cut. The winter, however, was unusually severe. The men's hands froze; the earth turned to stone; the canal cut was filled almost daily with fresh batches of snow. Problems of supply mounted. Out of frustration, the men called a strike. Harvey responded by closing the kitchen. The strike ended abruptly.

In the warm months of 1854, work seemed to progress more rapidly, and Harvey felt he was on schedule. He kept bringing in new men to replace those who left, and the big ditch kept growing as the second and final winter for the project closed down.

When ice formed on Lake Superior above the canal, Harvey sent a crew of engineers to study the possibility for dredging a channel. Their report was a shock; a stone reef lay offshore, blocking entrance to the canal. The engineers were gloomy; the entire project seemed doomed. It would take several months and $250,000 to remove the rock.

Harvey then thought of a radical solution. He conferred with his engineers; they said the plan would never work. He called in his blacksmiths; they, too, were doubtful. He wrote his company and asked for the sum of $250,000; they sent him $30,000.

That did it. He would have to try the plan on his own. He would build a heavy gravity punch that would drop from a barge on the reef. It would be slow work, but it might crack the rock enough to remove it by dredge.

That winter Harvey started constructing the big hammer. He forged the tip from a four-inch bar of steel, getting the blacksmith shop so hot it burned down in the process. He had a huge oak beam cut for the handle of his hammer, and a raft built to float it. A steam engine was mounted on the raft to raise the hammer after each drop.

When spring came, he immediately started work with the punch. On the first blow, the main shaft broke under the three-ton weight, and the punch gurgled out of sight into ten feet of water. A new and heavier shaft was made; the punch was retrieved; and work started again. This time everything held, and the punch began to work. The rock reef first chipped; then bigger chunks began breaking off; then the entire ledge started breaking down under the repeated blows.

Harvey's hammer was able to do the job. The tip of that hammer, blunted by several months of laborious pounding, was preserved and lies today in the small museum at Sault Ste Marie.

With the problem of the reef solved, and the canal and locks nearly completed, there only remained the removal of the cofferdam for the project to be completed. In mid-April 1855, while an army of curious onlookers watched, the cofferdam was cut away, and the first waters of Lake Superior flowed into the locks and up to the gates. Surprising everyone, including disaster-conscious Harvey, the gates held, and the Sault Ste Marie Canal was proclaimed a success.

The canal was dedicated on June 18, 1855, a full six weeks before the deadline for completion. The first vessel through was the *Illinois*, the same ship that had carried Harvey and his crew north two years earlier. It took seven minutes to complete the journey to Lake Superior. Then the *S.S. Baltimore* locked through into the lower river. In July the downbound *Columbia* carried a hundred tons of Marquette Range iron ore through the locks. This was the first of thousands of such journeys as western Lake Superior iron deposits were opened to commerce.

That commerce became more and more important as trouble began to brew in the land. When the Civil War finally broke out in April 1861, the British government moved to prevent Canada's involvement along the Great Lakes boundary. Union ships on the Lakes were not permitted to pass through the Welland Canal or down the St. Lawrence River. The Union had thrown a blockade around all Confederate ports, and Britain feared that Great Lakes ships might aid this naval effort.

Since Great Lakes ships could not go to the war, the war came to them, a Civil War engagement taking place on the very same waters where Perry was victorious over the British in the War of 1812. This Civil War engagement, however, was shrouded in secrecy. Some called it a simple act of piracy, but stronger evidence soon indicated it was actually a Southern military plot.

The events leading up to the affair started at a Detroit River dock on Sunday evening, September 18, 1864. The steamboat *Philo Parsons* was tied there ready to run down river the following morning, then to angle southeast across Lake Erie to the Ohio shore. It carried mail, freight, and passengers, and served Middle Bass and Kelley's Islands before continuing on to Sandusky Bay.

It was a hot evening, and Walter Ashley, clerk of the boat, stood at the rail, finding such breeze as he could. He watched idly as a well-

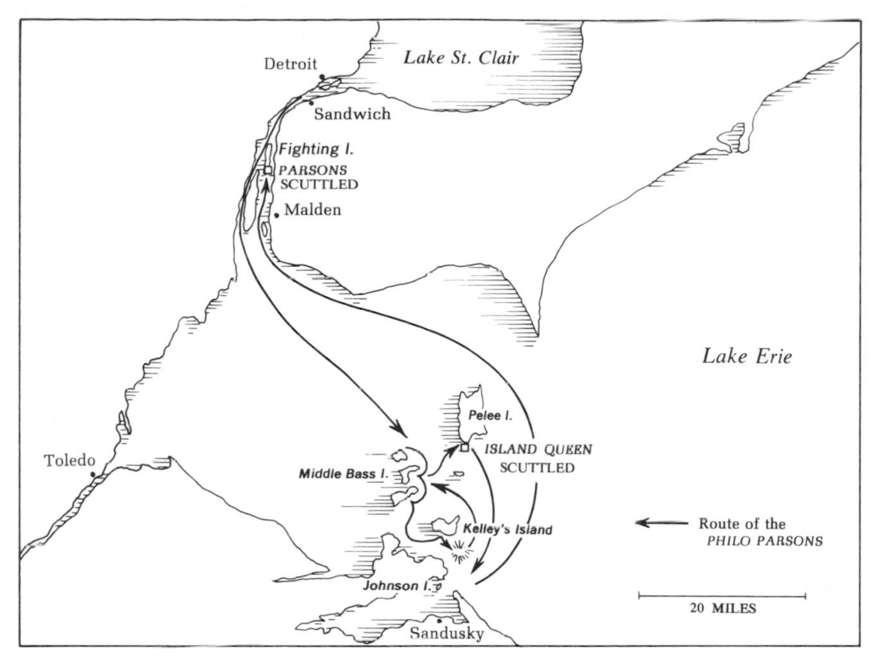

During the Civil War a group of Confederate sympathizers pirated the steamboat Philo Parsons *on Lake Erie. Their plan was to capture a federal prison on Johnson Island. They took over a second steamer,* Island Queen, *which they ran on a reef and scuttled. The* Parsons *sailed on to Johnson Island, where the federal gunboat* Michigan *lay at anchor. But failing to receive a prearranged signal from confederates, the pirates returned to Detroit, scuttling the* Parsons *near Fighting Island.*

dressed young man threaded his way between the piles of freight on the dock, then stepped up the gangway. On board the man introduced himself as Bennett G. Burley. After chatting a moment, he asked Ashley if the boat could sail across the river the next morning to pick up a group of his friends at Sandwich, now the city of Windsor, Ontario. Ashley agreed to make the stop, and the young man booked passage for himself.

Next morning, the *Parsons* left her dock about eight o'clock and eased out into the river. She crossed to Sandwich and stopped as planned to pick up Burley's friends. They were well dressed and appeared to be young men off on a holiday, carrying no baggage aboard the *Parsons.* The steamer then ran down to Malden and made a scheduled stop for more passengers. About twenty-five men, roughly dressed and carrying a large old trunk, boarded the vessel at this point and dispersed themselves about the decks. Captain S. F. Atwood said later that he thought these twenty-five might well be "skedaddlers," men who had slipped away to Canada to avoid service in the Union forces. It being the fall of 1864, perhaps they felt that the war was about over and they could return home. The passenger list now totaled about eighty, half of them women. The ship slipped her lines and headed out into Lake Erie.

If the new passengers had seemed unusual when they boarded the *Parsons*, it was soon forgotten as the ship continued on its way. During that day, stops were made at several islands, finally arriving at Middle Bass Island where Captain Atwood went ashore to spend the night with his family. After dropping Atwood, the ship sailed on under Ashley's charge. It stopped briefly at Kelley's Island and by four o'clock was well on its way to Sandusky to spend the night.

At this point, three of the men who had boarded the boat in Canada, including one who had gotten on at Sandwich, approached Ashley, drew out revolvers, and announced that they were taking over the vessel. Ashley and his crew were unarmed and offered no resistance. At the same time that this was happening, the men who had carried the trunk on board once more collected around it. Flopping open the lid, they drew out pistols and hatchets, then dispersed once more to control all the key positions aboard the boat. Ashley was forced to hand over all his own and the ship's cash.

Under command of the pirates, the ship now followed a somewhat erratic course, indicating that either the men were uncertain what to do with their prize or they were playing for time. After running down the lake half an hour, they turned back to dock at Middle Bass Island. They had been there only a few moments when a second steamer, the *Island Queen*, came to dock and tied up beside the *Parsons*. Apparently this was not part of the pirates' plan, but once the *Island Queen* was alongside, they boarded her, took over the ship, and herded all her passengers aboard the *Parsons*. Several shots were fired during the seizure, but the engineer of the *Island Queen* was the only person seriously wounded. After mulling over the situation, the pirates announced that the passengers could go ashore on Middle Bass Island if they promised not to communicate with anyone for twenty-four hours. In view of the large number of women aboard, all the passengers agreed to this bargain, and they were put ashore. Then as darkness fell, the *Parsons* backed away from the dock with the *Island Queen* lashed to her side, heading for open water. Some distance out, the captors cut the pipes and turned the *Island Queen* loose to her fate. She settled on a reef off Pelee Island.

The *Parsons* then headed for Sandusky, under cover of darkness, and cruised to a point off Johnson Island. At that time, the island was a federal prison for captured Confederate soldiers. In the bay, guarding the island, stood the *U.S.S. Michigan*, the only Union gunboat on the Great Lakes. The *Parsons* hesitated in the area for a time, cruising back and forth in the darkness. When it failed to receive a prearranged signal from the *Michigan*, it turned and steamed back toward Detroit. Near dawn the *Parsons* was scuttled at Fighting Island in the lower Detroit River. The pirates dumped the crew on the island and disappeared into the Canadian mainland.

This incident created an immediate sensation in the North, but the background of the entire incident unfolded only very slowly. The seizure of the *Parsons* was claimed by the men who participated in it to be part of a combined land-and-sea plot designed to free Confederate troops in four Union prisons. One prison was near Chicago; one at Columbus, Ohio; one near Indianapolis; and the last was the camp at Johnson's Island, protected by the *Michigan*. A total of 23,000 Confederate soldiers were held in the four prisons. The plan called for a network of Confederate sympathizers in the North to carry out raids to free the prisoners simultaneously. Southern agents near each of the prisons would direct the men after their release, and the whole action was to take place on the evening of September nineteenth.

One Charles H. Cole, posing as an oilman from Titusville, Pennsylvania, had command of the Sandusky part of the conspiracy. He laid the groundwork for his coup by acting as an easy-going entertainer with a particular friendliness for officers of the *Michigan*. He stayed at the West House, a Sandusky hotel, where he represented himself as secretary of the Mount Hope Oil Company.

His part in the plot was to prepare a lavish dinner for his acquaintances aboard the *Michigan*. During this affair the officers would receive drugged wine, and the ship would then be commandeered by Cole and his followers. They would signal the *Parsons*, cruising offshore, and together the two forces would converge on the island and force the entrance into the prison. All the Confederate prisoners would then be armed to raid the countryside as they returned to Southern territory.

That morning Cole supposedly wired Chicago members of the plot as follows: "Close out all stock in the Mount Hope Oil Company before three o'clock today. Be prompt."[1] This was the signal to release the Confederate soldiers held in the Chicago prison.

In Sandusky Harbor, however, Commander J. C. Carter of the *Michigan* said that he received the following telegraph dispatch from his Detroit commander in the early morning hours: "It is reported to me that some of the officers and men of your steamer have been tampered with, and that a party of rebel refugees leave Windsor tomorrow with expectations of getting possession of your steamer."

Carter said that he received another dispatch soon afterward describing the planned seizure of the *Parsons* and implicating the friendly Mr. Cole. Carter immediately sent a contingent ashore to arrest Cole, who was taken aboard the *Michigan* and held there as a prisoner of war. That night as planned, the *Parsons* stood offshore, waiting for Cole's signal; and as planned, Cole was aboard the *Michigan*. But the plot never came off. The drugged wine was dumped into the bay; the men who had captured the *Parsons* awaited the signal in vain.

Cole was tried and condemned to hang, but his sentence was commuted, and he later escaped to Canada, thence to Mexico, finally settling in Texas.

The young man who had stepped aboard the *Parsons* at Detroit, Bennett G. Burley, was captured in Canada and extradited to stand trial in Ohio. Ironically, it was the *Parsons*—which had been raised and restored to service, as was the *Island Queen*—that was used to carry young Burley from Detroit to his trial in Ohio. Because of legal complications, however, the jury was unable to agree on a verdict, and Burley went free. Another one of the group who seized the *Parsons*, John Yeats Beall, was captured in Niagara City, New York, in December. He was tried before a military commission in New York, sentenced, and hanged within two months of his capture. John Wilkes Booth, an intimate of Beall, made several unsuccessful attempts to prevent the execution. Some said Beall's hanging preyed on Booth's mind and that his failure to save his friend's life turned his thoughts toward the assassination of President Lincoln. Lincoln was shot less than two months after Beall's execution.

After the Civil War, a thriving pleasure-boat trade developed on the Great Lakes. Among many companies, the Detroit and Cleveland Navigation Company was long one of the mainstays of this summer-vacation traffic. The line ran freight, passenger, and pleasure steamers

[1] The details of this story are drawn from "Piracy On Lake Erie," by Charles E. Frohman, pages 172–180, Vol. 14, 1958, *Inland Seas* magazine, Cleveland.

throughout the Lakes from 1869 to 1951, providing eighty-two years of safe and pleasurable service in the Great Lakes region.

In the 1880's, the D & C joined forces with the Michigan Central Railroad, and the Grand Rapids and Indiana Railroad to build the Grand Hotel on Mackinac Island. That great rambling white structure still dominates the south face of the island, being visible to traffic crossing the Mackinac Straits bridge. The hotel was built as a mecca for travelers landing at the island on D & C vessels. It became renowned for having the longest veranda and the most spacious lawns of any hotel ever built. Socially, too, it was a gilt-edged marvel, being visited by kings, queens, and dignitaries. Financially, however, it long seemed doomed, losing money steadily from almost the day it opened. It changed hands several times, and twice it was nearly destroyed. Eventually it was purchased by the enterprising and flamboyant hosteler, W. S.

Around the turn of the century a thriving pleasure-boat trade developed on the Lakes. These two ships made daily runs from the foot of Woodward Street in Detroit, stopping along Lake St. Clair and Lake Erie. Women dressed in the fashion of the day—long white dresses and big floppy hats.

Michigan Historical Commission

Woodfill, who has converted it into a prosperous, going concern. Woodfill, a key figure in the development of the Straits Bridge and reconstruction of Fort Michilimackinac, has backed various other successful developments in the Straits area.

Another famous vessel in the pleasure-boat trade was the old *Britannic*, a steamer of the Montreal and Cornwall Navigation Company. The *Britannic*, which traveled from Montreal to Kingston on the St. Lawrence River, took five days for the journey, charging a total sum of twenty-five dollars for passage and board. The relaxed life aboard this old, slow, charming vessel attracted thousands of vacationers during its many years of operation.

Many, many other ships took part in this Great Lakes traffic, including the popular *Tashmoo* of the White Star Lines, long known to travelers in the Detroit area; the *City of Cleveland* of the D & C; the *Alabama*, the *North America*, and the *South America*. Most of these vessels, however, dropped out of service as automobiles and airlines more and more took over transportation, thus closing a delightful interlude in the Great Lakes story.

The decades around the turn of the century were also a time of a flourishing Great Lakes community life. On Saginaw Bay, for example, most families had sailboats for the practical purposes of commercial fishing, freight hauling, or transportation. When it came time for play, however, such boats were used extensively for duck hunting, sport fishing, and for racing to community picnics. When Bay Port invited Sebewaing to a picnic, Sebewaing would come, all of it, in small boats, racing the fifteen miles along shore for a prize of free beer to the winner. Sebewaing was a community of people with names like Schultz and Schneider, and promises of free beer were clear inducements to victory. No holds were barred in the race, and all boats started on equal terms. If the larger boats sailed faster, they also required deeper water, which meant a longer course to skirt the islands. It took sailing skill to win in a large boat.

To win in a small boat required large supplies of nerve in addition to skill. The route from Sebewaing to Bay Port is cluttered with obstacles, and it took a knowing skipper to find the way through the tangle of shifting bars, mudbanks, and islands. If the wind was off the bay, there would be enough water close to shore so that a man could sail the channels, which cut like a maze through the miles and miles of marsh grass and cattails. But those grasses and cattails stood eight feet tall, and cut off all view of surrounding landmarks. Either the

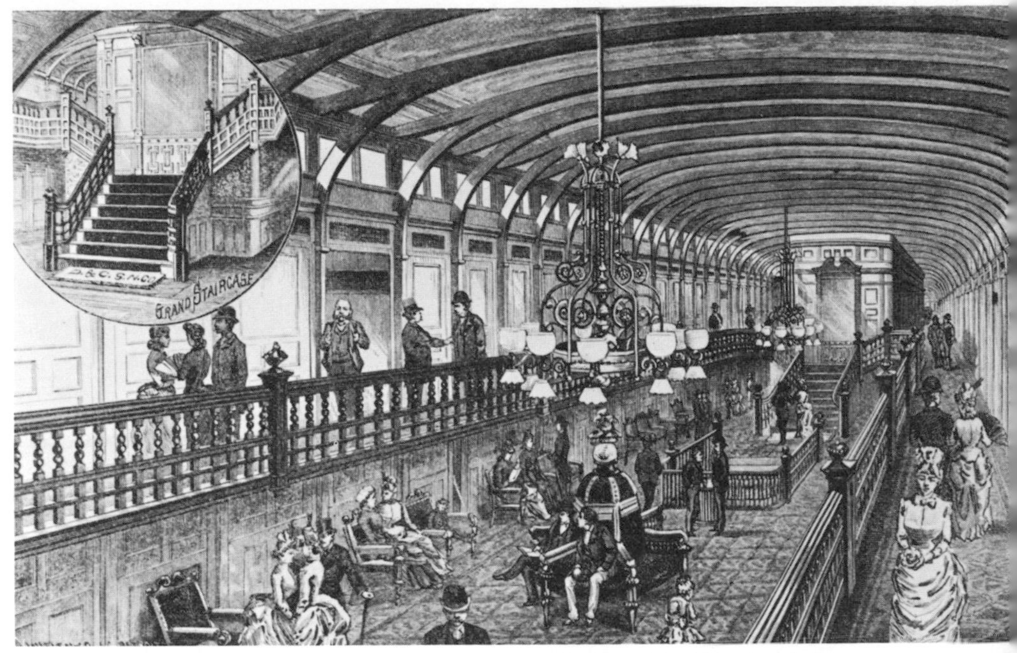

The Great Lakes Historical Society

The grand saloon on the City of Cleveland *shows the opulent construction of such pleasure boats. This steamer was one of the Detroit & Cleveland Steamship Company's leading vessels.*

navigator must have the course mapped in his head or he was soon lost and out of the race.

If wind was not pushing the water toward shore, the smaller boats had to skirt the marsh bank and sail a tricky route offshore. There, all would seem to be open water and clear sailing, but the bay shore slopes very slowly in this region, and hidden beneath those open waters was another maze of confusing channels. The depth of water in the channels changed as the speed of the offshore wind changed, adding to the frolic. This was where nerve came into play. To win the race, a man had to take calculated risks. He had to scrape bottom now and then in cutting corners, but he had to avoid going aground. With all sails crowding the boat along as fast as possible, any miscalculation would strand the boat solidly on a bar or mudbank and remove it from the race completely. Imagine the plight of hungry, thirsty sailors, stranded and stewing under a July sun while friends and neighbors were miles away, toasting their ineptness with free beer. Perhaps on the return

The Great Lakes Historical Society

Launching a Life-Saving Service boat in the nineteenth century. Founded in 1878, the Life-Saving Service saved many crews from storms on the lakes. In 1915 it became part of the United States Coast Guard.

trip some sympathizer might carry out their anchor and help them kedge off the bar. Such a loss of race and face sapped a man's confidence and robbed him of his nerve. Such a community life offered rich rewards in friendships and social unity, but it also demanded a high level of competence. A sailor who did not know his water was no sailor at all, and the next week found the chastened skipper out among the shoals, testing the water's depth, looking for his lost dignity.

These races are only a sample of the life that flourished along the shores of the Great Lakes. Every bay area and shore community has its own collection of stories and memorable characters. Life along the big blue water is such a mixture of land and sea that it is difficult for any town or community to remain ordinary for very long. Many inland towns have only a pallid portion of the past, yet along the Lakes it is only necessary to question one or two oldtimers in a bar or along some rotting fish dock to bring out a trickle of stories. Given encouragement, such a trickle may grow into a steady stream punctuated by long pauses for chuckling and discourse among wonder-rapt listeners.

Such men may tell you about the Great Storm that hit the lakes in 1913, if you ask them. Many storms have aroused these lakes to violence in historical times, but none compares with that of 1913. The old men in small villages may provide varying accounts of what happened, as they saw it happen, but one man took time to collect all these stories into a book, *Freshwater Fury*, by Frank Barcus.

About ten o'clock on the morning of Friday, November 7, 1913, the United States Weather Bureau issued the following bulletin to all its stations in the Great Lakes area:

> HOIST SOUTHWEST STORM WARNINGS 10 A.M. STORM OVER UPPER MISSISSIPPI VALLEY MOVING NORTHEAST. BRISK TO HIGH SOUTHWEST WINDS THIS AFTERNOON AND TONIGHT SHIFTING TO NORTHWEST SATURDAY ON UPPER LAKES. WARNINGS ORDERED THROUGHOUT THE GREAT LAKES.

On the Great Lakes, 1913 had been a pretty good year. The shipping season started fairly early and went well. There had been a few summer gales, but nothing out of the ordinary. It might yet be a record shipping season and with the year nearly over it behooved all freighter captains to get another load of ore or coal or grain moved across the Lakes, if possible, before the winter lay-up.

So no one paid much attention when the two red-and-black flags were hoisted at life-saving and weather stations that November morning. Those flags had been seen many times before. They seldom meant very much to big ships; to ore and coal boats; to tugs and barges built solidly for heavy lakes work. The sailors of the Great Lakes, after all, had three hundred years of experience in their background. There were always storms in the fall of the year, some worse than others. Sailors of these seas knew what to expect this time of year and they went on with loadings and unloadings, with preparations for the last trip of the season.

At Ashland, Wisconsin, and at Port Arthur, Ontario, the weather that morning was chill and moody, the sky filled with dark, brooding clouds. At the Soo locks, business as usual was under way. A long string of ships was locking through on the voyage down, each filled with grain or ore, and headed for some port on the lower Lakes. Other ships were passing through on their way up, empty, or loaded with coal or freight for Marquette, Fort William, or Duluth. It had started as snow. At Chicago, Detroit, and Cleveland, more ships were fueling for last runs of the season, and in those down-lake ports, the storm warnings must have looked very much out of place. The main weather center that was building the worst storm in Great Lakes history was still far to the north, moving slowly out of Hudson Bay. Ports on the lower Lakes went about their business. The storm flags flapped slowly in the chill wind.

At 10 o'clock on Saturday, November eighth, the Weather Bureau instructed all Great Lakes stations to continue the storm warnings at least another twenty-four hours. That meant the two red and black flags would continue to fly, old warnings now, looking less important than when first hoisted. All across the Lakes, ships continued moving.

By this time, however, one part of the storm had already hit western Lake Superior and had, in a matter of seconds, reduced the *L. C. Waldo*, a 472-foot ore boat, to a floating hulk. The *Waldo* was headed from Two Harbors, Minnesota, to Cleveland with a load of iron ore. Early Saturday morning and practically without warning, she was struck from behind by a series of massive waves that nearly rolled the big ship over. Her captain and mate were in the pilot house, and because of severe cold, spray on the windows had caked to ice. The two men were navigating blindly, using compass and wheel, trying to keep the ship off Keweenaw Point to their right. Captain Duddleson recalled that he heard the roar of the first wave coming, one which he knew was much bigger than any other. He felt the ship's stern begin to lift, but not soon enough. Like a tremendous falling wall, the wave dropped on the ship, carrying away the pilot house and cabins in one wash, smashing them to kindling. The captain and mate dove for their lives through a hatchway and miraculously escaped being swept overboard. The boat soon swept ashore on Keweenaw Point, a total wreck. Her crew was saved.

A less happy ending, however, came to thirteen other large ships which sank, capsized, or were otherwise lost, in all cases with some loss of life, and in most cases, with all hands.

The *Waldo* had been blown ashore and broken in two by daylight on Saturday, November eighth. From there the storm moved eastward across the length of Lake Superior, crossed directly over Sault Ste Marie, and by Saturday night, moved south to Alpena, Michigan. As it moved, winds from the northwest increased, lifting the waters of Lake Superior into a mighty rolling sea. The winds that hit the *Waldo* Saturday morning were said to be of hurricane force. However, a deceptive change now occurred. The wind seemed to diminish and on northern Lake Huron that Saturday night, velocities reached only forty miles an hour. The storm looked like a normal November blow. It had moved along the length of Lake Superior from west to east. Now as it began moving south into Lake Huron, it seemed to be moderating. Like countless other storms, it looked as though it would keep moving generally east. In three or four days, it should roll down the St. Lawrence Valley and blow itself out in the North Atlantic.

In the Detroit *News* that Saturday afternoon, a small item appeared at the bottom of the front page:

> BIG WIND BLOWS STEAMER ASHORE
>
> Algonac, Mich., Nov. 8—A southwest gale blowing here this morning drove the sand steamer *Mary* aground just above the southeast bend of the St. Clair River. The *Mary* is owned by the Malcomson-Houghton Company of Detroit.

But that was all. Notice of the *Mary's* plight was the only storm news in the paper. Word of the *Waldo's* disaster had not yet reached lower ports. Radio was almost unknown, and so temperamental as to be almost useless. Weather forecasting was young and inexperienced

More than 250 sailors were lost during the Great Storm of 1913. Circles on the map show where some of the larger ships went down.

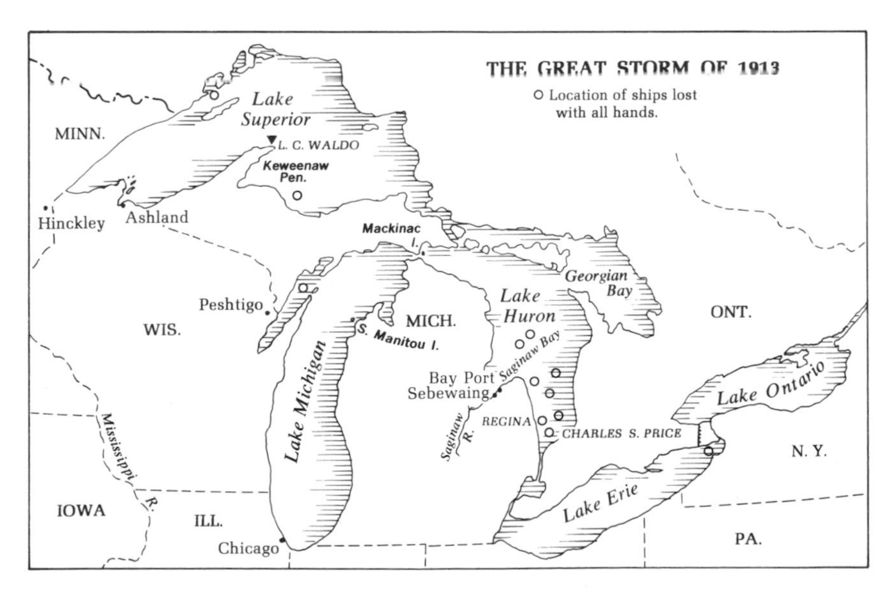

—the continued butt of public jokes. Depth indicators were in use but unreliable. In short, ships plowing through Lake Huron were essentially cut off from the world and followed their separate courses until too late. The storm continued to grow through the hours when it should have diminished. By the time these sailors realized they were in a virtual hurricane, they had no choice but to fight it through.

For it was truly a cyclonic hurricane that hit the Lakes that weekend, a type of weather previously unknown to these waters. The wind shifted from northwest to north to northeast during the storm and kept growing in strength. Changes in wind direction came very suddenly, so that waves, which had started rolling in one direction when the wind began, soon were hit by winds from another direction, became confused, and then were far more deadly. Ship captains who survived said at times they were pounded by waves from several directions at once, so that normal safety maneuvers were meaningless. The winds on Sunday were seventy miles an hour, enough to make waves so high and heavy that they swept away superstructures on many ships caught in the storm.

The heaviest losses occurred on lower Lake Huron. In a section known as "the Pocket," eight large ships with crews totaling 194 men were lost with all hands. For many weeks afterward, the Huron shoreline was littered with bodies, ship wreckage, and cargo flotsam.

One of these eight ships flipped over so fast air was trapped under the hull, keeping it afloat like an upturned bottle. No one knew what ship she was until days later, when a diver slithered down the side of the hull and read the name, upside down, *Charles S. Price*. To further confuse the situation, bodies of the crew from the *Price* were found wearing life jackets from the *Regina*, also lost in the storm. When last seen, the *Price* and *Regina* were fifteen miles apart, headed in opposite directions. Marine experts reasoned that somehow the two ships collided during the blinding snowstorm, at which time there was an exchange of crew or life jackets. No one survived from either ship, and the truth of the matter remains entombed at the bottom of Lake Huron.

Elsewhere unusual measures were taken against the storm. In at least one case, these proved their worth; in another, they proved disastrous.

The steamer *Illinois* was headed from Northport, Michigan, to Chicago. When the storm hit her near South Manitou Island, she put into the deep bay on the east side of that island. With no dock avail-

Fred W. Dutton and the Great Lakes Historical Society

During the Great Storm of 1914, the worst in Great Lakes history, the heaviest losses occurred in lower Lake Huron. Eight large ships and 194 lives were lost in this section, known as "the Pocket." The J. H. Sheadle, *above, was one of two ships that made it through the Pocket during the height of the storm. Good sailing and plain luck carried her crew to safety.*

able, the captain drove the ship's prow onto the beach, tied lines to the biggest tree in sight, and rode out the storm in safety, chugging his engines slowly to keep his position on the shore. When the winds finally fell, he cast off and continued on to Chicago, arriving three days late but undamaged.

Not so lucky was the crew of the engineless barge *Plymouth*, criminally abandoned by her tug in Green Bay. Like the steamer *Illinois*, the seven men on the *Plymouth* used unusual measures against the storm. Abandoned, and without power, they lashed themselves to their boat to prevent being swept overboard. Days later, when life savers finally reached the barge, they found a silent and grisly spectacle. All seven men were dead, still lashed to their ship, frozen in place.

Somehow during the height of this incredible storm, two ships made it through Lake Huron to their destinations. The *J. H. Sheadle* left Fort William loaded with grain, plowed right through the storm on Lake Superior, and continued down Lake Huron into the eye of the hurricane. At the Soo, the *Sheadle* went through the locks behind the *Carruthers* and ahead of the *Hydrus*—both those ships sinking with all hands. All three were headed for Port Huron, and all experienced the worst part of the storm together. Good sailing and plain luck helped the *Sheadle's* master, S. A. Lyons, accomplish what seemed impossible. He realized he could not negotiate the St. Clair River at Port Huron, so he turned his ship back and forth several times, first running ahead of the storm, then plowing back into it. These maneuvers saved his ship and crew. When the storm dropped on Monday morning, he ran the *Sheadle* into the safety of the river.

The other survivor was the *J. F. Durston*, bound up Lake Huron loaded with soft coal. The *Durston* also passed through the center of the storm that Sunday night, but arrived at Mackinaw City safely. Her captain said later he simply headed her into the seas, and the ice which formed on hatches, windows, and doorways sealed the ship against swamping. Like an ice-covered bottle, the *Durston* wallowed through.

It was the most damaging storm that ever hit the Lakes, and the loss shocked the nation. When it was over, seventy-one large ships, most of them in the 400- to 500-foot class, were sunk, stranded, broken, or had suffered severe damage. Most of the loss occurred on lower Lake Huron, but Lakes Superior, Michigan, and Erie also recorded losses. A total of 251 sailors are known to have died, but additional losses have always been suspected. Countless small craft were destroyed.

Even though this is known as the Great Storm, the Great Lakes have always been dangerous waters. From the mysterious disappearance of the *Griffin* in 1679 down to the present time, these waters have carried a deceptive look that betokens calm acceptance of sailors and their ships. In fact, they are highly unpredictable, and the roll of Great Lakes tragedies and mysterious losses is long.

The ocean sailor may think it ludicrous to regard these inland seas as troublemakers. After all, the Lakes are small bodies of water compared with the ocean. But difficulty arises from the circumstances of their location, size, and shape. Storms sweeping overland can change course and pounce on the Lakes unexpectedly, stirring them to a froth in a short time. This was how the Great Storm caught so many ships off guard on Lake Huron. Under storm conditions, the Lakes usually produce short-length, choppy waves, rather than long rolling combers characteristic of the ocean. Lake waves thus have steeper sides, break more easily, do not allow a ship a chance to rise and slide naturally with the roll of the water. Such short waves are caused by the relatively short distances over which they have a chance to grow and by the comparative shallowness of the water. Given long, open stretches of deep water, short waves caused by sudden storms can smooth out into long waves. On the Great Lakes, there is not room enough to develop such moderation. The sudden brutality of lake storms, together with this abrupt wave action, has caught many ships unaware and foundered them only half-battened down. There is the further consideration of the narrow waters available for running. An ocean ship may take a storm on her hip and roll along ahead of strong winds for many days, but the Great Lakes provide no such opportunity. All these dangers have given to sailors who know the Lakes a rightful respect.

Stories about ships lost on the Great Lakes in other storms are manifold, but the worst single accident of all occurred on the calm waters of Chicago Harbor. There, at a dock where Clark Street crosses the Chicago River, stood the passenger steamer *Eastland* on the morning of July 24, 1915. The time was about seven o'clock, and the *Eastland* was loading employees of the Western Electric Company and their families. The morning was crisp and breezy; the sun was already well up; and the day promised a lovely sail to Michigan City. A steam calliope on the stern tootled through tunes of the day. More people crowded aboard. By seven-fifteen, twenty-five hundred persons were aboard the ship; the gangplank was hauled up; and the lines slacked off. Slowly the *Eastland*, pulled by a tug, edged away from the dock. At the same time she began to tilt slightly to port. Someone noted that the stern lines had not been freed, but the tug was pulling them taut, and they could not be released. It was now about seven-twenty. The tilt of the *Eastland* increased a bit more. The calliope rattled on. Finally the tug was backed down to release the dock lines. Despite this the *Eastland* continued to tilt, a slope that now was becoming alarming. Some deck chairs edged sideways. Still it remained a festive holiday, right up to the time a few startled cries of concern broke out. That was the trigger, and absolute pandemonium smashed the festive air, sending passengers into screaming panic.

Long-skirted women and men in sailor straws clung desperately to railings, ran clumsily looking for children, trying to keep from the rising water. Slowly the *Eastland* settled sideways in twenty-one feet of water. Hundreds of spectators on the dock and along Clark Street stood by in horror and watched helplessly. Some said the ship took five minutes to go over; some said ten. But time, seemingly, had stopped, and when it started again, the water was filled with milling, screaming passengers. A few nearby boats moved in and began clumsy

Eugene Herman Memorial Picture Collection

Passengers climbed out onto the upturned hull of the Eastland *as she capsized in Chicago Harbor on the morning of July 24, 1915. Most of the survivors had been on the upper decks, but as this photo was taken, passengers trapped in the decks below were helplessly drowning. More than 800 people perished in this disaster—the worst in Great Lakes history.*

rescue efforts. The starboard side of the *Eastland* remained out of water, and everywhere along its length passengers clambered like ants for footholds. A few pitiful lines were thrown from the dock. Some who could swim the few feet to the dock were helped out quickly; others were pulled under by panic-stricken nonswimmers.

Rescue efforts took time to organize, and then trucks and ambulances rolled through Chicago's Loop for hours, loaded high with sheet-shrouded forms. Armories and school gymnasiums were turned into temporary morgues, where long rows of bodies were laid out. Doctors worked at the scene for hours, checking each stretcher as it passed. Finally darkness fell on that tragic day, and the *Eastland* lay on her side like a great dead fish, white belly exposed under a blaze of shore lights.

For days newspapers across the nation ran lists of the dead and missing. As the loss was mourned, President Wilson appointed a court of inquiry headed by Judge Kenesaw Mountain Landis. Surviving officers of the ship were arrested, including the captain, after being rescued by police from a frenzied lynching attempt at the scene. Of the 2500 persons aboard the *Eastland* that morning, 835 lost their lives. Most of those killed were on lower decks, trapped as soon as the ship began to roll over.

Inquiries raged back and forth through the courts for years. All possible explanations were considered, including overcrowding, the rush of passengers from side to side, the unreleased dock lines, the seaworthiness of the craft. But the United States Circuit Court of Appeals in Chicago finally ruled that the blame lay on an engineer who had neglected to fill the ballast tanks before the passengers were loaded that morning. With air in her lower tanks and a heavy load of passengers on top, the balance of the boat was destroyed and over she went.

Other heavy losses of life on the Great Lakes have occurred in more standard fashion—through fires, collisions, and sinkings. The list of the ten worst disasters in Great Lakes history reads as follows:

1. *EASTLAND*—July 24, 1915. Losses, 835 lives.

2. *LADY ELGIN*—September 8, 1860. This sidewheel steamer was a posh 300-foot passenger vessel. She was headed from Chicago to Milwaukee on Lake Michigan. About ten miles off Winnetka, Illinois, she was rammed amidship and nearly cut in half by a loaded lumber schooner. The accident occurred at night, and the schooner was un-

lighted, as was the custom at that time. This accident, however, forced a change in navigation law, thereafter requiring all vessels to be lighted. The schooner drifted away from the accident and did not aid in rescue work. Many of the passengers struggled to shore on wreckage, but tallies showed that 297 lives were lost.

3. *G. P. GRIFFITH*—June 17, 1850. This steamer was traveling from Buffalo to Chicago, making numerous stops between. Her cargo was immigrants. Off the present village of Willoughby, Ohio, on Lake Erie, the *Griffith* caught fire. Her captain tried to drive the ship to shore, but it stuck fast on a sandbar half a mile out in the lake. Being all-wood construction, the *Griffith* burned to the water and 285 persons died with the ship, about 30 surviving. This spectacular disaster forced Congress to pass new safety laws. But they came at the end of a decade in which an estimated 1000 persons died in a series of similar, if smaller, ship tragedies. The new laws helped, but the losses continued.

4. *MONTREAL*—June 27, 1857. Destroyed by fire on the St. Lawrence River near Lake Ontario. An estimated 250 persons were lost.

5. *PHOENIX*—November 21, 1847. Destroyed by fire on Lake Michigan with a loss of 200 to 250 persons.

6. *ATLANTIC*—August 20, 1852. This steamer sank after colliding with another ship in Lake Erie, about sixty-five miles west of Buffalo. Total loss of life unknown, but estimates ranged from 150 to 250 persons.

7. *ERIE*—August 9, 1841. En route from Buffalo to Erie, Pennsylvania, this sidewheel steamer suddenly exploded. Fire engulfed the ship in a short time. About 250 persons were aboard, and an estimated 150 perished, including a large number of immigrants bound for new lands in the west.

8. *PEWABIC*—August 9, 1865. This passenger steamer was sunk while greeting her sister ship, the *Meteor*, off Alpena, Michigan, in Lake Huron. The *Meteor* sliced into the side of the *Pewabic* and sank her in a few minutes with a loss of 125 passengers and crew.

9. *ASIA*—September 15, 1882. This propeller-driven steamer sank in Georgian Bay during a storm with a loss of 123 lives. Only 2 passengers survived.

10. *NORONIC*—September 17, 1949. This passenger steamer caught fire at her dock at Toronto during night hours. Most of the 524 passengers were asleep at the time, and though quick efforts were made to arouse them, 118 perished by fire, smoke, and drowning. The ship was a total loss.

Such heavy losses as these may never again strike the Great Lakes, unless the St. Lawrence Seaway develops a heavy passenger-vessel industry. At present passenger ships are passing out of use on the Lakes, and large numbers of persons are not so frequently exposed to possible disaster. Also large ships these days are mainly of steel construction, reducing the danger from fire. Better weather forecasting, use of radio, and more stringent safety regulations—all tend to keep loss down.

But nothing can be done to quiet the Lakes when tornadoes boil up out of hot July afternoons, or rolling northerlies pound in late November, when some ships will always tempt the season for a final fall run. Such storms and losses stand as warnings and bring a realization that the Great Lakes are indeed a recreational delight and a resource whose worth we are just beginning to tap; but they are also untamed giants on whose waters it is best to paddle softly.

237
14
13
12
11
10
9

13

The Raw Material of History

TOWARD THE END of this many-century journey into the times and happenings of the Great Lakes, the trail of history trickles out, and current events take over—the raw stuff from which tomorrow's history will be made. Already, however, outlines of that history are beginning to take shape.

The Great Lakes have ended their role as a provincial waterway. They are no longer tucked away from world view, left to a home-bound destiny. With the opening of the St. Lawrence Seaway in 1959, the merchant fleets of the world found entry to the center of our continent.

The first such seaway actually came into existence in the late 1800's, when Canada constructed a series of shallow-draft locks on the St. Lawrence River above Montreal. These allowed small ships, with a draft up to fourteen feet, to travel back and forth from the Great Lakes to the Atlantic Ocean. Even though small, this seaway soon proved popular. In 1909 use of the entire Great Lakes waterway was

The iron industry has come a long way since the first iron was smelted in 1847. This ore boat is loading at a special dock at Marquette on Lake Superior. Rail cars above the dock dump their loads into the chutes, and the entire ship is loaded in a few hours.

Michigan Department of Conservation

formally opened to both United States and Canadian ships by the Boundary Waters Treaty. That treaty recognized that "all navigational boundary waters shall forever continue free and open for the purpose of commerce to the inhabitants and to the ships, vessels and boats of both countries equally." The treaty did not improve the locks on the St. Lawrence River, but it did cement shipping relations between the two nations. A fleet of "canalers"—freight boats small enough to squeeze through the locks—was gradually added to other traffic along the river. These carried freight in a thriving business between the Lakes and the tidewater at Montreal. Large ships, meanwhile, eyed the rich commercial possibilities of our continent and waited for bigger locks to open the Great Lakes.

After several years of talk and study, Congress finally passed a bill in May 1954, establishing the St. Lawrence Seaway Development Corporation. The corporation is owned by the United States government and operated under an administrator appointed by the President. A five-member advisory board, also appointed by the President, assists the administrator in policy work. Canada had set up similar enabling legislation somewhat earlier, and in August 1954 the two governments exchanged formal notes calling for development of the seaway. The locks were built over a period of five years, with a hydropower system added to serve the region.

In the first years after the St. Lawrence Seaway opened in 1959, business was modest, if not disappointing. World shipping did not make as much use of the waterway as hoped, and income from tolls lagged behind expectations. However, in recent years the seaway has experienced a steady increase in use, and is now beginning to fulfill earlier expectations. Where only twenty million tons of cargo moved through the seaway in 1959, its first season, that total had increased to more than thirty million tons five years later. Most of the cargo was in bulk commodities, such as iron ore, wheat, corn, fuel oil, barley, and coal. These six items accounted for more than two thirds of all seaway cargo.

In recent years about three thousand ships have moved up and three thousand have moved down the seaway each year, and the trend is toward use of larger ships. Canadian vessels carry about 60 per cent of the total cargo, while those of the United States carry less than 10 per cent. The flags of many nations are included in the remaining 30 per cent, and travelers now frequently sail from Chicago, Detroit, Cleveland, or Buffalo to ports throughout the world.

A few big ports have prospered most heavily from the seaway. Many small cities lack harbor or onshore facilities to handle large ships. But such a trend toward developing a few big ports has been underway for many years, and the smaller ports around the Great Lakes have long been headed toward a future of their own. Many which started as sawmill towns are being reborn for resort and recreation. The cool blue waters, sand dunes, and hot summer sunshine—all combine to lure big city dwellers away from their day's routine. Increasing recreational use of these northern shorelines and their small, delightful cities are a promise for future years.

Meanwhile in the bigger cities a case of megalopolis is setting in. An industrial-strip city is developing from Toledo through Detroit, Pontiac, Flint, and Saginaw to Bay City. Another is gradually being filled in from Detroit to Muskegon, taking in such rapidly growing

The St. Lawrence Seaway, opened in 1959, enables ocean vessels to make stops on the Great Lakes. The photo shows St. Lambert lock, the first of seven between Montreal and Lake Ontario. Montreal is in the background.

National Film Board of Canada

areas as Ann Arbor, Jackson, Lansing, Battle Creek, Kalamazoo, and Grand Rapids. A third extends from South Bend to Gary, Chicago, Kenosha, Racine, and Milwaukee. A fourth is developing in the south shore of Lake Erie, centered on Cleveland. Buffalo, Toronto, and Montreal are booming and spreading industries outward along the shore of their Great Lakes waters. All these industrial corridors are certain to become even larger as populations increase and use of the St. Lawrence Seaway expands.

Meanwhile more remote sections of the Great Lakes region have actually been losing population. This is particularly true in Michigan's Upper Peninsula and portions of northern Wisconsin and Minnesota. Lack of economic opportunity is cited as the main factor causing the decline, but most observers see the trend as temporary. Growing recreational activities such as hunting, fishing, skiing, and vacationing have already begun to reverse this pattern. Northern real estate is selling steadily for resort and retirement locations. Commerce from the development of the land's natural resources is also burgeoning, due to the seaway, new industrial techniques, and national economic growth.

Although copper mining has declined sharply, iron mining in parts of the Lake Superior region has passed through a complete metamorphosis. The Jackson Mining Company started in the 1840's by extracting surface lodes of ore. As these were exhausted, mining operations moved deeper, some shafts being driven several thousand feet into the ground. In the 1950's many of these deep mines in turn began to be exhausted, and mining companies started looking for new ore deposits. One very rich lode was found in Labrador, and the St. Lawrence Seaway, then under construction, soon made this ore available to Great Lakes furnaces. In response to this competition, Lake Superior companies began surface-mining operations once again, this time extracting so-called low-grade iron ores, mainly taconite. These ores are mined, then ground to a fine powder. By use of flotation and screening, the iron is separated from the surrounding rock. The recovery process, known as beneficiation, continues with the iron powder being formed into pellets about the size of marbles. These transport and handle easily. Savings in time and equipment at the blast furnace offset the somewhat higher costs of beneficiation, so that the pellets are now highly desired by the steel industry. The Lake Superior taconite reserves are believed to be very extensive, promising a long future on the Lakes for such mining and shipping operations.

The forests likewise have seen an increasing use with sound timber management now beginning to pay off. The forest was almost entirely stripped from the Great Lakes region during the period of early settlement and logging. Then forest fires raged in the dried tops and limbs left on the forest floor. Until the 1930's, no one had figured out how to stop such fires. In that decade the Civilian Conservation Corps camped a large number of men on those barren lands and set them to planting trees and controlling fires. This carpet of young growth began to hold moisture in the land, providing increased resistance to fires. Also, as the nation moved from the era of the plow horse to that of the mechanized tractor, heavy equipment became available for use against forest fires. By 1940 the Great Lakes states were greening up; water was being held in the soil; and it was safe to travel and build in the northern portions of the region.

At the same time, research developed new products and new markets for forest resources. The principle of "sustained yield" came into play, wherein the amount of timber cut does not theoretically exceed the amount grown. Because of new growth, Great Lakes forests are now providing wood-using industries with all the raw material they need. Aspen, for example, long considered merely a fast-growing weed tree, now sees heavy use in the manufacture of boxboard, pressed board, and other products. Some foresters now envision mammoth equipment that will plant and harvest commercial forests the way farmers plant and harvest grain. Meanwhile those who like to see green and growing forests need not despair. Under new management techniques, we will see large forests growing beside a sizable wood-products industry for years to come. Toward the end of this century, population growth will catch up to the forest's ability to produce, but at least until then—and probably much longer—we shall have trees in abundance to view.

The type of trees presently found in this region are generally fast-growing and short-lived. If not harvested, they simply fall down and rot. The problem is sharply different in the Northwest and West Coast states, where conservationists are waging a losing battle to save ancient stands of redwood, Douglas fir, and other trees that cannot be replaced in a short time.

Similarly, other resources of the Great Lakes region are coming into more meaningful use as modern resource management becomes more widely accepted. The white-tailed deer, for example, still is found throughout the Great Lakes region, being one of the most durable forms of wildlife on our continent. It has outlived mastodons, saber-toothed tigers, and other ancient creatures, and it continues to thrive despite civilization, heavy hunting, and the automobile. The automobile alone is pretty hard on deer. About five thousand car-and-deer collisions occur in Michigan each year, and the number is growing rapidly. Minnesota, Wisconsin, Ontario, Pennsylvania, New York, and Ohio have similar recorded accidents and losses. Mainly this is because deer are increasing in certain areas through changing land uses. Also, of course, traffic is increasing. But the increase in the number of deer has also come at a time when the human population is increasing and leisure time is becoming more available. Together these factors have made the Great Lakes region a deer viewer's and a deer hunter's paradise. The hunter, by moving from state to state, can now chase deer for weeks on end. But again, those who prefer their deer alive and on the hoof may rest easy. As with forest management, so it is with deer management; if deer are not "harvested," they out eat their range and die in periodic mass starvation. The loss of fifty thousand deer a winter, mainly to starvation, is not unusual for Michigan's Upper Peninsula alone, and other areas of the Great Lakes have suffered similar losses. Large-scale feeding programs to save these deer have never worked, because deer saved one winter merely increase the problem the following winter. For the health of the deer herd and its range foods, and to provide more recreation, the best approach is to increase deer-hunting opportunities. Nearly all states have moved in this direction in recent years, and the result has generally silenced earlier critics. Even some local chapters of the Audubon Society, which tends to include many people who find hunting distasteful, have come out in support of such programs, because of the benefits provided the deer herd.

But one of the most delightful natural-resource programs of the region has been the growing control of the destructive sea lamprey and consequent rebirth of the whitefish and lake trout fisheries. At some unknown time in the past, possibly in glacial times, the sea lamprey became established in Lake Ontario. The adult looks somewhat like an eighteen-inch length of dark gray garden hose, tapering toward the tail. Its head-end is like a circular suction cup, fitted inside with sharp grinding teeth. It fixes this suction-cup mouth against the side of a fish, then through a grinding action of its sharp teeth cuts a hole and sucks out the life juices. The fish may wrench and twist to get away, but the lamprey can usually hold on until the fish collapses.

During the first decades of this century, the Great Lakes were famous for production of superb whitefish, lake trout, and other species. Saginaw Bay walleyed pike was highly prized in New York, Cleveland, Detroit, and Chicago restaurants. These fish supported a thriving industry throughout the Great Lakes, and there seemed no limit to the amount of fish in sight. The Great Lakes were, by all counts, the world's greatest freshwater fishery, and their economic importance was felt throughout the entire region.

In the early 1930's, however, fish production began to decline, and fishermen in Lake Erie noticed long ugly scars on some whitefish. Other fish were caught in nets with lampreys still clinging to their sides. Soon the nets were coming up nearly empty of whitefish, and then rather abruptly their catch ended entirely.

Soon after, Lake Huron fishermen began to notice the same problem. The decline started first at southern ports, then moved to more northerly ones. Commercial fishing for both lake trout and whitefish soon collapsed in both Lake Huron and Lake Michigan. By 1945 supplies of these fish had been virtually eliminated from all except Lake Superior. The narrowness of the Sault rapids and restrictions of the canal and locks held lampreys out of that lake for a time. Gradually, however, they filtered past these obstacles, and by the mid-1950's were working westward through the lake. Total destruction appeared a certainty by 1960. Meanwhile, state and federal agencies started a frantic search for some solution to the lamprey problem. In the 1940's they developed a thorough study on the life and habits of the sea lamprey, looking for points of vulnerability. They found that the lamprey spawned only in tributary streams entering the Great Lakes, and research now centered on those streams.

A wide-ranging system of barrier weirs was placed at the mouths of the streams to keep lampreys out. That program soon proved a failure as barriers became clogged with debris washing downstream. Barriers also were washed out by flood, or became riddled with holes as floating logs ripped through them. Then electrical weirs were tried, composed of electrodes hung dangling in the water. These kept lampreys from moving upstream past the area and worked better because floating debris and logs could wash underneath. But power failures, periods of high water, and equipment problems showed that the effectiveness of these weirs was also limited.

Meanwhile serious study was under way at the United States Fish and Wildlife Service's Hammond Bay research station on northern

Lake Huron. There a search started for a chemical to destroy young lampreys while they were still concentrated in streams. Study had shown that lampreys placed their young, called ammocetes, in stream bottoms where they remained from three to eight years. Then they emerged as six-inch youngsters to move downstream for their destructive adult life. If a chemical could destroy lamprey young in streams, the problem would be licked at the source. The chemical had to be nontoxic to other fish and to humans, and had to dissipate soon after destroying the lampreys. This was a difficult assignment. Dozens of chemicals were tested without success. Then hundreds went through the involved screening process. Finally biologists had studied several thousand chemicals without success. The lamprey had by now de-

Michigan Department of Conservation

Commercial fishing is still an important, though small, industry on the Great Lakes. These Lake Huron fishermen are lifting smelt from a pond net.

Recreation on the Lakes. Dock fishing with cane poles is a popular, relaxing sport throughout the region. These enthusiasts sit on a breakwater at Grand Haven, Michigan.

Michigan Department of Conservation

stroyed Lake Erie, Huron, and Michigan fisheries, and about half of Lake Superior's lake trout were gone.

In the fall of 1957 researchers at Hammond Bay were startled to find a chemical which seemed, after so many failures, to do the job. They could hardly believe their eyes, but there it was—a highly complex chemical on a phenol base, expensive to produce, but it seemed to do the job.

As quickly as a supply of the chemical could be produced, it was given a field test on Little Billie's Creek near the Hammond Bay station in October 1957. The test was a complete success, killing not only young lampreys in study pens, but also hundreds of others hidden in the stream. Overjoyed by this triumph, the Great Lakes Fisheries Commission ordered full speed ahead on chemical treatment of all Lake Superior tributary streams. The GLFC was set up in 1955 as a Canadian-United States policy group to coordinate all Great Lakes lamprey work. The lampricide breakthrough was the first stroke of good fortune for the commission. Treatment of the streams would be a last-ditch attempt to preserve what remained of lake trout fishing in Lake Superior.

On both sides of the lake, as soon as the ice went out in 1958, the chemical treatment of streams got under way. It was a hard job. Log-clogged wilderness streams, remote from any roads, had to be treated just as thoroughly as short, dam-blocked creeks. All streams could not be treated in one year, or even in two, but by the end of 1961, all Lake Superior streams had been treated, and conservationists stood by to await results.

What they sought was not long in coming. In the spring of 1961, a spot census of lampreys at specific locations showed eighty thousand of the predators. One year later, the count at these same locations was down to about ten thousand, a dramatic drop of more than 85 per cent. Fishermen also reported a drop in lamprey numbers taken in test nets. By 1965, lake trout were again appearing in nets, and success of the program was assured.

As soon as chemical treatment of Lake Superior was completed, efforts turned to Lake Michigan. If all goes as planned on that lake, chemical treatment will take place on Lakes Huron, Erie, and Ontario later. The tremendous vitality of the Great Lakes as fish-producing waters will again be realized, and restaurants and kitchens across the land may soon know the delights of Great Lakes whitefish and lake trout. Baked, roasted, broiled, or fried in a pan, the delicacy of these fish can resist the destructive efforts of the worst cooks, while under the hand of even a minor chef, a modest little meal will rise to the level of *haute cuisine*.

Primarily sport fishermen will catch these fish in future years, with commercial fishing headed toward a secondary role on the Lakes. Each state sets its own fishing regulations, and each state owns the bottomlands of Great Lakes waters adjacent to its shores. Michigan and Wisconsin, for example, divide Lake Michigan down the center, with each state in full control of its own share. Indiana and Illinois control smaller sections on the southern end of the lake. All can develop their Great Lakes waters as they see fit. But as the population has grown around the Great Lakes, the pressing need for new recreational areas has become apparent. Coho salmon, a favorite of Pacific Coast sport fishermen, are being introduced into the Great Lakes, and if they take hold, will provide a whole new recreational activity for people in the region. New sonar equipment is being used to locate schools of fish. Fishing techniques and gear have improved steadily, and as lake trout and whitefish increase in abundance, recreational fishing is sure to boom. Some observers foresee really spectacular sport fishing and the birth of a large-scale charter-boat industry, similar to that of Florida and the Gulf coast. Commercial fishing, meanwhile, will probably harvest less desirable species from sections of the Lakes not used by sport fishermen. This dual "harvest" will raise the Lakes to a pre-eminent position as the most productive and spirited fresh-water fishery in the world, a natural-resource story that can be told with pride.

A less happy tale and undoubtedly the most worrisome problem now facing the Great Lakes is the matter of water pollution. The level of pollution, rising nearly everywhere, is particularly serious on Lake Erie. Highly detailed studies of Lake Erie show pollution is gaining rapidly. Both government agencies and the general public are growing more and more concerned, despite heavy effort by some to halt the trend. Walleyed and blue pike, two valuable fish, have virtually been eliminated from Lake Erie within the last ten years. Pollution is suspected as the prime cause for the loss. Dissolved oxygen levels in waters of the lake have dropped disastrously low over thousands of square miles. Fish and most fish foods, such as insect larvae, snails, certain midges, and minnows, all require minimum levels of this oxygen for life. Pollutants such as sewage are believed to be capturing the oxygen formerly available to these pike and their foods.

In 1907 studies showed a total of 133 parts of dissolved solids per 1,000,000 parts of water in Lake Erie. In 1961 this total was up to 183 parts per 1,000,000, with particularly heavy increases noted in chlorides and sulfates. What does this lead to? Here is a United States Fish and Wildlife Service statement on the subject: "Lakes are essentially transitory things on the geological time scale, and as they age they change. The aging process of a lake is usually so slow and subtle that it frequently goes unnoticed in a lifetime of man. When lakes are used for the disposal of industrial and human wastes, the aging process may be greatly accelerated as has been thoroughly documented in Lake Zurich in Switzerland and Lake Washington near Seattle over the past fifty years. Never before, however, has such a dramatic process of accelerated aging been detected in a lake the size of Lake Erie." The report continues: "In the last forty-five years, mean annual water temperatures have risen almost two degrees Fahrenheit . . . the abundance of mayfly larvae [an important fish food] has reduced from 400 to 10 individuals per square meter . . . sludge worms have increased many fold . . . caddisfly larvae have been reduced almost to the vanishing point." The lake bottom, the report concludes, "is polluted to the extent that the status of the entire lake as a useful producer of fishery products is uncertain."

Meanwhile another writer noted that hearings in Chicago "showed that the lower end of Lake Michigan is but one step removed from a cesspool. Industrial waste and inadequate treatment of sewage by some communities have raised the pollution level to dangerous heights."

But just how serious will pollution become? Certainly, as population has increased, pollution has followed close behind. An average city resident today uses about 150 gallons of water daily. To make a ton of steel requires 25,000 gallons while a ton of paper requires 50,000 gallons. Filtration and cleansing systems that rehabilitate such used water have lagged far behind national abilities to pollute. Rapidly increasing urbanization in the Great Lakes region seems to assure a continued increase in this difficulty. If the United States runs true to form, the situation will get far, far worse before public indignation calls a halt. At that time, however, it may be too late to correct the situation.

It is a puzzling anomaly when one looks at American history to see that we must apparently destroy our most vital and valued natural possessions before we realize their worth. Such was the case with certain wildlife species, including many now extinct or near extinction. One, for example, is the bald eagle, symbol of our nation, now declining rapidly in the contiguous forty-eight states because of water pollution. So have we abused our forests, our land, our water, and the air we breathe. So have we hard, unyielding chemical pollution in every major river system of the nation, and so it may be that in our own time the "total" pollution and wreckage of the Great Lakes will occur.

But the long-run hope is that the United States is coming alive to the values of its natural resources, among the most precious of which are the Great Lakes. Wrapped in history, steeped still in the freshness and uncertainty of the recent frontier, faced with new and destructive forces that only man himself can control, the Great Lakes are not less a part of our natural heritage than the Grand Canyon or the California redwoods or the Rocky Mountains. Water, unfortunately, is like trees in being more susceptible to man's excesses. Water by belonging to everyone, belongs to no one. Its champions are few, its enemies all of us together. Thus far, the Great Lakes have dominated the history of all the men who have come upon them; and perhaps they can withstand the onslaughts of new millions. But a hollow sadness lies at the end of our long voyage if we must drop anchor in a mass of sludge.

It remains to be seen whether the Federal Water Quality Act of 1965 can turn the tide of pollution. That act will pump $380,000,000 into the fight against pollution, and much of the money will be put to use on the Great Lakes.

In the meantime, there are memories to recall and mental pictures to catalogue. For those who have never toured the Lakes, the time was never more ripe.

Fall is a golden season around the Lakes, one of the few regions in the world where the colors of autumn come to a full richness. The winter is a still white hush—when you are far enough inland not to hear the murderous pounding frenzy of the Lakes' waters. Once or twice in history, Lake Superior has been frozen over its entire surface for brief periods of time. The northern portions of Lakes Michigan and Huron are generally frozen shut for several months in winter, blocking all ship traffic through the straits. These are intriguing sights

Wide, sandy beaches, found along the shores of the Great Lakes, are typical of this glaciated country. Conservationists are fighting to preserve some of these dune areas for state and national parks before they are turned into industrial or residential sites. This scene is on Lake Michigan near the Michigan-Indiana border.

Michigan Department of Conservation

for any who have not seen them. Spring is always a time of riotous color, wild squally weather, and the sudden deep warmth of quiet days. Then virtually you can hear the push of new life coming up all around.

And summer? Well, summer is the time for work and the time for the Great Lakes, week after sunny week, when ships and people are most numerous on these waters. It is actually possible to *swim* in the Great Lakes—unlike oceans where swimmers, so called, spend most of their time breaking breakers. The fresh water of the Lakes is still refreshing and clean in most places, and not sticky like seawater. If someone breaks a bottle on the beach, the bits of glass are frosted and the edges softened by wind-driven sand within a season. Dozens of kinds of shore birds and of water and land animals strive mightily to remove dead fish, garbage, and other organic debris from these shores. And they may yet win the battle. At least they keep busy, and watching them at work is always a joy.

These then are the current events that may someday become part of Great Lakes history. Use of the St. Lawrence Seaway will expand, while big cities grow larger and small ones thrive as resort and retirement locations. Natural resources of the region will prosper under improving management policies, while water pollution grows with the times. And finally, for those of us who are sometimes depressed by the idea that all the world must march in step with progress, there will be one last saving grace. We can never quite hope to conquer the Lakes entirely. They will always be able, when minded, to roar and roll and tear apart man's puny constructions.

Without doubt, they are the biggest, broadest, and bluest lakes in the world, and they can be the most destructive. They have carried fierce tribal war parties, intrepid explorers, religious zealots. Colorful voyageurs have sung to these lakes, and lonesome traders in small canoes have cursed them. A capsule of all human history can be found here, from the most primitive stone-age people through the first use of metal and agriculture to the coming of the white man and modern civilization. Man's history started here before the modern Great Lakes had completely formed, and a very large share of Canadian and American history has taken place on and around their waters. If population centers are any measure of an area's importance, this Great Lakes area leads, and will lead, the continent. They are still the greatest inland seas in the world and are not only the Great Lakes, but the Greatest Lakes.

Michigan Department of Conservation

A late afternoon in early November suggests the cold brutality of Lake Superior. The ribs of an old schooner lie in the foreground.

Index